WITHDRAWN

Interest Groups and
Campaign Finance Reform in the
United States and Canada

Interest Groups and Campaign Finance Reform in the United States and Canada

Robert G. Boatright

THE UNIVERSITY OF MICHIGAN PRESS

Ann Arbor

Copyright © by the University of Michigan 2011
All rights reserved
Published in the United States of America by
The University of Michigan Press
Manufactured in the United States of America
♾ Printed on acid-free paper

2014   2013   2012   2011   4   3   2   1

A CIP catalog record for this book is available from the British Library.

Library of Congress Cataloging-in-Publication Data

Boatright, Robert G.
    Interest groups and campaign finance reform in the United States
and Canada / Robert G. Boatright.
        p.   cm.
    Includes bibliographical references and index.
    ISBN 978-0-472-07144-9 (cloth : alk. paper) —
    ISBN 978-0-472-05144-1 (pbk. : alk. paper) —
    ISBN 978-0-472-02675-3 (e-book)
    1. Campaign funds—United States.   2. Campaign funds—Canada.
3. Pressure groups—United States.   4. Pressure groups—Canada.
I. Title.

JK1991.B59   2011
324.7'80973—dc22   2010043191

Contents

Acknowledgments

This project has a long and complicated history. From 2002 through 2004, I was part of a research team at the Campaign Finance Institute that was exploring the effect of campaign finance reform on organized interests. I had the privilege of being in Washington, within a few blocks of all of these groups' headquarters, as they were planning their strategies for the 2002 and 2004 elections. As part of the Institute's research team, I spoke with the leaders of almost all of the major American organized interest groups. I and my co-investigators on this project (Institute director Michael Malbin, Mark Rozell, and Clyde Wilcox) contributed two chapters to books on campaign finance reform. As part of a completely separate Campaign Finance Institute project, however, I took an interest in the Canadian political contribution tax credit. My correspondence about the credit with Lisa Young led to an invitation to a conference on Canadian party finance reform held at the University of Calgary in 2006; there, several Canadian political scientists encouraged me to apply for a research grant to do the same sort of interview-based work on Canadian groups. My work in Canada convinced me that the only way to make sense of the pile of material on American groups I had accumulated was to use it not simply to look at American campaign finance law but to look at the incentives for and constraints on American interest groups in a comparative context.

At the Campaign Finance Institute, I am deeply indebted to Michael Malbin for his mentorship regarding my thinking about interest groups, his patience in reading through so much of the material here, his ability to get in touch with virtually anyone that matters in Washington, and the support he has provided. Mark Rozell and Clyde Wilcox were also instrumental in helping me to think about the role of interest groups in contemporary American politics and in lining up interviews with the various groups. Steve Weissman shared with me his extensive knowledge of many of the finer points of federal law governing advocacy groups and campaign finance. And although he left the Institute before I arrived there, Richard Skinner's earlier work on the interest groups project was invaluable in helping me figure out what to ask the groups. Although this project has evolved substantially since my departure, the component of it concerning American groups would have been impossible without financial support and intellectual guidance from the Institute.

On the Canadian side, my travel to Ottawa, Toronto, and Halifax was covered by a research grant from Foreign Affairs Canada. Marc Jacques of the Canadian consulate in Boston helped me to formulate the proposal and to get the Canadian side of the project started. Throughout my work on this project, Lisa Young answered all of my questions about Canadian politics, from the most basic to the extraordinarily complicated; Harold Jansen, William Cross, and Jonathan Malloy also provided important feedback on the project, helping me to identify groups with which to speak, to make sense of Canadian election data, and, most important, to enjoy my travel in Canada.

I owe a substantial debt as well to all of the group leaders who agreed to sit down for interviews with me. Many of the American group leaders submitted to not just one but two or three interviews. Although each of the Canadian group leaders spoke with me in person only once, many of them educated me about relatively basic features of Canadian politics, fielded follow-up questions, and read drafts of my summaries of our interviews.

Chapter 5 is a revised version of material that I originally wrote for an article published in the *Canadian Journal of Political Science* in 2009. Portions of chapters 3 and 4 appear in *Election and Party Finance in Canada: Consequences for Democracy,* edited by Lisa Young and Harold Jansen. I gratefully acknowledge the permission given by Cambridge Journals and the University of British Columbia Press to reprint this material here.

I have had the good fortune to receive unusually helpful comments on this material from colleagues and at conferences. Neil Burnham, William Crotty, Michael Heaney, James McHugh, Steve Schier, and Tim Werner provided feedback. My colleagues in the government department at Clark University have also been a valuable resource. Paul Posner and Valerie Sperling fielded my questions about the comparative politics literature, Mark Miller helped with questions on the courts, and department chairs Beverly Grier, Sharon Krefetz, and Mark Miller helped ensure that I had the funding and research support needed to keep this project afloat. I am also thankful to Jeff Biggs and the American Political Science Association Congressional Fellowship Program for enabling me to travel to Ottawa as part of my fellowship in 2000. At the time, I had no idea that I would be writing a book on Canada a few years down the road, but this visit certainly made my return trip in 2007 much easier.

I could not have asked for a more supportive editor for this project than Melody Herr. She has been an enthusiastic supporter of this book since I sent her the proposal, cheerfully fielding all of my questions about the manuscript while never failing to remind me to write the book that I want to write. Thank you as well to Susan Cronin, Kevin Rennells, and the rest of the University of Michigan Press staff.

One of the pleasures of doing research is always the opportunity to visit new places. My children, Jacob and Dara, ages eight and three, remain skeptical that it is possible to get on an airplane and be in another country within two hours. I wasn't able to disabuse them of their skepticism during this project, but maybe next time I will be able to bring them along. Jacob also has been duly impressed by the existence of a copy of my earlier book on the living room bookshelf. I hope that both of my kids will learn that the task of writing a book is nothing compared to the task of trying to be a good parent and that the pleasure of holding a copy of one's book pales in comparison to the pleasure of seeing one's children running about the house.

Finally, I am always a bit dubious when I read in the acknowledgments of others' books claims that the writers' spouses carefully proofread the book manuscripts or debated the finer points of those books. It seems to me that it is enough to subject one's spouse to the various inconveniences of being married to an academic without making these sorts of requests. I did not presume to force my wife to acquaint herself with American and Canadian campaign finance laws, and I am sure she is thankful for it. It is enough for me to know that she would have done so had I asked. Instead, Audrey helped with this book, perhaps more than she knows, simply by always being there for me.

Author's Note

One of the perils of writing an academic work about contemporary politics is the risk that a book starts to become out of date the moment it appears in print. In both the United States and Canada, campaign finance law is very much in turmoil. Canada's prorogation crisis of late 2008 added an unexpected twist late in the writing of this book, and the U.S. Supreme Court's *Citizens United v. FEC* decision was handed down the day before I had expected to submit my final draft of the manuscript. I have incorporated these two events in the book as best I could, but both will continue to have profound and perhaps unanticipated effects on interest group activity in the next few years. I encourage readers to consult the book's Web site at www.press.umich.edu for my thoughts on how interest groups' election strategies have changed since the book went to press.

Throughout this book, I use the term *campaign finance* in referring to the receipts and expenditures of both American and Canadian politicians. This is a concession to American readers; the more common term in the Canadian literature is *party finance*. Students of comparative political financing have noted that the United States is among the few nations where most political spending is directed toward campaigns and have argued that *party finance* is a more accurate term insofar as much of the money raised by candidates and parties in Canada and other Western democracies is used for purposes other than election campaigns (see, e.g., Nassmacher 2009). While such observations make sense, I have retained the use of *campaign finance* simply because it will be more familiar to most readers. Similarly, I use the term *interest groups* in reference to both American and Canadian organizations; I avoid the Canadian term *third parties* because it has different connotations within American politics.

Finally, I do not convert Canadian spending amounts in this book into American dollars or vice versa. For readers wishing to make direct comparisons, the annual average exchange rates of relevance to this book, as provided by the Bank of Canada, are:

    2000: $1.00 US = $1.49 CDN
    2002: $1.00 US = $1.57 CDN
    2004: $1.00 US = $1.30 CDN
    2006: $1.00 US = $1.13 CDN
    2008: $1.00 US = $1.07 CDN

(*Source:* Bank of Canada, http://www.bankofcanada.ca/en/rates/ exchange_avg_pdf.html)

List of Acronyms

AA-EVP	Animal Alliance–Environment Voters Party
AARP	American Association of Retired Persons
ABC	Associated Builders and Contractors
ACT	America Coming Together
AFL-CIO	American Federation of Labor–Congress of Industrial Organizations
AFSCME	American Federation of State, County, and Municipal Employees
AFT	American Federation of Teachers
AJS	Americans for Job Security
BCRA	Bipartisan Campaign Reform Act
BIPAC	Business-Industry Political Action Committee
BQ	Bloc Québécois
CAW	Canadian Auto Workers
CBM	Citizens for Better Medicare
CCCE	Canadian Council of Chief Executives
CEA	Canada Elections Act
CFIB	Canadian Federation of Independent Businesses
CLC	Canadian Labour Congress
CME	Canadian Manufacturers and Exporters
CTF	Canadian Taxpayers Federation
DCCC	Democratic Congressional Campaign Committee
DSCC	Democratic Senatorial Campaign Committee
EEA	Election Expenses Act
FEC	Federal Election Commission
FECA	Federal Election Campaign Act
FTA	Free Trade Agreement
HRC	Human Rights Campaign
IUPAT	International Union of Painters and Allied Trades

LCV	League of Conservation Voters
MP	Member of Parliament
NAACP	National Association for the Advancement of Colored People
NAFTA	North American Free Trade Act
NARAL	National Abortion and Reproductive Rights Action League
NCC	National Citizens Coalition
NCLR	National Council of la Raza
NDP	New Democratic Party
NEA	National Education Association
NFIB	National Federation of Independent Businesses
NOW	National Organization for Women
NRA	National Rifle Association
NRCC	National Republican Congressional Committee
NRLC	National Right to Life Committee
NRSC	National Republican Senatorial Committee
NVF	National Voter Fund
P2	Prosperity Project
PAC	Political Action Committee
PC	Progressive Conservative
SEIU	Service Employees International Union
UFCW	United Food and Commercial Workers
USW	United Steelworkers
VWF	Voices for Working Families

Introduction: Interest Groups and Campaign Finance Reform—A Natural Experiment

"What's most important is that we elect a president with the proven ability to bring Democrats and Republicans together to get results so we can stand up to special interests."
—Barack Obama, *November 27, 2007*

"Maybe I've just lived a little too long, but I have no illusions about how hard this is going to be. You are not going to wave a magic wand and have the special interests disappear."
—Hillary Clinton, *February 25, 2008*

"I understand who I work for. I don't work for a party. I don't work for a special interest. I don't work for myself. I work for you. I've fought to get million-dollar checks out of our elections. I've fought lobbyists who stole from Indian tribes. I fought crooked deals in the Pentagon. I fought tobacco companies and trial lawyers, drug companies and union bosses."
—John McCain, *September 5, 2008*

"Canadians replaced an agenda designed to make the government strong with a government committed to making the country strong. Conservatives heard the desire for change. We understood. And we responded. To those unrepresented by lobbyists and special interests: we hear you. To those who have longed to reform our democratic institutions: your time has come."
—Stephen Harper, *January 25, 2008*

The 2008 American presidential election featured two candidates who had a history of working to reduce the power of interest groups in American elections. One of Republican nominee John McCain's landmark achievements during his twenty-two years as a senator was the passage of the Bipartisan Campaign Reform Act (BCRA), also known as the McCain-Fein-gold Act. BCRA placed new restrictions on corporations' and labor unions' ability to donate to the parties and to engage in broadcast advocacy, or "electioneering," regarding candidates for office. Although Democratic nominee Barack Obama had been in the Senate for only four years, he, too, had been active in placing new restrictions on lobbyists, and Obama touted his support for a 1998 Illinois law restricting campaign contributions from lobbyists.

In principle, both Obama and McCain supported reducing the role of interest groups in campaigns. Yet the two could neither prohibit substantial spending on their behalf nor agree on any sort of joint effort to discourage groups from spending money on the 2008 election. Both denounced the activities of the "527 groups" that had played such a major role in the 2004 presidential campaign, but, as was the case in previous elections, neither could do anything about the fact that independent groups made some of the nastiest attacks on the candidates. A group calling itself the Our Country Deserves Better PAC put together an advertisement in which actors playing Mahmoud Ahmadinejad and Fidel Castro mocked Obama's lack of foreign policy experience. Democracy for America, an offshoot of Howard Dean's 2004 presidential campaign organization, aired an advertisement speculating about the secrets in McCain's health records. MoveOn.org parodied drug prevention public service announcements in an advertisement encouraging viewers to talk with their parents about their potential Republican sympathies and the damage those sympathies might cause. And the American Issues Project spent an estimated three million dollars on a television advertisement linking Obama to former Weather Underground member William Ayres and then further comparing the Weather Underground's activities to the September 11 attacks.

Both candidates may well have been sincere in denouncing such advertisements, but they could do little to stop these groups. Likewise, Obama could do little to stop the AFL-CIO from spending an estimated two hundred million dollars on the 2008 election, and McCain was generally powerless to stop the Chamber of Commerce, the National Rifle Association, and other Republican-leaning groups from spending money to support him or to criticize Obama. While much of the media focus in 2008 was on the massive amounts of money spent by the candidates and the parties, interest groups were very much a part of the election. And they played such a prominent role despite the fact that BCRA was the most consequential piece of campaign finance reform legislation passed in almost thirty years and despite the fact that labor unions, business associations, and many advocacy groups had fought BCRA tooth and nail on the grounds that it would limit their freedom of speech in campaigns.

On September 8, 2008, less than two months before Election Day in the United States and more than two years after the first American presidential campaign committee was formed, Canadian prime minister Stephen Harper dissolved Parliament and called an election for October 14. Harper, like McCain and Obama, was also on record decrying special interests' role in elections. And like McCain and Obama, Harper could claim credit for passing legislation restricting group influence in elections. The Federal Accountability Act, passed by Harper's Conservative Party in 2006, prohibited labor unions and business groups from contributing to political parties. The Accountability Act was the successor to the 2003 Canada Elections Act (CEA) amendments passed by Jean Chrétien's Liberal Party, which restricted corporate and labor contributions to token amounts. Chrétien's government had also passed separate legislation curtailing the ability of "third-party" groups, or nonparty political organizations, to spend money on advocacy. During the 2008 election, however, neither Harper nor his competitors had to think very much about group spending in the election because there was virtually none. In fact, a perusal of election-related articles in the *Globe and Mail*, Canada's leading newspaper, turns up not a single article detailing group spending on the federal election. Of course, Canadian interest groups had views on the election; they were not completely silent about these views, but they did not spend enough money to attract the attention of the national media.

The campaign finance reform laws passed in the United States and Canada in the early 2000s look, on their faces, to be quite similar. And the organized interests in these two countries are quite similar. Many American labor unions are in fact internationals, with locals in the United States and Canada. Many of the advocacy groups active in the two countries are either identical (for instance, the Sierra Club and Focus on the Family are active in both the United States and Canada) or maintain extremely close ties (as is the case for the National Rifle Association in the United States and the National Firearms Association in Canada). Business groups, too, either bear the same names (both nations have a Federation of Independent Businesses and a Chamber of Commerce) or are functionally similar. And finally, both nations have a long history of political rhetoric about restraining interest groups. Yet the consequences of these similar reforms for similar groups could not be more different. What accounts for these differences?

In this book, we shall consider this fortuitous pairing of campaign finance laws as a sort of natural experiment. The timing of these two laws and the generally similar political culture of these two countries (at least with regard to the role of groups in politics) enable one to hold culture and legislative changes constant and look at political institutions' effect on interest group activities. Political institutions ultimately shape group activities and do so far more thoroughly than do changes of the scale of BCRA or the various amendments to Canadian campaign finance law. Laws that have the same ostensible purpose have different effects because of factors that are often seen as being outside the purview of debate over campaign financing. It does not necessarily follow that reform is bound to be inconsequential. Those who expect major changes from campaign finance reform must, however, either temper their hopes according to the way in which larger institutional rules and structures create a demand for money or pursue decidedly more radical reform to reshape interest group money's role in the political system.

This perspective is rarely available to those who study campaign finance reform or the role of organized interests in politics. American political science has a long history of work studying interest groups' changing role in politics, and some work has compared the effects of campaign finance reforms in the states on the behavior of politicians, parties, and interest groups. Yet political institutions tend to be taken as a given. Observers have argued for at least fifty years that interest groups are to a degree shaped by politicians to meet their ends, but we cannot see how institutions shape groups simply because we cannot posit any sort of counterfactual in looking at groups. We cannot say, for example, what American interest groups would look like were Congress organized differently, were parties stronger, were there more than two parties, and so forth, simply because we cannot observe any such state of affairs.

The coincidence of American and Canadian campaign finance reform enables us to compare different institutional structures. It allows us, for example, to ask whether interest groups behave differently in systems where parties maintain a high level of discipline as opposed to those with low levels of party discipline. It allows us to look at the effects on interest groups of having elections held on a regular calendar or of having elections called by the government or brought about by a vote of confidence. It allows us to look at the electoral calculations of interest groups in two-party and multiparty systems. And it allows us to do so while holding the interests and their cultural salience somewhat constant.

One could make these sorts of comparisons without having any sort of catalyzing event. In fact, many Canadian studies of interest groups have routinely begun with comparisons of the American and Canadian interest group systems. Yet the focus here should not simply be on how groups operate, which is a moving target. Interest groups change their political strategies regularly, in response to changing political circumstances, the emergence of new issues, or new developments in communications technology. Groups also change when they are ordered to do so through the passage of new laws regarding their activities. The common themes of the American and Canadian reform packages allow us to hold another feature constant—the changes imposed on group activity. The focus here, then, is on how groups acting to influence different types of institutions respond to a shared change in their legal status and their permissible election activities.

In this book, I draw on interviews with the political directors of the most politically active American and Canadian interest groups to present a story of how groups in the two countries behaved before the most recent round of campaign finance reforms and how these groups have responded to these reforms. The claims made by these political directors go beyond merely presenting data on aggregate contributions or aggregate spending and show how groups' strategies are altered by reform, what these groups' options have been since the passage of reform, and what sort of communication has taken place between groups in the two countries. While American groups have become more partisan and more political, focusing on mobilization, on bundling individual contributions, and on expanding their use of the Internet, Canadian groups have distanced themselves from the parties, engaging in some limited mobilization but largely stepping back from the political arena. Similar reform laws have brought about very different results. The story told by these group leaders illuminates politicians' role in shaping group activities and shows some of the unintended consequences of reform. Is there a danger in having too much reform, too much restriction on group activity? Likewise, is there a danger in doing too little to restrain groups? The comparison presented here provides some insight into these essentially normative questions.

This book is, therefore, a comparative study of reform in two countries, but it deliberately seeks to compare two countries that are alike in many important ways. How alike they are, however, is a controversial question. Accepting the premise of this book—that comparing the effects of campaign finance reform in the United States and Canada has merit for understanding how political institutions shape group options—requires accepting (1) that the two nations' reform laws are similar, (2) that the two nations share important characteristics of political culture, and (3) that the two nations' institutions are quite different. In other words, similar laws, similar cultures, different institutions. The second of these claims is the most controversial—Canadians do not always like being told they are like Americans, and vice versa—but it is important to address this claim before looking at the groups themselves. In the remaining pages of this introduction, I provide a rudimentary defense of these claims, explain how these claims are useful in setting this book up as a sort of natural experiment, and explain how the book examines the consequences of this experiment.

Similar Laws

John Kingdon's (1984) "garbage can" model of policy-making states that when confronted with a political problem, policymakers will quickly peruse existing proposals to address this problem and implement the proposal that seems the best fit to their immediate circumstances. Proposals may linger for years, waiting for a "policy window" to open up, and the ultimate policy chosen may not necessarily be the best fit for the problem. It need only bear the appearance of being a good fit to the problem facing policymakers. At any given moment, numerous proposals may exist in the world of think tanks or as legislation introduced but never taken up by congressional committees or subcommittees. Broadly speaking, interest groups have only two options for influencing elections—they can contribute directly to parties or candidates, or they can engage in independent activity designed to aid one candidate or party at the expense of another. It is no surprise, then, that American and Canadian campaign finance reforms have worked from a similar palette—any reform will be aimed at influencing permissible amounts or sources of contributions or at encouraging or discouraging particular types of speech.

Given the ease with which political actors in the United States and Canada can observe each other's activities, it is also unsurprising that tactics developed in one country may also be implemented in the other or that reform movements in one country find some currency in the other. One country's reforms can easily make it into the other country's "garbage can," to be considered in the other country when circumstances warrant. According to some observers, this process occurred following the passage of BCRA. As I recount in chapter 3, during the 1990s, both Canada and the United States engaged in lengthy investigations of political financing. In the United States, this inquiry took the form of congressional hearings regarding the fund-raising practices of the Clinton administration and a series of legislative proposals by Senators John McCain, Russell Feingold, and others. In Canada, the Lortie Commission, appointed by the Mulroney government, recommended a variety of restrictions on campaign contributions. Yet the ultimate passage of reform laws in both countries followed a catalyzing event that did not quite fit the specific reforms implemented. In the United States, scandals involving the political contributions of the Enron Corporation finally broke the Senate filibuster that had prevented a vote on the McCain-Feingold proposals. In Canada, the Gomery Commission report on kickbacks and illegal contributions to the Liberal Party also made reform laws seem an attractive option.[1] In neither case did the catalyzing event have anything directly to do with legal political activities of the parties or of interest groups; in both cases, however, the passage of comprehensive reform laws seemed an attractive option.

In chapter 3, I also provide details on the specific provisions of the laws enacted in the United States and Canada. Here, it is sufficient simply to note that the laws bore a substantial resemblance to each other. In the United States, BCRA prohibited "soft money" contributions by corporations, labor unions, or individuals to the political parties and prohibited corporate or labor funds from being used for independent broadcast advocacy that named a federal candidate during the two months preceding the general election. In Canada, the 2003 CEA amendments limited corporations or labor unions to contributing a total of only $1,000 per year to local party organizations or candidates. BCRA was passed in 2002 and took effect the day after the 2002 election; the CEA amendments were introduced on January 29, 2003, and took effect the following June. At roughly the same time, the Canada Elections Act of 2002 limited independent groups from spending more than $150,000 on political advocacy during any election period. There are many technical differences, but the intent and major components of the laws are the same.

These laws are not entirely about groups; they are about the recipients of political contributions and the beneficiaries of political advocacy as much as about those who make contributions or engage in independent advocacy. The laws are, however, substantially similar—so much so that former Canadian prime minister Joe Clark (2004) remarked that "Canada has a new policy because the United States has an old problem." In Clark's view, Canada has few of the campaign finance troubles of the United States, but given the political problems of the Chrétien government, changes in American law provided the Canadian government with a convenient means of signaling that it cared about campaign finance law despite the fact that American-style legislative changes offered an imperfect fit for the regime's problems. Whether or not Clark's assessment is fair, it indicates that the similarities between the two changes are more than just accidental.

Similar Cultures

Clark's comments suggest that the two sets of reforms do not fit the two countries equally well. This phenomenon may be attributed to cultural factors or institutional factors. In the most controversial aspect of this comparison, I contend that the two laws address quite similar strains in the two nations' political cultures. In other words, in all the ways that matter for this project, Canadian and American culture are the same.

Although this claim might seem unremarkable to Americans, these are fighting words within some circles in Canada. As Nevitte (1996, 3) has noted, Canadians have been primed by debates over their constitution and over free trade with the United States to examine the ways in which their culture is distinct from that of America. There is a strong left-populist strand within Canadian culture, perhaps best exemplified by one of Canada's largest citizen groups, the Council of Canadians, which has continually pointed to value differences between the United States and Canada. This argument is borne out in Canadian popular literature; for example, Michael Adams's (2003, 2) best seller, *Fire and Ice: The United States, Canada, and the Myth of Converging Values,* begins with the contention that "for all of the pressing of Canadian noses against the glass of American prosperity and achievement, we cherish our separateness." In Adams's view, the United States is a far more individualistic, far less tolerant, and, post–September 11, far more self-absorbed and security-conscious society than Canada. Likewise, in his 2003 book, *The Border: Canada, the U.S., and Dispatches from the 49th Parallel,* James Laxer alleges that there is a lack of shared social experiences among different classes of Americans and that there is a much greater sense of community within Canada. These books second the received wisdom of American sociologist Seymour Martin Lipset (1991), who argued, among other things, that Canadians are more law-abiding and collectively oriented than Americans, more trusting of their government (and of authority in general), and less concerned with individual rights.

Culture, however, is a messy term, as are the conventional distinctions made by public opinion researchers between attitudes and values. Some observers, such as political scientist Nelson Wiseman (2007), deny that

Canada has any such thing as a national culture—instead, the country has as many as five different regional cultures. For that matter, the United States also exhibits similar regional variation in culture; Grabb and Curtis (2005) argue that one cannot compare the United States and Canada without acknowledging that this comparison actually includes four distinct political cultures—the U.S. North and South and English-speaking and French-speaking Canada.[2] In addition, as Nevitte (1996, 2002) and Dalton (2004) contend, it is nearly meaningless to talk about cultural differences within a two-country framework or at one point in time; appreciating how "different" or "similar" the United States and Canada are requires asking, "Compared to whom?" That is, are the two countries more similar than different when compared to other Western democracies? On what dimensions? And are they growing apart, growing closer together, or moving in parallel directions?

The claims made by Lipset and in the popular media have support both in public opinion data and in historical treatments of the two countries' origins and development. For the purposes of this study, the greater union density within Canada, the large role played by Christian conservatives within the United States, and the larger role played by antitax groups within the United States have historical roots and are symptomatic of long-standing national differences. However, American and Canadian citizens have over the past few decades exhibited attitudes and values that should lead politicians to take similar steps in the arena of electoral reform. Whatever underlying differences exist in national values, Americans and Canadians have exhibited a greater desire for political participation, a growing distrust of politicians, and a growing sense that organized interests wield too much power—at the same time as citizens in these two countries are turning to groups to press their demands on government.

In general terms, this trend has been characterized as an increase in the "democratic deficit"—a growing gap between citizens' expectations of government and the performance of government. As Dalton (2004) notes, this trend exists within most Western democracies. Both Nevitte and Dalton argue that beginning in the 1960s, increasing education and income levels in these countries corresponded to an increasing cynicism among citizens about what government could do at the same time that citizens became more confident in their ability to understand political decisions. In technical terms, this phenomenon meant that citizens displayed a growing sense of internal efficacy but a declining sense of external efficacy (Nevitte 2002). In practical terms, all of these nations exhibited declining voter turnout, decreased faith in all governmental institutions, and decreased faith in nongovernmental institutions such as churches and labor unions. Citizens dealigned from political parties, creating more volatility in election results and an increased public receptivity to less conventional political ideas, as exemplified by the growing appeal of direct democracy in both the United States and Canada. At the same time, however, both the United States and Canada exhibited high levels of systemic support—that is, as critical as citizens might be of individual politicians or political parties, overwhelming numbers endorsed democracy and their nations' basic constitutional principles (Nadeau 2002).

How are these trends in citizen values manifested in attitudes toward politics? Two characteristics shared by Americans and Canadians are relevant here. First, public satisfaction with politicians and organized interests has declined precipitously in both countries. Majorities of the respondents in the American National Election Studies biennial survey have reported that they "trust the government in Washington to do what is right most of the time" or "just about always" only once since 1972. More than 40 percent of respondents agreed that "quite a few of the people running the government are crooked" in every election cycle during the 1990s, although the percentage agreeing with this statement declined slightly to approximately 35 percent during the 2000s. In each of these years, between 48 and 76 percent of respondents agreed that "government is pretty much run by a few big interests looking out for themselves."[3] Other questions regarding trust in government show similar responses. On these issues, Canadian respondents are no different from Americans. Roese (2002, 152) documents similar trends among Canadians—the percentage of Canadian Election Study respondents who said that they "can trust the government in Ottawa to do what is right most of the time" or "just about always" declined from 58 percent in 1965 to 33 percent in 1993, and the percentage who argued that "quite a few of the people running the government are a little crooked" increased from 24 percent to 45 percent over the same period. The trends and even the percentages are virtually identical.

Second, some sort of institutional reform would seem like an obvious response on the part of government in both nations. Respondents tend to blame interest groups for many of these problems. Hibbing and Theiss-Morse (2002, 99) report that 59 percent of the respondents in their 1998 survey contend that interest groups have too much power, and Canadians appear to share this sentiment. Limiting the role of interest groups in campaigns would thus be an obvious response and indeed was one of the major arguments made by the (Canadian) Reform Party. Many observers have cautioned that reform will have little effect on the underlying trend—Dalton (2004, 187) has argued that electoral reforms have had little effect in Western democracies and may even breed greater cynicism; Nevitte (2002) has contended that prior changes have not influenced public sentiment in Canada; and Grant and Rudolph (2004, 5) have summarized a vast array of American literature contending that while citizens support reform, they fail to notice the consequences of specific reforms. Yet despite the fact that citizens do not rank campaign finance reform as a high priority, substantial majorities in the United States have voiced support for many types of reform, including limiting contributions, abolishing political action committees, and limiting spending (Grant and Rudolph 2004; Hibbing and Theiss-Morse 2002, 97). Americans and Canadians tend to be cautious reformers—Nevitte (1996, 101) reports that 82 percent of Canadians and 76 percent of Americans support gradual rather than radical reform of political institutions.

Are these patterns signs of a shared political culture? The issues on which I have focused do not address the broader debates about the "Americanization" of Canadians or a general convergence of values, but they do indicate that the reforms described here were aimed at addressing similar concerns about the linkages between citizens and government. The public's demand for reform and citizens' receptivity to reforms that limit the role of groups in politics are similar enough that one can reject the notion that groups somehow had greater permission to flout the new laws in one country than in the other. Groups and politicians in the two countries confront similar public attitudes toward their activities and can be expected to operate with similar concerns about how the public will evaluate their actions.

The lone cultural difference that requires elaboration here is the greater propensity of Americans to frame their responses to questions on government and on groups with reference to partisanship. Although Nevitte, Dalton, and others have noted a growing political polarization between left and right in both countries, Americans exhibit a stronger propensity than Canadians to think about partisan leanings when evaluating their political leaders (Nevitte 2002). Grant and Rudolph (2004, 53) present a "group-centric" theory of support for reform, demonstrating that, for example, those who identify labor unions as their most disliked type of interest group tend to be more likely to support curtailing group influence when they are asked whether, to continue the example, "we need new campaign finance laws to reduce the power of labor unions" than when they are offered the question without a specific group reference or with reference to a group about which they have a more favorable opinion. Nevitte's claim would suggest that a similar experiment in Canada would yield more ambiguous results, but one can interpret the claims of Lipset and Meltz (2004, 79) that trends in union support are similar in the two countries as a sign that Canadians also exhibit a degree of group-centrism. American groups may, then, benefit from a certain level of trust or slack that enables them to maintain the support of some of the public while developing creative strategies to circumvent legal restrictions. In highly charged elections such as those of the 2000s, American groups may have found it worthwhile to be more political than did their Canadian counterparts. This difference might be said to have less to do with culture than with the circumstances of particular elections.

Different Institutions

The notion that institutions and institutional rules shape the behavior of all political actors—politicians, parties, interest groups, and citizens—is a standard beginning point for rational choice theory. Institutions are, of course, malleable. That is, individual choices shape institutions as well. It is a chicken-and-egg proposition to argue that groups shape institutions or that institutions shape groups. Most rational choice treatments of electoral activity, however, note that the wrangling over institutional rules is more of an inside game, that it is less visible to the public than are the debates over issues or candidate platforms that dominate elections. Any discussion of group change must insert itself somewhere in the ongoing back-and-forth of changes in institutional rules and changes in public policy. In other words, to argue that American and Canadian groups adopted different types of election strategies in response to changes in campaign finance law is to place the institutional change before the change in group behavior. However, doing so adds the acknowledgment that groups have preferences about what sorts of institutional changes would benefit them and that these preferences, in turn, are shaped by the institutional status quo ante—that is, the rules in existence before the enactment of reform laws and the ways that groups behaved under the prior laws. One could even take the story further back in time, but doing so would further complicate what is already an intricate tale of reform and group response to it.

In chapter 1, I discuss the most consequential institutional differences between the United States and Canada for the purpose of this study. While the two nations' reform laws can be seen as a form of institutional change, both were relatively modest in scope. The features that matter most in structuring group behavior—bicameralism, the existence of an American executive branch elected separately from the legislature, the election calendar, the manner in which parties organize the legislatures in the two countries—are far too well entrenched to be touched by changes in campaign finance law. Campaign finance laws are regulations governing the procedures by which institutions operate, as are components of the constitution mandating what institutions shall exist, but one set of laws is far smaller and more malleable than the other. It makes sense, then, to separate "big" institutional laws (the laws that create the institutions themselves) and "small" rules (such as the rules of campaign finance) and to treat the big laws as far less malleable than the small ones. So while the big laws can in theory be changed, they are more fixed than the small ones. When I refer here to institutions, then, I am referring to the existence of different types of governing bodies—the Congress, the House of Commons, the presidency, and so forth—and the basic electoral procedures that are used to select the members of these bodies, such as the first-past-the-post system, the election calendar, or the means by which parties achieve the ability to govern or organize the legislature.

To briefly summarize the argument as it pertains to institutions, the story is as follows: there are four institutional variations of note here. First, both nations have a first-past-the-post electoral system.[4] The consensus in the rational choice literature is that a first-past-the-post system leads to a two-party system. Such has historically been the case in the United States but not in Canada. Canada has traditionally had two major parties and one to three minor parties that win seats in Parliament, and the strength of these parties varies across the country. Canadian groups that seek to have an impact on who governs must be more strategic and less sincere in choosing among parties to support than is the case in the United States. Second, American politics tends to have a variety of access points because of the separation of powers—different parties may control the House, the Senate, and the White House, and group success in one chamber may not lead to success in another. Canada nominally has a bicameral system, but its Senate is rarely relevant except in unusual circumstances, and Canada does not have a directly or independently elected executive; its legislative and executive branches are fused. There are effectively far fewer meaningful access points than in the United States. Third, American elections occur on a fixed schedule, while Canadian elections can be brought about by a confidence vote or at the discretion of the prime minister. Because the governing party can be brought down at any time, members are expected to support the party on most votes, and individual legislators' policy positions and views become far less important than in the United States. Correspondingly, Canadian parties cannot stray from the "responsible party" model, and party discipline is far more important in Canada than in the United States. An American group may care about currying favor with individual legislators, but Canadian groups do not benefit from doing so. And fourth, the greater regional variation in party support and the lack of connection between provincial and federal parties is both a cause and a consequence of a more decentralized form of federalism in Canada than exists in the United States. Even some Canadian national groups may prefer to work in a piecemeal fashion with sympathetic provincial legislatures, while American groups with a national focus are drawn to form relationships with national parties and to see their alliances with state-level and national parties as one and the same.

A final set of rules, which I will treat as an institutional constraint although it is less about institutions than it is about rights, is embedded in the two nations' constitutions. The U.S. Supreme Court has equated interest group advocacy with free speech and has been reluctant to impose limitations on group expenditures for this reason. To take matters back to the Constitution, the First Amendment states that "Congress shall make no law . . . abridging the freedom of speech." There are no explicit qualifications to this statement. Section 2 of the Canadian Charter of Rights and Freedoms, conversely, holds that one of the fundamental freedoms is the "freedom of thought, belief, opinion and expression, including freedom of the press and other media of communication." The Charter prefaces the establishment of this freedom, however, by stating in section 1 that it "guarantees the rights and freedoms set out in it subject only to such reasonable limits prescribed by law as can be demonstrably justified in a free and democratic society." Most Americans would likely find this proposition valid as well, but the existence of this phrase, known as the "explicit limitations clause," has caused constitutional interpretations of group speech rights in Canada to feature far more scrutiny of these "reasonable limits" than has been the case for American courts (see Manfredi and Rush 2008, 17). The results in Canada have been, among other things, more stringent hate speech laws, greater emphasis on allowing equality in political expression, and, most consequentially for our purposes here, greater restriction on group advocacy spending. These rules and their interpretations may be more malleable than the institutional arrangements summarized previously, but because no one on either side of the party finance reform debate in Canada argued in favor of changes to the Charter itself and because no one involved in the campaign finance debate in the United States sought to amend the Constitution itself, these provisions can also be taken as a fixed part of the institutional landscape.

We have, then, far more variation in institutional arrangements in this comparison than we have in the campaign finance laws themselves or in the general cultural attitudes that shape these laws as well as the public's attitudes toward the role of organized interests in politics. Thus, any variation in interest group activities following the enactment of campaign finance laws is far more likely to be a consequence of institutional differences than of cultural factors or different components of the laws themselves.

Campaign Finance Reform as a Natural Experiment

This book is hardly the first to use the United States–Canada comparison to hold cultural features somewhat constant while focusing on how policy changes play out in two different countries. Relatively casual comparisons of this sort are made by politicians all the time—in the United States, the most familiar such comparisons are made in regard to health care and to prescription drug laws. There is also a substantial Canadian popular literature concerning differences between Canada and the United States; most of this literature tends to identify particular differences in social or economic policy and to make normative claims about whether the difference is or should be shrinking. More rigorous comparisons have been made from the Canadian side as well, focusing on health care, education, and economic policy (see, e.g., Heath 2001). These studies often refer to the political dynamics in the two countries, in some cases drawing attention to features such as the Electoral College or the role of the Senate in the United States or discussing party collusion or the role of the Senate in Canada.

The framework here is also common in comparativists' work on social movements and interest groups. Sperling (1999), for example, analyzes the development of women's groups in Russia with an eye toward governmental policies of recognizing certain groups and allowing international aid for groups. Sawer (2004) compares women's movements in Canada and Australia, noting the role of federal funding for women's groups and conservative groups in group development. A voluminous body of work compares labor unions' lobbying strategies, including studies of union politics in Latin America (Murillo 2001), Western Europe (Erne 2008), and Eastern Europe (Ost 2006), and a similarly large body of work compares business associations' lobbying in different nations (see, e.g., Woll 2008). Many such studies have addressed both culture and institutions, as is the case in Mainwaring's (1988, 1991, 1992) work on party development in Brazil and other Latin American countries.

The comparison here is somewhat easier to make for two reasons. First, changes in campaign finance law address election procedures, which are easier to identify than changes in, say, health care policy. Procedural changes are both a consequence and a cause of the behavior of political actors, so one can steer clear of all of the messy details of policy implementation or the growing pains of any sort of new social policy. To extend the health care comparison, any sort of comparative study would have to combine extensive quantitative work within each country, identifying different subpopulations affected by each policy, with qualitative work that cannot help but get only a few (hopefully) representative pieces of the problem. Zuberi's (2006) work on American and Canadian poverty policies illustrates this approach—Zuberi combines quantitative data on welfare programs with case studies of similar cities in each country (in his case, Seattle and Vancouver), but his approach does not pretend to be comprehensive. In contrast, the smaller universe of groups substantially affected by campaign finance reform can enable one to draw from all of the affected groups and make more of a claim to include all of the major participants.

Second, the shared stimulus in this study is relatively uncommon in the literature on campaign finance. Three major comparative campaign finance literatures exist. First, numerous comparative studies, particularly in Europe, have examined the effects of public funding or other campaign finance restrictions, including the work of Scarrow (2004, 2006, 2007), van Biezen (2004), Hofnung (2006), and Fisher (2011).[5] A growing literature examines the relationship between party development and campaign finance laws in Latin America (Mainwaring 1991, 1992; Posada-Carbo 2008), and the National Endowment for Democracy, the International Anti-Corruption Conference, and the International Institute for Democracy and Electoral Assistance have published conference reports considering variations in campaign finance laws across different nations. Because campaign finance data are publicly available in many Western countries, these types of approaches can make detailed quantitative comparisons of different types of laws. What they lack, again, is a common stimulus—it is possible to conduct pre- and postreform analyses for individual countries, but it is not possible to make comparative pre- and postreform studies simply because it is rare for similar reform packages to coincide as precisely as they do here. It is possible to get the comparative dimension or to address policy change, but it is rare that one has the opportunity to do both.

A second comparative campaign finance literature addresses reforms in the American states.[6] Many such studies have analyzed the effects of different types of campaign finance reform laws on elections and legislatures (see, e.g., Gross and Goidel 2003; Hamm and Hogan 2004, 2008; Malbin and Gais 1998; Squire et al. 2005). In many instances, states have adopted reforms such as public funding, tax credits, contribution restrictions, or other features that have been discussed at the federal level, and state-level studies can provide insight into the consequences of these laws. An added benefit of these studies is that many of the American states that have enacted new reform laws have done so within a similar time frame. The stimulus, then, is somewhat similar. The added piece in this study is the variation in institutions. State-level comparisons can hold many important features constant, and the sources of variation that exist—which party controls the legislature, what the campaign finance laws were prior to reform, and so forth—can be more precisely isolated and used as independent variables. Yet some of the basic features that are easy to take for granted in American studies—such as the existence of a two-party system or a bicameral legislature with an executive branch—are clearly consequential features but do not vary substantially in the state politics literature.

A third type of literature of relevance to this study is the emerging American literature that compares the responses of parties, politicians, and groups to the major reform landmarks in American political history. Here, the relevant comparisons are within the same system but across time. In his study of changes in American interest groups' election strategies, Franz (2008a) argues that interest group strategies are influenced by the political and legal context of each election cycle. Franz also argues, as do I, that interest groups respond to politicians' demands for different types of campaign assistance and that changes in campaign finance law are a codification of different types of demands. Likewise, Parker (2008; see also Parker and Coleman 2004) argues that political eras can be categorized according to the types of resources needed for election campaigns. For Parker, the post-BCRA political environment represents a fourth era of campaign organization in which interest groups have a newfound ability to act independently of politicians and parties. While Parker's book is not solely about interest groups, he provides a substantial role for extralegal developments—for tactical changes by groups that originate not because of changes in the law but because of experimentation and learning by groups. These authors, as well as La Raja (2008), subscribe to the "resource theory" of campaigns, in which groups, parties, and candidates adapt their strategies according to the types of resources they possess or can attain. While I do not dispute the usefulness of such a theory in understanding American politics, such studies are limited in that the basic institutional structures in which groups operate remain relatively constant across time periods.

This study builds on these literatures but does so to highlight the role that institutional structure plays in creating and sustaining campaign-oriented interest groups. While I hope that this book will be of use to comparativists, I have deliberately framed my argument to address contemporary American campaign finance debates. The important details of both nations' reform proposals should be familiar enough to American audiences that readers can focus on the incentives politicians provide to groups in the two countries. The similar nature of the two countries' reforms brings about a number of questions of importance both in a comparative context and in the context of American and Canadian politics. In the American case, what effect would greater party discipline have on groups' activities? What effect does divided government have on groups' activities? What effect would more stringent restrictions on group speech, more comprehensive public funding, stricter contribution limits, or the abolition of political action committees have on group activities? In the Canadian case, how would reform intersect with fixed election dates, relaxed party discipline, or a greater role for the Senate? For that matter, what will be the effect of a rollback in campaign finance laws, such as the *Citizens United* decision in the United States or the proposed curbs on public funding of parties in Canada? This study uses similar campaign finance reforms to look at the potential future interactions of reform and institutional changes and at the next steps in the reform agenda.

The groups and their policy goals should likewise be sufficiently familiar that readers can focus on the context in which groups seek to achieve their goals. The possibility of close relationships between American and Canadian groups, the shared cultural and policy framework of group activities, and, in some cases, the need simultaneously to develop proposals in both countries to address shared problems or border issues enables one again to ask several questions pertinent to the interest group literature. How closely do groups in different countries observe each other's electoral strategies? To what extent do groups learn from their allies or their competitors in developing responses to changes in their permissible activities? How do small variations in campaign finance law affect groups? And how do campaign finance laws intersect with institutional arrangements in shaping groups' decisions about electioneering, contributing, or collaboration? Holding the groups themselves constant or at least identifying similar group types enables one to hold the group or issue context, the cultural context, and the type of reform constant while varying the institutions.

This type of endeavor is necessarily qualitative in nature. In contrast to most comparative campaign finance studies, the precise laws, pre- and postreform, regarding contributions or independent expenditures are similar enough that one can make general claims about their intent or scope, but they are not similar enough that simply providing financial data will be particularly illuminating. What matters instead are the groups' views on what they could do before reform, what they can do following reform, and what factors influenced changes in their activities. The universe of prominent groups in electoral campaigns in the United States and Canada is small enough that I have included enough groups from each country to come close to providing a comprehensive account of groups' response to reform. An added benefit of the qualitative approach here, however, is that readers can get a flavor for individual decisions, particular types of group innovations, and the issues and personalities that shape interest group activities in the United States and Canada. This is not a story about individuals or individual groups per se, but individual choices and innovations matter even in a context where broader, impersonal institutional arrangements shape choices.

Outline of the Book

This book addresses two basic questions. Part 1 of the book comprises three chapters that address the causes of reform: How much of a role did groups play in bringing about reform in the United States and Canada, and how did the two nations' reform proposals address group activities of the 1980s and 1990s? Chapter 1 summarizes the relationship between the American and Canadian interest group literatures, with a particular focus on pluralist and neopluralist arguments about the ways in which politicians have sought to use interest groups to further aims and to shape legal options. Both the American and Canadian interest group literatures have used this notion as a starting point, but differences in the two countries' political institutions have pushed interest groups in different directions. In the American case, interest groups have traditionally had numerous ways to influence elections, while the more closed Canadian system has left organized interests in a more subordinate position in their relationship with political parties. Chapter 1 also summarizes the major theoretical variables to be considered here. Assessing the consequences of reform requires distinguishing between group responses to reform, group responses to political events, and evolving group adaptations and technological innovations. Identifying differences between responses in the two countries also requires distinguishing between the effects of political culture, political institutions, and political events in the two countries and accounting for the fact that groups within each system have contacts in the other country and can learn about their political options from observing events across the border.

In chapter 2, I document the development of interest groups' roles in elections in both countries during the 1970s, 1980s, and 1990s. In both systems, the perception that interest groups had acquired inappropriate means of influencing elections had gained wide currency by the end of the 1990s, but the extent to which groups had in fact gained a major role in election politics differed substantially in the two systems. In America, group spending, whether through contributions or independent expenditures, had grown to the point that groups indeed had a major voice in presidential and congressional elections by 2000. Canada's groups had many of the same options as American groups, but the nature of Canadian elections had led groups to be far less able and willing to influence elections except in extraordinary circumstances. By the time that reform legislation had been implemented, the somewhat weaker American legislation was presented as a means of curbing a trend that was quite observable to the public, while the Canadian reform legislation, which closed off many avenues of group spending, was seen as a means of forestalling a trend that had not yet actually come to pass. That is, the American legislation was at most a means of tempering group activities of which politicians may have disapproved but that were nevertheless seen as being at least somewhat legitimate, while the Canadian legislation was a means of preventing Canadian politics from becoming too much like American politics. Chapter 3 describes the two nations' reform packages and the degree to which they addressed group activities. While neither reform package was solely or even primarily about these activities, the two packages were ostensibly aimed at curbing some group practices seen as harmful to the political system, to candidates, and to parties.

The second, more central question of this book, addressed in chapters 4–8, is how groups adapted to these reforms. Chapter 4 provides data on changes in overall group spending and candidate and party fund-raising.

These data show the systemic consequences of reform but do not necessarily capture the less measurable changes in group activities. Accordingly, chapters 5 and 6 draw on interviews with political directors of labor unions, business associations, and advocacy groups in the United States and Canada to assess the changes in interest groups' election-related activities during the 2000s. Chapter 5 addresses changes in American interest group behavior during the elections surrounding the 2002 implementation of BCRA, with some attention as well to the 2006 and 2008 elections. Chapter 6 addresses changes in Canadian group activities in the elections before and after the 2003 passage of the CEA amendments, the most substantial of the Canadian reform packages, with some attention to subsequent legislative changes and to the 2006 and 2008 Canadian elections. These chapters address the first set of theoretical distinctions—that between changes inspired by new campaign finance laws and those brought about by political circumstances or ongoing group innovations. Chapter 7 brings these two chapters together to assess differences between group responses in the two countries and the reasons for these differences.

Chapter 8 returns to the "democratic deficit" paradigm and the discussion of public sentiment regarding interest groups to draw some normative conclusions. What can one nation learn from the other about the proper role of groups in elections? Are either country's reforms worth emulating in the other country? And what are some of the consequences of limiting or redirecting groups' election activities? The comparison I present here ultimately brings us back to questions of political values. Despite a decade's worth of effort to change groups' role in electoral politics, it would be difficult to argue that these reforms have changed the way citizens view interest groups. In both countries, it may well be that only the most dedicated observers have noted profound changes in the role of groups in political campaigns. Yet much clearly has changed, and not all of these changes correspond to the rhetoric of the politicians who implemented the two countries' reform laws. In the end, the American reforms may provide a cautionary tale about the dangers of too little: a reform effort that began in the early 1990s left reformers exhausted and may have sapped politicians' will to undertake more meaningful and more urgently needed campaign finance reforms or to strike back when the Supreme Court invalidated components of the law. The Canadian reforms, conversely, may provide a cautionary tale about the dangers of doing too much: Canadian interest groups now largely sit on the sidelines in federal elections, and as a result, politicians and parties rather than the public dictate the issues at stake in campaigns.

Part I | The Roots of Reform

1 | Interest Group Studies in Canada and the United States

Within many subfields of political science, it has been possible to make advances in our knowledge of political institutions and behavior without placing the United States in a pivotal role. For example, many of the classic works on political parties, such as those of Duverger or Michels, have made enduring contributions to our knowledge of political parties as a feature of democracy despite the uneasy fit between American parties and those of other countries. The same cannot be said, however, about the study of organized interests—or at least the American and Canadian literature considered here provides no evidence of this phenomenon. Even early observers of American politics such as Alexis de Tocqueville (1966, 193) have contended that organized interests are a peculiarly American phenomenon. When one peruses Canadian literature on interest groups, one is struck by the fact that many of the basic claims made about interest groups are derived from studies of American interest group politics and that much of what is known about the role of formally recognized non-governmental groups in politics is derived from the studies of, among others, Americanists E. E. Schattschneider, David Truman, Robert Dahl, and V. O. Key. Each of these studies began with a consideration of group politics within the framework of American political institutions, but perhaps because few other countries have as sustained a history of officially recognized groups within their political systems, these studies have been taken as starting points in looking at other countries in which groups subsequently developed independently of the party or class system.

Within the study of American politics, one striking claim in the early literature on interest groups was that groups tend to be created—or at least to be recognized—by politicians in ways that advance politicians' interests. Early in his landmark study of parties and groups (1964), Key discusses the dependence of groups on government. While Key begins by noting the centrality of parties to American politics, he quickly points out that one must understand group interests before seeking to understand parties:

> The exercise of the power of governance consists in large degree in the advancement of legitimate group objectives, in the reconciliation and mediation of conflicting group ambitions, and in the restraint of group tendencies judged to be socially destructive. (17)

This claim wound up not being central in the 1950s pluralist literature, although it did become important for the "neopluralists" of the 1970s (Smith 2008, 22), who argued that politicians used groups strategically to communicate with the public. While this claim might be said to apply to groups in a general context—for example, to regional groups, ethnic groups, linguistic groups, classes, and so forth—Key and others writing after him applied this perspective in a slightly more narrow fashion to formally constituted nongovernmental organizations such as labor unions, business associations, and later what Berry (1999), a strong proponent of this neopluralist framework, denotes as "postmaterialist" groups such as environmental or civil rights organizations.

In this perspective, government has the ability to define the legal means by which groups can engage in politics and to alter the laws governing group activities when such alterations advantage those within government. Within the areas of legislative politics or electoral politics, such laws include defining the legal parameters of lobbying, campaign contributions, organizations' tax statuses, or organizations' rights to discuss political affairs with the public. Within twentieth-century American politics, some observers have taken the encouragement given by government to the formation of various interests, such as the Chamber of Commerce (Wilson 1981, 58–59), the prohibition on direct corporate or labor contributions to politicians, and the creation of political action committees to be political decisions aimed at the advantage of those whom these groups would support.

Yet while many students of interest groups generally accept the neopluralist conception, this perspective is rarely made explicit in studies of campaign finance or of interest groups' role in campaigns. In this chapter, I call attention to the common starting point of American and Canadian interest group studies, summarizing the role political institutions in the two countries have played in the development of the two nations' interest group literatures. Because of the greater role of political parties in the Canadian system, Canadian studies have stayed far closer to Key's original conception of groups as entities serving politicians than have American studies. Scholars have drawn on many examples of ways in which Canadian politicians have exerted control over groups, either restraining their activities or defining which types of group activities (or even which types of groups) are legitimate. These literatures provide the key to understanding two salient differences in the adaptations by groups in the two countries to changes in campaign finance law: first, why American reforms have only imperfectly sought to redirect groups' political activities, while Canadian reforms have sought to restrict them; and second, why American reforms have had little effect on those groups that wish to engage in electoral politics, while Canadian reforms have encouraged a framework in which many citizens see groups as an alternative to electoral politics.

To begin this argument, I consider three major areas of inquiry regarding interest groups: groups' acquisition and use of resources, groups' relationships with politicians, and groups' relationships with the public. Throughout, I begin with what is known about American groups before moving on to consider how our understanding of American groups can be enriched through comparison with Canada.

Group Resources

Within the American interest group literature, the most common resource categories are money, membership, and to a lesser extent group reputation. A group that has substantial financial resources but few members, for example, may effectively distribute money to politicians or conduct advertising campaigns, but it cannot necessarily influence elections by inspiring members to vote. Conversely, groups that have a large membership base but little money may influence election outcomes inexpensively (by encouraging members to support particular candidates) but may not have the ability to provide financial assistance to candidates. And a group with a reputation for policy expertise or for adherence to a particular point of view may influence politicians and sympathetic voters simply by virtue of endorsing a particular candidate or policy proposal. In some instances, groups with different types of resources can work closely together—for example, smaller groups can signal their preferences to wealthier groups, or coalitions between different group types can divide up the ways in which candidate support is provided.

One paradigm that seeks to distinguish group activities according to these resource characteristics is the "push/pull" distinction (see Boatright et al. 2003, 2006; Malbin 2003). This paradigm distinguishes between money that is "pushed" into the system by partisan or ideologically charged groups and money that is "pulled" into the system by rent-seeking politicians. This distinction roughly parallels the distinction often made between influence-seeking and access-seeking groups in politics. This paradigm also maps neatly onto different types of groups. Table 1.1 shows the Boatright et al. distinctions between group types according to their resources and their willingness to use their resources either directly to support political candidates or to advocate for issues independently of candidates.

This push/pull paradigm provides a convenient means of mapping political reforms onto group types, but it contains the assumption that within the American system, politicians can pick and choose among groups and advantage or disadvantage particular group types. This paradigm has not traditionally been used to analyze governmental control over group resources. A more common paradigm is the "hydraulic theory." In this theory, money, like water, will continue to seep into the political system. Reforms can change the direction that the money takes, but it will eventually seep back into the system through loopholes in the law. Arguments in favor of this theory range from those of reform advocates such as John McCain, who believe that reform will be needed at regular intervals to repair leaks in the system, to those of libertarian critics of group regulation, who have argued that the best means of addressing the role of money in politics is to provide clear channels for it to take and then to try to maximize transparency and provide voters with the tools to observe the flow of money into the system (see, e.g., Smith 2001, 220–25).

One can adjudicate between these two theories in two different ways. First, one cannot simply assume that wealthy organizations will be major political contributors or that large organizations will necessarily have politically active members. As table 1.2 shows, it is difficult to draw a line from any particular group type to its political activities.[1] Many of the same organizations appear in each column, but important differences exist. Some of the largest groups in terms of membership (such as the AARP) do not engage in elections at all; some of the most influential groups, such as the American Israel Public Affairs Committee, are neither large nor wealthy in comparison to the other groups in the table. And many groups that have substantial resources adopt a relatively bipartisan strategy, giving small contributions to many candidates, while others spend heavily on independent advocacy. Whatever type of resources one is considering, they alone do not dictate political activity if the group is not motivated to engage in a particular type of politics.

TABLE 1.1. Group Resources and Political Activities

	Business/ Industry	Peak Business	"Shell" Group	Labor Union	Issue Advocacy
Membership	Individuals (restricted class)	Corporations	Often undisclosed; generally corporations	Individuals—generally involuntary	Individuals—voluntary
Financial resources	Large or small—depend on size of business	Generally large	Generally large	Generally large but depends on size of union	Large or small—depends on size of group
Type of resources	Generally hard money	Hard and soft money	Primarily soft money	Hard and soft money; mostly soft	Hard and soft money; mostly soft
Campaign contributions	Frequent; cannot bundle	Frequent; cannot bundle but often institute giving programs	None	Frequent but a small percentage of budget	Frequent but a small percentage of budget
Advertising	Infrequent	Frequent	Frequent; generally sole purpose of group	Frequent for larger unions	Frequent
Member communications	Frequent but of limited use given size of membership	Frequent but of limited use given agreement among members	Infrequent	Frequent; useful because members may not always subscribe to union position	Frequent but of limited use given agreement among members
Mobilization (of non-members)	Can work to mobilize employees	Can work to mobilize member corporations' employees	Frequent	Infrequent	Frequent

Source: Adapted from Boatright et al. 2003.

TABLE 1.2. Rankings of Interest Groups in Selected Categories

(1) Most Effective Interest Groups	(2) PAC Receipts	(3) PAC Contributions	(4) Independent Expenditures	(5) Internal Communication Costs
National Rifle Association (NRA)	Service Employees International Union (SEIU)	National Association of Realtors	SEIU	AFT
American Association of Retired Persons	EMILY's List	AT&T	MoveOn.org	AFSCME
National Federation of Independent Businesses (NFIB)	MoveOn.org	IBEW	National Association of Realtors	SEIU
America-Israel PAC (AIPAC)	American Federation of State, County, and Municipal Employees (AFSCME)	Operating Engineers' Union	Club for Growth	National Abortion Rights Action League (NARAL)
American Association for Justice (AAJ)	American Federation of Teachers (AFT)	American Bankers Association	AFSCME	Change to Win
AFL-CIO	International Brotherhood of Electrical Workers (IBEW)	NBWA	EMILY's List	National Association of Realtors
Chamber of Commerce	National Association of Realtors	Airline Pilots Association	AFT	National Education Association
National Beer Wholesalers Association (NBWA)	NRA	National Auto Dealers Association	Life and Liberty PAC	National Right to Life
National Association of Realtors	International Brotherhood of Teamsters	AAJ	Defenders of Wildlife	Culinary Workers
National Association of Manufacturers	Laborers International Union of North America (LIUNA)	International Association of Firefighters (IAFF)	IAFF	Machinists' Union

Source: (column 1), 2001 *Fortune* Power 25; Birnbaum and Newell 2001; (columns 2–5), Center for Responsive Politics, www.opensecrets.org (data for 2008 election cycle).

However, if one draws a line in the reverse direction—from political activities to group characteristics—campaign contributions, advertising expenditures, and independent expenditures clearly map onto particular types of groups. Table 1.3 notes some of the patterns in which types of groups appear in each column of table 1.2. The descriptions in table 1.3 show that groups seek niches in their political activity that correspond closely to the types of resources the groups command.

To what extent can these American categories be used to make general claims about interest group politics in other nations? The motivations for political activity and the politicization of group members should be roughly similar in other democratic countries. Businesses, for example, can be ex-

TABLE 1.3. Group Strengths by Type

Group Type	Examples	Rankings	Resource Strength
Labor unions	SEIU AFSCME AFT	Well represented in PAC receipts, independent expenditures, and communication expenditures	Membership, money— these tend to be large organizations with large treasury funds
Trade associations	National Association of Realtors NBWA National Auto Dealers Association	Well represented in PAC contributions	Money—these groups tend to contribute to sympathetic candidates but rarely take an overtly partisan stance
Peak business associations	U.S. Chamber of Commerce NFIB	Ranked high for effectiveness	Money, reputation— these groups can spend money on elections, but their spending is often a signal of sentiment with the business community
Advocacy group, large membership	MoveOn.org NARAL NRA	Ranked high for effectiveness	Membership, reputation
Advocacy group, small membership	EMILY's List Club for Growth	Some ranked high in independent expenditures, PAC receipts	Money—membership in these groups involves a commitment to contribute to the group and to candidates

pected in other countries to have similarly large resources but to lack the motivation to tie themselves to a strong ideology or to a particular political party when there is the risk that that party may not always hold power. Similarly, organized labor is likely to have a large membership base but one that is not in itself always prolabor (see Freeman 2003). And because individual members join precisely to advance the group's issues, issue groups may have dependable members and an incentive to educate the public about their issues, but these groups should vary in size and in the degree to which they wish to connect themselves to a particular political party. In broad strokes, then, these characteristics ought to be generalizable.[2]

However, the activities linked to particular group types are not necessarily options in different countries. One might argue, for example, that advocacy groups may wish to educate the public about particular politicians' actions on issues of concern but may not necessarily have the legal means to do so or may not have the same means in different countries, or politicians may not provide the public with the information necessary to draw these connections.

Groups and Politicians

The American Perspective

Dating back to the *Federalist Papers,* the conventional American view has been that organized interests are a potentially harmful but unavoidable feature of politics. It is not uncommon for politicians to rail against "special interests," but more often than not, politicians define such interests primarily as those that oppose the politicians' own interests. During the explosion of interest group studies in the 1950s, many political scientists argued that groups could, in fact, be beneficial to politicians by aggregating the diffuse, often uninformed views of citizens, by providing heuristics for politicians in their decisions, and in providing technical expertise to which politicians might not otherwise have access. This theme remains a major thread in lobbying literature.

Politicians have at times encouraged the creation of groups for just such purposes. Beyond the creation of interest groups, the creation during the 1970s of political action committees (PACs), specifically for the purpose of providing group contributions to politicians, has often been read as a means by which politicians encouraged a particular type of group formation. A flurry of literature during the 1970s bemoaned the rise of PACs, arguing that American politicians were now more dependent on groups than on parties (for a review, see Sabato 1984). By the late 1990s, however, many political scientists argued that PACs provided a means by which group support for politicians could be diffused and that the soft money reforms of 1979 enabled parties to reassert control over groups (see, e.g., Parker and Coleman 2004). Politicians might be more dependent on groups in general but were not necessarily beholden to any one group or type of groups; too much depends on circumstances, popular support for an issue, a legislator's reelection prospects, and a host of other factors (see Baumgartner and Leech 1998, 128–34; Smith 1995). With the rise in party discipline within Congress during the 1990s and the increasing polarization between the parties, many groups were forced to take sides—or at least were encouraged by politicians to take sides. Groups were not necessarily subservient to the party organizations, but many of the more prominent groups became part of one or the other party network. By this point, talk about any opposition between groups and parties had become a thing of the past.

PACs proliferated during the 1970s, however, with their numbers growing from 608 in 1974 to 2,551 in 1980 (Ornstein, Mann, and Malbin 2002, 106). The number of PACs continued to grow, albeit at a slower pace, until it topped 4,000 by the early 1990s. It would be a stretch, however, to contend that more than a small number of these PACs sought to direct congressional activity. Most research on PACs contended that they were a means of ensuring access to members of Congress. The chairman of the Democratic Congressional Campaign Committee during the 1980s, Tony Coelho, is often credited with having persuaded business PACs that the Democrats would be the majority party for the foreseeable future and that PAC contributions would ensure continued access to congressional leaders (Jackson 1988, 82–87). Research on the link between PAC contributions and legislative outcomes or legislative voting has yielded decidedly mixed results (for a summary, see Baumgartner and Leech 1998, 136), a fact that supports the notion that politicians may have more control over PACs than PACs have over politicians. Similar arguments have been made about soft money contributions to the parties.

During the 1990s, many previously bipartisan PACs became more willing to side with one party. Part of the switch from Democratic support to Republican support by PACs in general may have simply been a desire to support the majority party, and part of this switch may have reflected some degree of ideological sorting—Republican-leaning groups may have given a slightly larger percentage of their money to Democrats because they were the majority party during the 1970s and 1980s, but when Republicans gained control of Congress in 1994, these groups tilted more heavily toward the Republicans than they had previously tilted toward the Democrats. Another reason for this switch, however, may have been politicians' increased demand for money. The average amount of money raised by successful House candidates doubled from $407,000 in 1990 to $840,000 in 2000.[3] Candidates' demands for PAC contributions increased partly because elections became more expensive but also partly because those who aspired to advance within the party saw fund-raising (and subsequent redistribution of that money to the party committees or to other members' campaign treasuries) as a means of doing so. In addition, the Republican Party, following Coelho's strategy, applied more pressure to groups to donate heavily to Republicans. Many of the larger groups that became more partisan and more political during the 1990s, such as the National Federation of Independent Businesses, may well have done so because they were seeking to play by the majority party's rules.

In short, one can read the existence of many American interest groups and the support they provide to politicians as a function of the demand for group support from politicians. Many basic institutional features of the American political system encourage groups to engage in election politics but discourage groups from becoming too closely allied with one party. First, the American party system is sufficiently decentralized that groups seeking to have an effect on legislation tend to support candidates, not parties. Second, interest groups that value access to politicians cannot help but notice that more than 90 percent of House and Senate incumbents are reelected; groups thus are likely overwhelmingly to support incumbents. Third, the level of party discipline is weak enough that almost all but the most partisan groups tend to support candidates of both parties. And fourth, groups that care about particular policies generally can look to many members of Congress to advance their interests on these policies. Committees and committee chairs have substantial opportunity in drafting or amending legislation, and many members who have introduced prominent pieces of legislation on particular issues become active on these topics not because they are in positions of power but simply because they have taken an interest in these issues.

This quick outline of events suggests that groups became more partisan in the 1990s because they were pushed to do so by politicians. In some cases, groups may have been directly encouraged to do so, as was the intention behind the K Street Project.[4] In the case of many advocacy groups, the motivation may have been a lack of sympathy from one party or the other. American interest groups have rarely been viewed as being entirely above the fray of partisan politics; the claims by Canadian parties that contributions are a "civic function" and a means of merely showing support for the existing political system would certainly ring hollow to American ears. Yet the literature on PACs suggests that if one is to explore changes in the relationships between groups and politicians, one should look beyond campaign contributions.

In so doing, one cannot avoid being drawn further into the thicket of distinctions in how the American tax code treats organized interests. The groups that have traditionally been the most active in American elections have been those that have adopted somewhat complex structures. 501(c)(4) organizations, which are permitted to conduct issue advocacy as long as this advocacy is directed at educating the public, were among the biggest spenders on campaign advertisements during the 1990s. 501(c)(5) organizations (labor unions) and 501(c)(6) organizations (business associations) also can play a role that stops short of direct political advocacy. Groups organized to comply with Section 527 of the tax code are permitted to engage in political advocacy as long as they do not coordinate their activities directly with candidates. Many of the larger interest groups maintain multiple funds—for example, many advocacy groups maintain a (c)(4) fund, a PAC, and a 527 fund.

Ongoing American interest groups (as opposed to funding conduits such as temporary coalitions or the 527 groups that appeared in 2004) have an incentive to be political but not necessarily partisan. They have a brand-name reputation to protect and a defined nongeographic constituency to represent, two goals politicians do not necessarily share. Although some prominent groups do not maintain PACs or have a policy against making campaign contributions, most groups see contributing to politicians as a relatively benign activity that ultimately has little effect on election outcomes but that entitles these groups to some consideration from lawmakers. When groups have taken on a role as extensions of the parties or party factions or as part of an extended party network, they have generally done so to meet the demands of politicians or to address areas in which the parties have proven deficient. To the extent that the American public has taken a dim view of groups' role in the political process, it has done so arguably as a consequence of politicians' appeals. Both parties tend to denigrate the role of groups in politics and to cast themselves as defenders of individuals' rights and benefits, but the groups that have been a staple of politicians' appeals have allied with their opponents. Teachers' unions and "big labor" have tended to be criticized from the right, while business groups have tended to be criticized from the left.

The fact that both parties have encouraged group formation and depended on groups for support has tended to blunt politicians' desire to restrain groups in general rather than simply to restrain groups with which they disagree.

The Canadian Perspective

The relationship between groups and politicians is somewhat less clear in the Canadian case, in part because the major parties have been more disciplined than American parties and have been less dependent on groups for campaign support. Canada has a less clear separation of powers than is the case in the United States. The Canadian executive branch is integrated into and responsible to the legislature. The Canadian prime minister is the leader of the party with the most seats in the House of Commons, and executive branch officials are appointed by the prime minister (see Savoie 1999, 87). Although Canada has a Senate, it is far less powerful than the U.S. Senate. Canadian members of Parliament (MPs) are elected in the same fashion as U.S. House members—that is, they represent geographically defined districts, known in Canada as ridings—but their electoral success has more to do with support for the party than for the individual MP (Blais et al. 2003). While most MPs reside in their ridings, they can change ridings, or the party can protect its leaders by having them run in safe districts. As in other parliamentary systems, the governing party usually holds the majority of seats; in the rare instance where no party holds a majority, the party with the most seats in the House of Commons forms a minority government.[5] Canadian elections are not held at fixed intervals, as in the United States; they are called by the governing party at least once every five years or are brought on by the governing party's defeat in a vote of confidence in the House of Commons. Although Parliament passed legislation in 2007 establishing a four-year election cycle (with the next election scheduled for 2009), this did not stop Prime Minister Stephen Harper from calling an election in 2008, and elections can still be triggered by a confidence vote.

The fact that elections have not occurred on a fixed calendar has several important consequences for interest groups. American interest groups can operate with clear electoral goals in mind and can steadily work toward those goals, but Canadian groups cannot. Canadian groups and parties alike are also unable to maintain an ongoing professional political staff. According to some observers, many consultants to Canadian groups and parties consequently tend to be Americans; the Canadian system is not conducive to sustaining a consulting industry (Cross 2004, 111). This system also ensures that the governing party can generally choose the terms of an election; contentious issues are subject to debate only if the governing party chooses to use an election as a referendum on a particular set of policies. For the most part, Canadian parties have avoided seeking to wage elections in this manner; the 1988 election, in which free trade with the United States was the main issue, is the major exception to this pattern.[6] Canadian interest groups thus have fewer opportunities to appeal to the public or the electorate than do American groups (Engelmann and Schwartz 1975, 143).

Another consequential difference is that MPs are expected to support their party on most votes. Although party leaders have declared some votes (often on social issues such as abortion or same-sex marriage) to be "free votes," in which MPs vote their conscience, not the party line, these votes tend not to be on major policy issues, and the outcome is often clear in advance (Smith 2005, 83). Incumbent MPs have a small "personal vote" (see Blais et al. 2003; Ferejohn and Gaines 1991), but this vote is smaller than in the United States and is primarily a consequence of constituency service or of a reputation for policy expertise, not a consequence of deviation from party positions. Interest groups, then, may seek to attack a particularly visible MP but cannot influence individual members' positions by doing so. Interest groups thus have little incentive to lobby individual members (Engelmann and Schwartz 1975, 143), less incentive to target individual MPs for support or opposition than is the case in the United States, and even less incentive to work with members of parties other than the governing party. Interest groups thus seek to work with the cabinet or the bureaucracy, two avenues that steer them away from electoral politics. Presthus (1973) claims that this approach is one of "elite accommodation," with groups joining the parties in seeking to influence decisions outside of the electoral arena.

This arrangement has been shaken somewhat by changes in the fortunes of Canadian parties. The system that prevailed from the 1920s until the 1993 election was generally referred to as a "party brokerage" system, in which the Liberal Party and the Progressive Conservative Party sought to ward off divisive conflicts in part to avoid exacerbating the geographic conflicts between Quebec, Ontario, and the western provinces.[7] One important corollary to the brokerage concept is that the parties did not cultivate enduring voter identification with the parties (as have American parties) and have reversed their positions on major issues frequently enough that despite high levels of party discipline, the two major parties have not maintained consistent ideological distinctions.

During the 1990s, the Progressive Conservative Party splintered into two parties, the predominantly western and populist Reform Party and the rump Progressive Conservative Party. This split enabled the Liberals to govern without unified opposition from 1993 to 2004. The Reform Party changed its name to the Canadian Alliance Party in 2000, and in 2004, the Progressive Conservative Party and the Canadian Alliance Party merged to form the Conservative Party, somewhat unifying the opposition. A series of scandals within the Liberal Party enabled the Conservative Party to establish a minority government in 2006. The formation of the Reform Party was abetted by the work of several conservative interest groups, most notably the National Citizens Coalition and the Canadian Taxpayers Federation. The Conservative Party is more conservative than were the Progressive Conservatives but has tacked more to the center than did the western populist parties and groups that preceded it.

Canadian and American interest groups also operate in strikingly different legal environments. Young (2004) has contended that the U.S. Supreme Court's *Buckley v. Valeo* decision equating contributions with free speech has no clear parallel in Canada and has almost singlehandedly placed the two countries' campaign finance reform movements on different trajectories. As Manfredi and Rush (2008) argue, some Canadian Supreme Court justices, most notably Beverly McLachlin, have advocated the *Buckley* approach, but it has not held sway in decisions limiting party expenditures, legitimating public financing, or restricting interest group advocacy. When this legal framework is coupled with Canadian majority party's ability quickly to pass sweeping legislation, the difference in groups' abilities to influence decisions regarding financing becomes evident. Much of the debate regarding the passage of BCRA, for example, revolved not only around the wisdom of the law itself but also whether it would satisfy a Supreme Court that, thirty years later, still largely accepts the *Buckley* decision. Some aspects of reform in Canada, including the restrictions on group advocacy and eligibility of minor parties for public financing, have been shaped by Supreme Court decisions, but the legislative hearings on the 2003 CEA amendments included little discussion of the Court's potential views on the reforms.

A final salient difference is the degree of federalism in Canadian policy-making and consequently in group structure and activity. On many issues, most notably labor laws, provincial governments have more jurisdiction than does the federal government. Literature on Canadian interest groups often posits a multiplicity of access points for groups, but such arguments differ substantially from those made in the United States. The "multiple crack" theory (Schultz 1980; Thorburn 1985, 53) of Canadian interest group politics posits a large number of potential access points, but they are institutional access points, not, as in the case of American groups, individual access points. Insofar as regional differences and regional conflict in Canada are greater than in the United States, some observers have seen the absence of strong, centralized groups as evidence that groups are not politically relevant (Engelmann and Schwartz 1975, 149; Tuohy 1992). The greater strength of Canadian provincial governments relative to American state governments also can lead groups to downplay national strategies. Consequently, groups may mobilize members at the local or provincial level but demobilize them on federal issues (Kwavnick 1975; Thorburn 1985). In many instances, groups are more concerned with provincial elections than with federal elections. American groups have at times turned to state politics to achieve ends denied them at the federal level—the Web-based peak business group strategy discussed in chapter 5, for example, has been adopted in state-level legislative and judicial elections, and at the time of BCRA's passage, there was some discussion that state parties might become conduits for large corporate or labor contributions. The shifting of money from the federal to the state or provincial level is, however, nowhere near as common or as explicitly mentioned by American groups as it is in Canada.

These basic institutional differences have led to an interest group system that is less active, less powerful, and certainly less partisan than is the case in the United States. Canadians tend to see the American system as a looming specter whenever political changes are introduced. For example, some Canadians saw the intense interest group activity in the divisive 1988 free trade debate as a worrisome sign that the country's elections were becoming more like American elections (Sharpe and Braid 1992, 180). Canadian campaign finance debates at times refer to American PACs as harmful to the political system (see, e.g., Pross 1992, 174). And within the Canadian labor community, the financial ties between labor unions and the U.S. Democratic Party are often held up as a cautionary tale in the sense that the American two-party system encourages groups to ally themselves with parties but does not necessarily offer groups something in return (Neumann 2006). To the American observer, Canadian interest groups can appear weak, and the major Canadian parties can appear lacking in strong ideological commitments, but Canadian politicians and group leaders tend to see virtue in these arrangements. Canadian groups have remained weaker than American groups because Canadian politicians do not need groups working for them; party leaders can use the parties to advance their goals.

If one is to zero in on the patron/client relationship between Canadian parties and groups, perhaps the most illuminating place to begin is the indirect comparison between the United States and Canada presented by Leslie Pal (1993). For Pal, American interest groups exemplify for Canadians the dangers of groups adopting a confrontational stance toward government. Nonetheless, he argues, the Liberal Party under Pierre Trudeau saw the diffuse free-for-all of American group politics of the 1960s and 1970s as a means of moving past the enduring two-group conflict between francophones and anglophones or between Quebec and the rest of Canada. Pal's history of federal funding of groups in Canada argues that the ruling party observed the confrontational stance taken by American groups such as the National Organization for Women (NOW) and sought to co-opt emerging social movements by providing them with federal funding. This goal, Pal argues, served higher purposes than merely channeling group activities; given the emergence of Quebecois nationalism, support for nationally based groups enabled the government to argue that a multiplicity of diverse groups—including women's groups, ethnic associations, and language groups—was a part of Canada's national identity. That is, Canada is a multicultural rather than bicultural nation. Much of the discussion of the National Action Committee, Canada's largest feminist organization for much of this time, has focused on the degree to which funding constrained groups' ability to work against government goals or to engage in electoral activity (see Young 2000). Although Pal does not argue that the government overtly limited groups' political activities—and in fact argues that many groups, particularly ethnic groups, became *more* political after receiving government funding—he notes that at a minimum, groups now had allies within Parliament and remained focused on their immediate issues of concern instead of searching for new issues that might be helpful in raising funds (see also Pross 1975). To draw two American comparisons, several American groups (most notably the Chamber of Commerce) had their origins in federal funding programs, and during the 1970s, several groups were in effect created by federal antipoverty programs. Such groups, however, generally maintained a narrow issue focus while they continued to receive funds; they did not cast about (in the manner of contemporary groups such as MoveOn.org) for issues that would mobilize the public or encourage contributions. In sum, Pal's argument shows that many Canadian groups were set on a different path from their American counterparts in the early 1970s, and this development has continued to shape groups in more powerful ways than do campaign finance laws.

On a rhetorical level, several noteworthy differences exist between Canadian and American interest group studies of the past several decades. First, it is not infrequent to see Canadian interest groups presented as threats to the political parties. While some of the 1970s literature on party decline in the United States engaged this idea with reference to PACs, it is no longer seriously argued that U.S. interest groups compete with the parties for the allegiance of citizens. Yet Carty, Cross, and Young (2000, 93) contend that the proliferation of interest groups over the past thirty years in Canada has been a direct threat to the parties because groups can give citizens political voice without engaging in the regional compromises or brokerage that characterize political parties (see also Paltiel 1989a, 1989b; Young and Everitt 2004, 22–23). The parties have often responded by creating or encouraging internal caucuses to represent such issues (Carty, Cross, and Young 2000, 111) or, for governing parties, by appointing ministers in charge of advocacy portfolios (Galipeau 1989). Archer and Whitehorn (1997, 3) argue that during the 1980s, interest groups usurped the traditional party prerogative of establishing national priorities and strategies for confronting political issues. And MacKenzie (2005, 7) asserts that groups can and do entertain the option of becoming political parties. In the American case, some women's groups, environmental groups, and labor unions have toyed with the idea of establishing parties, but few have put the strategy into practice. In Canada, apart from the relationship between the Canadian Labour Congress and the New Democratic Party, the Green Party, the Christian Heritage Party, the Family Coalition Party, and the Feminist Party originated from interest groups, and the Reform Party had a relatively synchronous relationship with populist citizens groups such as the Canadian Taxpayers Federation and the National Citizens Coalition. Thus, there is some reason to envision Canadian interest groups as more of a threat to the parties, and if one contends that the brokerage function performed by the Liberal and Progressive Conservative Parties is (or was) necessary to hold together different regional factions in Canada, interest groups may well be seen as a threat to Canadian unity itself.

Some of the antigroup rhetoric clearly stems from politicians' experiences. Canadian politicians simply do not need interest groups as much as American elected officials do. Few Canadian interest groups have the resources to contribute to candidates, and as noted earlier, politicians have not seen businesses or labor unions that do contribute as interests. For many Canadian politicians, interest group activity in campaigns is often devoid of issue content, a means of making personal attacks to which an individual MP cannot respond. The "focused interventions" by interest groups in the 1980s that Pross (1992, 172) summarizes seem to have more to do with taking down individual members of Parliament than with advancing particular causes. As chapter 3 shows, attack ads aired late in the campaign season were a concern for American politicians and were the source of a few incumbents' losses in the 1990s. Because Canadian election campaigns are far shorter than American campaigns, the danger of an unanswered attack ad is even more acute.

Second, rhetoric surrounding groups has been much more extreme or ideological in Canada than in the United States. In the wake of the extensive support provided by the Canadian government for groups during the 1970s and 1980s, much of the rhetoric of the Reform movement took aim at "special interests" as groups that received advantages over individuals (see Laycock 2002, 38). According to Laycock, conservative activists sought to define equality as a matter primarily of individual, not group, rights, even though some of the most prominent actors in the Canadian Right during this time were groups themselves, such as the Canadian Taxpayers Federation and the National Citizens Coalition. The crucial difference was that these organizations comprised activist individuals—that is, the groups aggregated the views of citizens, not of members of distinct racial, ethnic, linguistic, or sexual categories. Such rhetoric is a feature of American politics as well, but American politics at least tacitly recognizes the legal standing of groups in politics. The Canadian debate takes place, however, in a context where sizable percentages of citizens claim to trust groups more than they trust political parties and where at least one category of groups—regional groups—is recognized as being an important component of Canadian identity (see Blais and Gidengil 1991).

In summary, then, the comparison between American and Canadian groups can inform the study of both nations in two different ways. First, the institutional and political arrangements of the United States and Canada push groups to take different approaches toward government. Second, both nations share a suspicion about interest group politics, but the Canadian case presents a clear example of how a distrust of groups is reflected in political arrangements. Canada has had more success than has the United States in limiting groups' role in politics. While Canada has had the ability to observe American interest group politics and draw lessons from the role of American groups, the institutions of Canada have enabled the country to develop a role for groups that reflects much of the antigroup rhetoric, while American discussions either have less impact or reflect a greater degree of insincerity in that politicians may decry group influence but ultimately fail to do anything about it.

Groups and the Public

Another strand of research on interest groups has focused only secondarily on the supply of group resources to politicians or the demand for group resources from politicians. Particularly among 501(c)(3) and 501(c)4 groups in the United States, much of the activity that might be defined as political is directed at shaping public opinion, not necessarily at directly influencing elections or politicians' decisions.

This arena has seen some of the more illuminating direct comparisons between American and Canadian groups. Schwartz (2006) considers the development of agrarian populist movements in the United States and Canada during the first half of the twentieth century. She notes that the Canadian populist movement coalesced around a political party (the Co-operative Commonwealth Federation), while the American movement's legacy is less clear. The past four decades have seen tensions with the Co-operative Commonwealth Federation's successor, the New Democratic Party (NDP), about how closely to ally itself with labor. The NDP has traditionally provided a formal role for union leaders in party governance. In the United States, the Democratic Party can be seen as maintaining a somewhat similar symbiotic relationship with organized labor, but this connection has never reached the sort of formal relationship that has occurred in Canada. The less formal arrangement may in part reflect the preferences of both the party and the unions, but it also no doubt is encouraged by Americans' somewhat lower regard for labor unions. While labor can effectively communicate with its members in the United States, it has had less success in communicating with the public, and the message of a party directly tied to labor undoubtedly would face similar obstacles. The NDP has defused such criticism in part because labor comprises a larger segment of the Canadian population as well as in part because it has pointed to periods of successful governance in some provinces and, more important, provinces other than those with the highest levels of union density.

Second, Hoberg (1997), Van Nijnatten (1996, 2003, 2004), and Pierce et al. (1992) have addressed the activities of environmental groups in the two countries. Pierce et al. hold the issue (acid rain) constant and consider adjacent areas of Michigan and Ontario to limit geographic effects. The authors find that despite a generally positive attitude toward groups on the part of Canadians, the ultimate political role of environmental groups remains murky; American groups appear to engage in virtually every aspect of politics to a greater degree than do Canadian groups. Local and provincial Canadian groups have maintained an issue-based focus in part because they are less likely to extend their activities into electoral politics, while groups that have played a greater role in national politics have done so primarily through endorsements and establishing reputations and only secondarily through direct political activism.

The third and perhaps most thoroughly analyzed comparison involves feminist movements within the United States and Canada. Young (2000), Vickers, Rankin, and Appelle (1993), Dobrowolsky (1998, 2000), and Black (1992) present studies of Canadian feminist groups that frequently refer to American groups. Sawer (2004) and Chappell (2002) also compare Canadian and Australian women's groups. All of these studies note that women's groups frequently shared information on their political strategies. According to Young, Canadian women's groups are difficult to disentangle from women's caucuses within the parties; the presence of such caucuses within each of the parties (except for the Reform Party) ensured that feminist issues rarely became partisan issues; and, with the exception of the 1988 election, women's groups were rarely major players in election politics. Despite the increased marginalization of the National Action Committee during the 1990s, women's groups in Canada ultimately had more success in many of their objectives than did longer-lasting American groups such as NOW. Young contends that the polarization of feminist issues in American politics ensured that a countermovement appeared fairly quickly, while in Canada, although antifeminist groups eventually appeared, they had nowhere near the clout that, for example, Phyllis Schlafly's Eagle Forum had in stopping the ratification of the Equal Rights Amendment.

These three comparisons show that groups' appeals to the public may eventually yield political benefits, but many participants in environmental groups, feminist groups, or social justice groups surely are not thinking first and foremost about their actions' effects on individual politicians. They are likely thinking more broadly—about changing citizens' minds, about influencing social consciousness regarding their issues of concern. These comparisons also show that lessons from one country cannot easily be applied to the other. In some cases, this is a slow process—a movement in one country brings about different results than a movement in the other because of small alterations to groups' structure or goals as their ideas work their way through the political process. In others, this process can be faster and more deliberate; within the feminist movement, many Canadian activists rejected American strategies long before they were played out within Canadian politics. In each of these cases, Canadian groups appear closer to the social movements that spawned them; the degree of institutionalization, for better or worse, is lower than it is among American groups.

Many of the most prominent groups in these arenas in both the United States and Canada are not known for their lobbying or for their clout in elections. In the United States, NOW remains a major advocate for feminist causes, but its PAC is somewhat of an afterthought, raising a mere $191,000 in 2004 and contributing just $43,000 of this money to politicians. Greenpeace, among the best-known environmental groups and the largest environmental group in Canada, has a high profile in the United States but does not maintain a PAC and is not regarded as an important player in American elections. For both groups, political activity is something to be carried out independent of election politics and fund-raising.

The line between American electoral politics and issue advocacy is fuzzy, however, as numerous proponents of regulating group activity can attest. One of the most important causes of BCRA was American groups' exploitation of this ambiguity. Likewise, the line between political and nonpolitical group spending has also been ambiguous. Tax-exempt 501(c)(3) and (c)(4) organizations are not permitted to make politics their primary activity, but few (c)(4) organizations provide the sort of transparency in their spending that eases investigations of this aspect of their operation.[8] Particularly for complex organizations, political money can be segregated into other funds to allow a group to maintain tax-exempt status or to allow tax deductions for contributions. And a third problematic area for American courts has been the determination of whether an interest group is coordinating a strategy of appealing to the public with the actions of candidates who would benefit from the group's strategy. The Federal Election Commission has launched several investigations into alleged coordination, with mixed results. In many instances, however, direct communication between groups and politicians is simply not necessary. Politicians can observe groups' activities, and groups can observe politicians' activities.

While politicians clearly have less control over group communications with the public than over group contributions to politicians, these American examples show that interest group communications with the public during election campaigns are replete with strategic calculations about how candidates will be helped or hurt by particular types of appeals. Groups here are allies of the parties—again, a part of an extended network of partisan activists—even if they are not exclusively in one political camp or the other. Institutional features are partially to blame. The regularity of American elections ensures that groups can plan their strategies around elections; even if a group does not want to be overtly political, it must take into account the political consequences of its communication with the public. The two-party American system ensures that what benefits one party hurts the other, so any issue-based appeal may be expected to have consequences. And recent political divisions, such as the narrow balance of power in Congress and the closeness of recent presidential races and corresponding need to consider the consequences of influencing the electoral votes of any state, ensure that groups must think through the consequences of appeals to the public.

Canadian groups engaging in any sort of advocacy work must also consider the political consequences of their actions, but just as the institutional constraints differ, so do the calculations groups must make. The fact that Canadian elections do not occur on a regular schedule means that groups cannot plan advocacy work around elections as easily as their American counterparts. Historically, Canadians have not perceived great differences between the two major parties, so any issue-based communication by groups will not necessarily have clear electoral consequences. Many Canadian groups have deliberately reduced their activities during elections to avoid giving the impression that they favor one party or the other. Exceptions exist—most notably the 1988 election—but they tend to be created by the parties, not by groups. Recent Canadian elections have also not been as consistently close or divisive as have American elections. Although Canada has now had three successive minority governments, throughout the 1990s the Liberals maintained a substantial edge over the other parties, and they did not face a strong, unified opposition party between 1993 and 2004. As many analysts have noted, the nature of party competition also differed dramatically across the provinces. During the 1990s, the Liberal Party competed against the Bloc Québécois in Quebec, against the Progressive Conservative Party in the maritime provinces, and against the Reform or Alliance Parties in Ontario; in western Canada, the Liberal Party in some instances ran a distant third to NDP and Alliance/Reform candidates. Groups seeking to communicate with the public thus needed to take into account a shifting array of parties, party positions, and potential beneficiaries or victims of their communications.

While some Canadian groups have practiced American-style issue advocacy and while enough Canadian politicians have worried about the consequences of such activity that these communications now have been restricted, many Canadian groups have worked to separate their appeals to the public from politics. Many groups believe that this strategy increases public acceptance of their message. One consequence, however, has been that some observers have argued that Canadian elections have become devoid of serious discussions of issues and have become captive to disputes over petty scandals or media discussions of politicians' personalities. In short, with the system loaded against issue-based communications by groups in elections, groups cannot influence elections but also cannot compel politicians to discuss issues that may be important to the public. This state of affairs may suit the interests of politicians as much if not more than do the extended partisan networks of politicians and groups in the United States, but the consequences differ strikingly. One system may breed heightened polarization, mobilization, and conflict, while the other may breed an issueless politics that can demobilize the public.

Changes in Interest Group Activities

A change in laws governing permissible interest group activities can alter group resources, the relationship between interest groups and politicians, and the relationship between groups and the public. Interest groups are, however, a moving target. That is, even if similar laws are passed at similar times, one must isolate changes in the law from changes that might have taken place anyway, changes that have come about for other reasons. In addition to legal changes, two reasons for evolving interest group strategies are relevant to this study—technological change or innovation and the historical or political context of group activities.

The economics of interest group advocacy changed substantially during the 1980s, 1990s, and 2000s as technological developments changed communications media. In the United States, interest groups shifted from a focus on broadcast television in the 1990s to a focus on cable television and Internet communications. This change was driven in part by declining television viewership and by the lower cost of targeting particular types of television viewers through cable channels and later by identifying types of Internet users. As the process of sorting the recipients of advocacy messages into particular niches became easier, groups could also fine-tune the content of their messages and could even begin to solicit contributions for themselves or candidates through new media.

Canadian groups can avail themselves of similar techniques, but they begin from a different place. Canada has little history of issue advocacy through television, in part because of its political ineffectiveness—as noted earlier, singling out particular legislators for praise or criticism makes less sense in Canada—and in part because of Canada's dispersed population. Group advocacy during the 1980s and 1990s was conducted primarily through the print media and was often aimed at the general public. In 1988, for example, some groups purchased advertisements in national newspapers to air their views on the United States–Canada Free Trade Agreement. Such advertisements may have reached many persuadable voters but sought to shape the policy debate and to influence media coverage as much as to communicate with voters. To take a more political example, during the 2008 prorogation of the Canadian Parliament, many groups also engaged in advocacy work discussing the suspension of Parliament, but given that groups could do little about it, their activities were again more about shaping discussion than about influencing politicians' actions (see Chase, Curry, and Clark 2008; Russell and Sossin 2009).[9]

Just as technological changes influence groups' options for communicating with citizens and with politicians, so political changes shape groups' motivations for communicating electoral messages. The polarization of American politics during the 1990s shaped groups' motivations for involvement in the electoral process. As the 2008 election showed, Democratic losses in 2002 and 2004 also inspired left-leaning groups and activists to work to redesign much of the party infrastructure. Led by organizations such as MoveOn.org, activist groups sought to exert pressure in the 2005 race for the position of chair of the Democratic National Committee and to lay the groundwork in recruiting candidates, identifying vulnerable Republican candidates, and compiling lists of party activists. Much of this work was accomplished through left-leaning blogs and through online fund-raising portals. Even earlier, many American groups were willing to put themselves into debt or to risk legal consequences for their activities because they perceived that their efforts might be pivotal.[10]

The lower degree of competitiveness for control of the Canadian government influenced groups' perceptions that political activities were worthwhile, but the fracturing of the PC Party, its reunification as the Conservative Party, and the Liberal Party's subsequent problems did not prompt a similar outpouring of group effort. Canada has had far more dramatic swings in the vote for its major parties over the past two decades than has the United States, but these swings may well work to the disadvantage of groups that seek to become involved in elections. It is difficult to imagine individual Canadian groups expecting that their issue might be pivotal when the major swings in partisan control, such as the 1993 disaster for the Progressive Conservative Party or the 2006 defeat of the Liberal Party, have been construed as referenda more on the competence of the governing party than on particular policy positions. The sort of incremental approach favored by American groups—a seat here, a seat there—would seem inapplicable either to influencing elections or to claiming credit after the election.

These three factors—legal changes, technological changes, and political changes—ultimately combine for groups, establishing a trajectory for the development of group politics and electoral activity. Subsequent chapters explore the relationship between these factors in the United States and Canada over the past decade, with special focus on the elections immediately before and after the passage of reform legislation. Many common themes emerge in the groups' responses, but the differences in group behavior speak to important differences between the countries.

Why Should We Expect Canadian and American Groups to Act the Same? Why Should We Expect Them to Act Differently?

At the risk of oversimplification, two factors explain why Canadian group responses might resemble those of American groups, and at least three factors—institutional, cultural, and historical—explain why responses to reform might differ in the two countries.[11]

The easiest argument for any similarities would be a contention that the two countries are similar in many relevant ways—despite differences in institutions, Canada and the United States share a first-past-the-post, geographically based system for electing legislators, and while cultural differences exist between the countries, political trends show more commonality than difference. A second explanation, however, also merits consideration—groups in Canada and the United States share information, observe each other's activities, and in some cases are formally connected.

For several reasons, however, divergence between the two countries might be expected. First, *institutional differences* shape group politics in the two countries. Canadian literature abounds with allegations that Canadian parties see interest groups as threats to their dominance (Archer and Whitehorn 1997, 3; Carty, Cross, and Young 2000, 93) and with accounts of co-optation of groups by the parties (Carty, Cross, and Young 2000, 111; Galipeau 1989; Pal 1993). Literature on American interest group politics often emphasizes the limited role of political parties and corresponding independence of legislators in making policy and therefore the numerous points of access within Congress for groups. The Canadian system is characterized by strong party discipline, which means that groups have little chance of influencing the actions of individual MPs. Canadian interest groups, then, have little incentive to intervene in elections and can be most effective, as Presthus (1973) has argued (see also Pross 1992, 42), in lobbying the cabinet or the bureaucracy than in appealing to individual MPs. In addition, the major "brokerage" parties in Canada historically have avoided taking contrasting stands on political issues to increase their ability to negotiate regionally based conflicts should they control government (Paltiel 1989a; Young and Everitt 2004, 22–23). This system provides groups few reasons to cement long-standing allegiances with the major parties. In the United States, ideological differences between the parties have created and reinforced group allegiances to the parties. Group-based interests in Canada are more frequently reflected by caucuses within the parties or by the formation of new parties than by the establishment of enduring nonparty organizations.

Second, despite my claims to the contrary in the introduction, *cultural differences* between the two countries may influence interest groups' role. Canadian interest group politics has been framed as a process of "elite accommodation" (Presthus 1973) in which groups are institutionalized through repeated informal contacts with political leaders. This theory corresponds to characterizations of Canadian culture as being (at least in the past) more deferential than American culture—as a culture in which groups have less interest in mobilizing the public behind issues or publicly airing group conflicts (Nevitte 1996). While Canadian constitutional debates of the past three decades have prominently recognized the multiplicity of groups present in the Canadian polity, in cultural terms a Canadian group is more likely to be defined according to geography than in terms of political interests (see Laycock 2002).

Third, *historical differences* between the two countries may have played a part in the development of interest groups. The major difference of note here is the level of state support for groups in Canada. The United States has never had such explicit government encouragement of groups; perhaps as a result, American groups have more consistently been involved in elections. The history of interest group activity in Canadian elections is

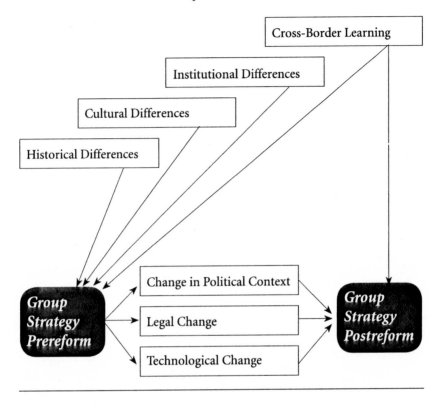

Fig. 1.1.   Influences on interest group strategy

therefore far more episodic than is the case in the United States. When Canadian groups have become involved in electioneering, the amounts spent have often been quite small, leading some scholars to argue that group advertising was geared more toward generating media coverage than toward swaying election results (see Carty and Eagles 2005).

In suggesting these broad theoretical categories, I do not mean to suggest that these three sets of differences are mutually exclusive. Culture shapes political institutions, institutions shape culture, both shape history, and so forth (see Lipset 1991). Institutional differences are perhaps the easiest explanation for many of the differences in how groups have responded to campaign finance reform, but I certainly would not rule out the possibility that political culture or the historical development of particular groups or issues in the two countries also matter. This book will examine three general explanations for group change and four different hypotheses (not including the claim to similarity, which is really a means of denying the potential impact of institutional, cultural, or historical differences) regarding reasons why interest group strategies in the United States and Canada might take similar or diverging paths. Figure 1.1 summarizes the variables in play, and subsequent chapters explore different means of evaluating and testing these hypotheses.

2 | Interest Group Politics of the 1990s and the Campaign Finance Reform Movement

The American and Canadian campaign finance reform bills were implemented at a time when citizens of both nations had developed substantial concerns that interest groups had come to play a far larger role than was the case during the 1970s and 1980s. Or, to put matters slightly differently, the two nations' campaign finance laws of the 1970s had immediate and to some extent predictable consequences in restraining group activities, but groups gradually found new ways of becoming involved in elections. The trajectory of groups' election-related activities did not necessarily take the same form in both countries, but parallels existed that are clearly reflected in the two nations' campaign finance laws of the 2000s.

In this chapter, I consider the changing role of interest groups during the 1990s. While BCRA and the Canadian reforms did not seek exclusively to limit or redirect group spending, the components of these laws that dealt with groups represented a clear response to legitimate concerns about group influence. Furthermore, to the extent that these laws adjusted the balance of party, candidate, and group spending, even some provisions not clearly directed at groups affected their ability to compete with the parties and with candidates for a voice in elections. This chapter sets the groundwork for considering the components of the nations' campaign finance changes, which are the subject of chapter 3.

American Interest Groups in the 1990s

Many American political scientists have spoken of the interest group "explosion" of the 1970s. In these accounts, the decade's reforms combined with the maturation of advocacy groups and social movements of the 1960s to bring about the institutionalization, often in the form of PACs, of a diverse array of organized interests. Studies of PAC behavior in the 1970s noted the use of independent expenditures, but the groups singled out—most notably, the National Conservative Political Action Committee—had stated intentions of effecting electoral change rather than ongoing issue niches (see, e.g., Sabato 1985, 96–107). Sabato's study of PACs' independent expenditures notes three explicitly political groups that spent in excess of $250,000 in the 1982 elections (the equivalent of $560,000 in 2009 dollars) and five issue-oriented groups and business groups (including the League of Conservation Voters [LCV] and the National Rifle Association [NRA]) that spent between $100,000 ($224,000 in 2009 dollars) and $250,000. Thus, some groups engaged in electoral activities, but their efforts were relatively small compared to what followed.

The 1990s were marked by an increased turn toward electoral politics by many of the largest interest groups. While the narrative presented here does not attempt to provide a comprehensive account of groups' role in politics during this decade, it does seek to situate the groups most affected by BCRA by illustrating their rapidly changing role, the ways in which this role brought about calls for reform, and the ways in which political strategies set in motion before BCRA put the groups on a trajectory that in many cases would lead them in directions that the architects of reform would not initially have predicted.

Increased Electoral Activity by Organized Labor

In a trajectory of group activities that precipitated the enactment of BCRA, the dramatic expansion in labor unions' political activity during the 1990s might be the best place to begin. Organized labor has several strengths in its political activity that render it unique among organized interests, and in the 1980s and 1990s, in response to the increasing electoral strength of the Republican Party, the AFL-CIO took advantage of all of these strengths. First and most notably, labor simply has more members than any other group type. As of 2000, organized labor comprised 13.4 percent of all workers, a figure that would continue to fall for the next several years but did so more slowly than it had fallen during the 1980s and early 1990s (Asher et al. 2001, 14; Bureau of Labor Statistics 2009).[1] Labor's 16.1 million members are unmatched by any other subset of organized interests. This number also ensures that if union members share political views, they can have the clout to influence a large number of elections without needing to speak to the broader public.

Second, labor has increasingly improved its ability to speak with a somewhat unified voice; despite occasional conflicts among union leaders, the majority of unions and union members belong to the AFL-CIO. At the time of BCRA's passage, approximately 80 percent of union members belonged to the AFL-CIO, which then comprised sixty international unions, spanning a wide variety of occupations. The antipathy between organized labor and President Ronald Reagan may have fueled a growing public sense that labor was in decline, but it also fostered a broader sense of purpose among labor union leaders and members.

Third, however, union members rarely have an option about joining; unlike advocacy group members, union members cannot automatically be assumed to share the views of their leaders, and occasional congressional efforts to implement "paycheck protection" laws that allow members to withhold the portion of their union dues used for political purposes have constantly worried union leaders. Many union members are not politicized, and a substantial minority of members have voted for Republican candidates even as union leaders have consistently supported Democrats. During the 1980s, Reagan and his successor, George H. W. Bush, garnered more than 40 percent of the votes of union members, and George W. Bush received 38 percent of the union vote in 2000. Between 1968 and 2000, only Jimmy Carter (in his first presidential campaign) and Bill Clinton (in his reelection campaign) received more than two-thirds of the union vote.[2]

Fourth, labor unions generally have had their greatest impact through internal communications and through soft money spending, not through their PACs. For example, while the AFL-CIO was spending an estimated $45 million on issue advocacy in 2000, its PAC, the Committee on Political Education, raised $1.74 million and spent $998,000. All 246 labor-affiliated PACs combined (including the PACs of union locals) contributed $52.6 million to candidates in 2000.[3]

Organized labor may have reached its high-water mark in terms of member mobilization in the 2000 election. Following the election of John Sweeney and his "New Voice" slate to lead the AFL-CIO in 1995, organized labor dramatically increased its involvement in presidential and congressional elections. Many observers have attributed the AFL-CIO's activism in the late 1990s to two linked factors: the Republican Party's success in the 1994 elections and Sweeney's leadership. Yet the roots of these activities extend even further back; as Dark (1999) contends, the seeds of today's politically active AFL-CIO lie in the Democratic Party reforms that followed the 1968 elections. During the 1950s and 1960s, labor's influence in candidate selection was frequently felt in the "smoke-filled rooms" of party conventions. Leaders of organized labor, for example, are said to have engineered John F. Kennedy's nomination in 1960, and Kennedy's choice to run in the primary in heavily Protestant West Virginia may have been a bid to convince labor leaders that he could motivate union voters as well as Protestants more generally. Under Sweeney's predecessor, Lane Kirkland, several large unions that had previously not been members joined the AFL-CIO; in addition, it expanded efforts to work with liberal advocacy groups, sought to couple its presidential endorsement with more extensive ground mobilization, and instituted a "face-to-face" mobilization program that trained shop stewards to meet with union members to discuss political matters (Dark 1999; Lichtenstein 2002, 249). Dissatisfaction with Kirkland, then, cannot necessarily be linked to his agenda for changing labor's political role.

Based solely on the amount of money labor spent under Kirkland, however, the implementation of this agenda seems to have been lacking. Following Sweeney's election, labor dramatically increased its spending on these activities as well as its efforts to reach out to nonunion members. In 1996, the AFL-CIO spent $10 million on internal communications, including appointing 131 coordinators to direct volunteers in congressional districts. The AFL-CIO also spent an estimated $25 million on radio and television advertisements, the majority of which criticized vulnerable Republican House members for prior votes on education, health care, and other issues that had been shown in surveys to resonate with the broader public. According to one estimate, this budget translated to an average of eight hundred airings in each of the targeted districts (Cigler 2000). As a point of comparison, the AFL-CIO spent only $3.3 million on media campaigns in 1994 (Francia 2006, 47).

This advertising campaign, coupled with AFL-CIO rhetoric about "taking back the House," attracted a substantial amount of media attention yet is not necessarily the most enduring legacy of labor's increased activism. The AFL-CIO's efforts did not help to elect a Democratic majority, although as Jacobson (1999) has shown, these advertisements were pivotal in defeating many of the eighteen Republican incumbents who lost. The ground campaign, however, was replicated and refined by labor and its allies over the next several elections. By 2000, labor was spending $46 million on election-related activities, but only $17.9 million of this amount went toward television advertising. Instead of relying primarily on advertisements, the AFL-CIO had developed a network of more than a thousand paid staff members plus many volunteers that registered voters and made direct contacts. One study estimated that in 2000, labor made more than 8 million telephone calls, sent 14 million pieces of mail and 60,000 e-mails, and distributed 2.5 million leaflets (Francia 2006, 60–65; see also Freeman 2003). This shift can be attributed in large part to the unions' measurements of the most effective means of communication.

In addition to their mobilization efforts, unions were also major soft money contributors to the Democratic Party in the 1996, 1998, and 2000 elections. According to PoliticalMoneyLine, the AFL-CIO contributed $776,251 in soft money in 1998, $760,000 in 2000, and $466,069 in 2002. All labor unions combined to contribute $10.3 million in in soft money in 1998, $30.3 million in 2000, and $35.9 million in 2002; almost all of these funds went to the Democrats. Internal dissatisfaction with the return on soft money contributions, however, led the AFL-CIO to tinker with its internal organization during the second half of the 1990s. Political director Steve Rosenthal, a longtime Sweeney protégé, had been appointed to lead the union's political wing when Sweeney became president. Rosenthal received more freedom than his predecessors, and he responded by dismantling the "marginal committees" that the union had maintained to oversee campaign contributions. According to political scientist Robin Gerber, Rosenthal made a conscious decision not to concentrate on raising PAC dollars, instead emphasizing educating and organizing members, activities that could be funded without drawing on PAC money (1999, 81–82). According to Gerber, the AFL-CIO also began identifying and mobilizing its members in competitive congressional districts, a task that previously had been left to the individual member unions. All of these activities centralized political power within the AFL-CIO to a greater degree than had been the case in the past.

The AFL-CIO also increased its activity in coalitions, a strategy toward which the union had begun moving under Kirkland. Under Sweeney, the AFL-CIO increased its involvement in coalitions with groups that advocated women's issues, civil rights, and the environment, including Citizen Action, the Coalition of Labor Union Women, the Labor Committee for Latin American Advancement, and Working Women Vote, among other organizations (Gerber 1999, 86). In 1996, the AFL-CIO began using college students as volunteers, and it later sought to organize graduate students on several campuses (Francia 2006, 61). This development reflects the AFL-CIO's changing membership and the relative strength of different groups, a desire for increased unity on the left, and the changing pedigrees of union leaders. As Dark (1999, 183) notes, "Many of the unionists involved in the New Voice coalition had cut their teeth on student, civil rights, and antiwar organizing during the 1960s. They were, in short, the descendants of the New Left, and the Sweeney victory now allowed this generation of activists to finally gain a secure position in the federation itself." But union leaders such as AFSCME's Larry Scanlon still criticized the AFL-CIO for failing to take a role in coalitions unless it was leading them (Moberg 2002).

Many of these changes occurred out of frustration with labor's waning political clout, and if one looks outside of the unions for results in the 1990s, the story is mixed. Organized labor enthusiastically backed Clinton in 1992, but the Clinton administration did not necessarily deliver everything that labor wanted. The issue with by far the highest profile for labor during the 1990s was free trade, in the guise of the North American Free Trade Agreement and the expansion of trade with China. On both issues, unions undertook substantial advertising campaigns, targeting congressional Democrats (albeit not in election years) as well as Republicans. On both issues, labor ultimately lost. According to David Moberg (2001, 28), during the Reagan administration, unions "headed for the bunkers, hoping that the Democrats could save them." When it became clear during the Clinton administration that labor simply lacked the votes in Congress and that the president would not help them on trade issues, unions were prompted to exercise far more independence from the Democratic Party than had previously been the case. Advertising campaigns, particularly those not undertaken close to the election, were run largely without the input of Democratic politicians. The end result of this growing independence was that although unions endorsed Al Gore early in the Democratic primary, the allegiance of the unions, particularly the industrial unions, was relatively tepid. The endorsement represented a pragmatic effort to bring the Democratic primary race to a quick conclusion. Following the 2000 election (and as he contemplated a 2004 bid), Gore appeared to command little support from the unions, and some observers believe that Sweeney's fervent backing of Gore prompted some dissatisfaction with Sweeney within the AFL-CIO (Judis 2000).

The Business Response

Business groups have been a part of the American political landscape as far back as the 1800s, yet political interest groups that represent business are of much more recent vintage. The first of the business association PACs were formed in the early 1960s, and they remain among the most influential—the American Medical PAC, the Business-Industry PAC, the National Association of Realtors PAC, and others (see Budde 1980). During much of the 1960s, 1970s, 1980s, and early 1990s, these organizations prioritized contributions to favored members of Congress, in part because of the Democratic Party's majority status in Congress through most of this period and in part because of direct outreach to the business community by Democratic leaders. With corporate PACs' desire for access to lawmakers, it was left to nonconnected PACs, such as BIPAC, to actually seek to change election outcomes in favor of business-friendly candidates.

Following the 1994 elections, business groups enjoyed substantially greater access in Congress than before, but few immediately began to change their political strategies. Business groups began to contribute more money to Republicans than had previously been the case, but this change was certainly to be expected given business groups' earlier support for incumbents. In fact, BIPAC senior vice president Bernadette Budde has contended that business became less involved in elections after 1994 because many corporations shifted their efforts from elections to lobbying (Nelson and Biersack 1999). The 1994 elections revealed a split between corporate PACs and association PACs. Some of the larger corporate PACs, for example, were surprised by the 1994 election, and even though they did not object to the Republican gains, they had not supported very many of the victorious challengers. Most notably, some observers have argued that AT&T's overwhelming loss in the vote on the 1996 Telecommunications Act stemmed from the company's tenuous ties to many junior Republicans and its lack of support even among members of Congress to whom AT&T had contributed (see Mutch 1994).

At the same time, several of the larger association PACs became more partisan and more political. In 1991, Jack Faris, a longtime Republican Party activist, became the president of the NFIB, and under his leadership, the group dramatically increased the size of its PAC (from $300,000 in 1992 to over $1,000,000 in 1996), increased the percentage of its money given to Republicans (from 86 percent in 1992 to 95 percent in 1996), and cemented its ties to the new House Republican leadership (Shaiko and Wallace 1999). The Chamber of Commerce followed suit by choosing former American Trucking Association president Thomas Donahue as its president and CEO in 1997, and BIPAC appointed a new and more politically aggressive CEO, former Senate sergeant-at-arms Greg Casey, in 1999.

In effect, no organized business effort to retain Republican control of Congress in 1996 took place until after the AFL-CIO had publicly announced its television advertising campaign and its intention to return the Democrats to majority status. A hastily convened series of meetings among leaders of the National Restaurant Association, the National Association of Wholesaler-Distributors, the Chamber of Commerce, the National Association of Manufacturers, the NFIB, and several smaller groups resulted in the formation of the Coalition: Americans Working for Real Change. The Coalition responded to AFL-CIO advertisements by running its own advertisements in thirty-seven congressional districts and may have helped to limit the effectiveness of labor's strategy (see Magleby 2000, 47–48). The Coalition included a site-selection committee, which analyzed AFL-CIO activity in each congressional district, studied the viability of the Democratic candidates and polling data in each race, and thereafter decided whether to run ads (Sandherr 2003). In this manner, the Coalition may well have functioned far more efficiently, in terms of the overall amount of money spent, than did the AFL-CIO.

When the AFL-CIO scaled back its advertising in 1998, however, the Coalition largely disbanded. Democratic gains in the 1998 and 2000 congressional elections put business groups on the defensive, but they had more difficulty responding to labor's new voter mobilization strategy than responding to its advertising strategy. Business groups dramatically increased their soft money contributions to the parties, particularly the Republicans, but this increase did not directly address labor's strategy.

Democrats gained four House seats in 1998 and two House seats and four Senate seats in 2000. Not all of the Democrats who won were conclusively antibusiness; for example, both Dennis Moore of Kansas, who defeated an incumbent in 1998, and Brad Carson of Oklahoma, who won an open Republican seat in 2000, won with substantial business support. But several of the priority races for business groups ended in defeat. Business groups spent $2.2 million on television advertisements in the 2000 Michigan Senate race, but Democrat Debbie Stabenow defeated Republican incumbent Spencer Abraham by sixty-five thousand votes (see Traugott 2003, 105). Similar narrow losses occurred in Washington and Missouri. Assessing the outcomes of 1998 and 2000, BIPAC's Greg Casey argued that businesses were too fixated on giving money to candidates and had failed to match labor in voter mobilization. In my 2002 interview with him, Casey singled out the Michigan race as a wake-up call to business groups: "We need to be as effective at being pro-us as [labor is] at being pro-them. I don't want to ape the unions, but they have done things effectively that we would be well served to try to emulate. We've got to come to the realization that their 42 percent turnout in Michigan was not just because they had the day off."[4]

Even as the Republican Party held off strong Democratic efforts to regain control of Congress in 1996 and 1998, then, business groups remained frustrated with their inability to counter labor's efforts. Given the very limited Democratic gains of these elections, this claim may appear disingenuous, but not until 2002 did business groups voice satisfaction at having outmaneuvered labor in mobilizing voters, marshaling resources to help in competitive races, and exerting enough control over elections to claim that they, not the Republican Party, had set voters' agenda.

Advocacy Groups Take to the Airwaves

While there is no simple story to tell regarding direct confrontation between advocacy groups and business or labor, advocacy groups on the left and right—but particularly on the left—had also come to play a more substantial role in electoral politics. During the 1990s, in response to change in Congress and to the growing number of competing interests, liberal groups increased the size of their PACs and lobbied aggressively on various legislative issues. Many of these groups also grew dramatically in membership during the 1980s and 1990s, and the total number of unconnected liberal PACs also grew (see Berry 1999, 145). Moreover, many of these groups capitalized on their name recognition in the media by very publicly endorsing candidates (Berry 1999, 97). But election retrospectives for 1994 and 1996 tend to discuss the role of conservative groups such as the Christian Coalition and the NRA, organized labor, or business groups. With the notable exception of the more explicitly political EMILY's List, observers credited few liberal groups with playing a major role in these election cycles apart from mailings and telephone calls to members. By 1998, some groups, perhaps in an attempt to emulate the AFL-CIO's 1996 electioneering strategy, had begun purchasing early television advertisements (Magleby 2000, 49–55). In 2000, many more of these groups had become more interested in electioneering communications and more able to purchase television advertisements.

The two most politically prominent environmental groups—the Sierra Club and the LCV—are typical of this trend. The Sierra Club was founded in 1892 but did not form a PAC until 1982, doing so largely out of concern about Reagan's policies (Cantor 1999). The PAC did not issue a presidential endorsement until the 1988 election. Prior to 1996, the Sierra Club's political activities were generally limited to endorsements and PAC contributions. The group dramatically expanded its direct mail fund-raising in 1996 and spent $3.5 million on voter education that year (Cantor 1999, 113). The Sierra Club purchased attack ads in the early 1996 Oregon Senate special election, seeking to help Democratic candidate Ron Wyden. In the 1996 and 1998 general elections, the group steadily expanded its issue advocacy spending, shepherding its resources to make large buys shortly before the election in competitive House races.

Similarly, the LCV engaged in fairly modest activities during the 1970s and 1980s. The LCV was founded in 1970 and has subsequently issued a National Environmental Scorecard discussing incumbent politicians' records. LCV has traditionally been a smaller, more Washington-focused group than the Sierra Club and has, as its name implies, been more concerned about politics than has the Sierra Club. LCV has been credited as far back as 1982 with independent expenditure and voter-contact work that made a difference in close House races (Sabato 1985, 97), but it expanded its efforts substantially in 1996. LCV expanded its professional staff in 1988 and opened field offices in several states. In 1996, LCV made an estimated $580,000 in independent expenditures, airing television ads in competitive Senate races that addressed local environmental concerns such as toxic waste and clean water (Mundo 1999, 124). Few of these ads directly referred to the Republican Party, but most aired within the final two months before the election. LCV also expanded its efforts to use voter files to profile voters for the purposes of direct mailings. In 1996, LCV also inaugurated its "Dirty Dozen" list, singling out members of Congress with particularly poor environmental records. This list generated a substantial amount of free media coverage, and in 2000 it was coupled with an "Environmental Champions" list of candidates with good environmental records, and a bundling program was developed.

This pattern of increased advocacy work was not distinctive to environmental groups. The National Abortion Rights Action League (now known as NARAL Pro-Choice America) followed a similar pattern. NARAL was formed in 1969, created a PAC in 1977, and provided contributions to incumbents throughout the 1980s. In response to adverse Supreme Court decisions, NARAL increased its membership in the late 1980s and initiated a three-million-dollar independent expenditure program in 1992 (Thomas 1999). This program involved more direct contact than did the environmental groups' programs, however; it consisted primarily of direct mail and telephone calls. In 1996, NARAL developed a poll-tested message aimed at the broader public. Its "Who Decides?" slogan, crafted to present a moderate, more libertarian message than other women's rights or abortion rights groups, was patterned after rights-based appeals made by groups such as the NRA (Saletan 2004). Like the Sierra Club, NARAL purchased advertisements in the Oregon special election, moving on to do advocacy work in twenty-two House races and seven Senate races.

Several other liberal advocacy groups followed this general pattern, if not the precise timing. Planned Parenthood largely eschewed electoral politics until 2000, when it expanded its independent expenditure work. The Human Rights Campaign, the largest gay and lesbian rights group, primarily focused on PAC contributions during the 1980s but began to turn to bundling and independent expenditures by the early 2000s. The NAACP inaugurated an independent expenditure program in 2000. And Handgun Control Inc. (now known as the Brady Campaign to Prevent Gun Violence) developed a "Dangerous Dozen" list, in emulation of the LCV, that singled out pro-gun-rights legislators and targeted independent expenditures against them in 1998 and 2000. Not all liberal groups followed this pattern—throughout this period, several explicitly political groups, such as EMILY's List, focused primarily on work for candidates—but advocacy groups had clearly become a larger force in congressional elections, if not yet presidential elections, by the close of the 1990s.

With one major exception, the NRA, conservative advocacy groups did not make the leap from grassroots advocacy work to independent expenditures and television advertising on quite the same scale as did liberal groups. Some antiabortion groups, such as the National Right to Life Committee (NRLC), increased their spending on mobilization and issue advocacy during this time, but evangelical groups such as the Christian Coalition never attained the same degree of institutionalization as liberal groups did during the 1980s and 1990s and were more inclined to focus on local politics, on appeals through churches, or on other more targeted efforts. As a consequence, although complaints were filed during the 1990s with the FEC about the political activities of groups such as the Christian Coalition, as BCRA inched closer to passage the stakes for conservative groups, again with the exception of the NRA and NRLC, were not quite as high as they were for liberals.

This is not to say that social conservative groups did not wield substantial power in American politics during the 1990s. Although Green and Bigelow (2005) note that the Christian Right had little legislative success during this time, they claim that the relative unpopularity among the general public of the agenda items of groups such as the Christian Coalition led these groups to seek to develop a network of activists without simultaneously appealing to the public. These groups often sought to develop power bases within state-level Republican Party organizations or to work in House elections rather than state-level campaigns. The emphasis on working within the Republican Party, however, or within the presidential campaigns of group leaders such as Pat Robertson and Gary Bauer, contributed to instability in groups' quests for resources. The movement never coalesced behind one or two durable groups. The Moral Majority, a leading group among evangelicals in the 1980s, disbanded in 1989; the Christian Coalition, founded in 1988, was in disarray by the 2000 election. Groups representing evangelicals remained prominent in the 2000 and 2004 elections but were not necessarily the same groups that had been major players in 1994 or 1996; that is, new groups took advantage of existing campaign finance laws, but ongoing groups did not adapt.

Resource problems also plagued the conservative groups whose strategies otherwise most resembled those of liberal groups. The NRA and NRLC, like social conservatives, maintained closer ties to the Republican Party than liberal groups maintained with the Democratic Party; testimony in the *McConnell* case revealed that NRLC had received large contributions from Republican Party organizations (O'Steen 2002), and the NRA had been the only advocacy group to make large soft money donations during the 1990s. Like social conservative groups, these organizations saw their resources decline even as politicians who championed their issues were ascendant. The NRA built up a large operating deficit during the 1990s, and the NRLC also saw its revenues decline. Up to this point, however, these groups had adopted a strategy of electioneering in states that were friendly to their issues and engaging in extensive grassroots mobilization, activist training, and get-out-the-vote efforts in more heterogeneous states such as Pennsylvania and Wisconsin (Gamerman 2000), where electioneering in more liberal urban media markets might provoke a backlash.

The NRA in particular followed the same trajectory of politicization as liberal groups. The NRA was formed in the late 1800s, did not establish a Washington lobbying office until the 1950s, and did not engage in significant political activities apart from lobbying until the late 1980s (Spitzer 1995). Factional conflict within the group during the late 1970s brought about a far more political, activist leadership, which sought rapidly to expand the group's membership lists and cement its relationship with the gun industry (Vizzard 2000). By 1992, the group was actively recruiting new members, spending an estimated $8.3 million on member communications (Spitzer 1995). The NRA was among the plaintiffs that filed suit against BCRA, but the group's opposition did not stem from the law's threat to circumscribe its activities because it depended less on electioneering than did other advocacy groups.

Literature on American political parties commonly asserts that the Democratic Party is much more reliant on group support than is the Republican Party (LaRaja 2008). The activities of advocacy groups, like those of labor and business, likely played into politicians' sense that groups ought to be restrained in their ability to shape electoral campaigns. Unsurprisingly, labor unions and business groups worked in coalition to fight BCRA, both before the law's passage and in subsequent court challenges to the measure. Perhaps paradoxically, the advocacy groups most affected by the law—those on the left—either supported BCRA or at least did not join the suit against it, while those on the right, whose tactics were less influenced by the law, joined the plaintiffs in the *McConnell v. FEC*.[5]

Canadian Interest Groups in the 1990s

In both Canada and the United States, groups that seek to be active during elections can choose either to provide financial support directly to candidates or parties or to engage in electioneering activities that may benefit particular candidates or parties but are undertaken independently of the candidates. The expansion in both of these activities in the United States has already been discussed, but the story of how Canadian groups took advantage of these options is far more episodic—more a story of short-term responses to the actions of politicians than of long-term organizational growth and adaptation.

In a general sense, Canadian groups have exhibited the same type of development as have American groups. Canadian organized labor has had similar difficulties in confronting the advent of free trade and the decline of manufacturing jobs (see, e.g., MacDonald 2003). Canadian business groups have become more political and willing to engage in advocacy work (Smith 2005). A similar boom has occurred among postmaterialist advocacy groups since the 1960s, as many of the studies on environmentalism and feminism discussed in chapter 1 show. And social conservatives, while not as major a political force as in the United States, have become more prominent in Canadian politics over the past two decades, particularly since the demise of the Progressive Conservative Party (Farney 2009). These movements have not, however, been clearly visible or measurable within election politics.

Prior to the enactment of the 2003 Canada Elections Act amendments, corporate contributions to the two major parties had comprised a substantial percentage of party revenues. Yet Stanbury's (1991) accounting of corporate contributions makes it clear that corporate contributions were to some degree pulled. Many corporations gave to both parties, although the largest corporate contributions rarely topped one hundred thousand dollars in any election cycle.[6] Fewer than 3 percent of Canadian firms made contributions, although an average of 40 percent of the five hundred largest firms contributed. Stanbury quotes one party fund-raiser referring to the obligation of corporations to "support the democratic system by making contributions that reflect the scale of their operations," indicating that parties viewed contributions as a relatively apolitical endeavor. The problem for corporations, according to Stanbury, was that the disclosure requirements established in 1974 as part of the Election Expenses Act ensured that corporations would be asked to give but told not to expect anything in return.

As in the United States, contributions from organized labor have been made more enthusiastically—they are pushed into the system by unions. While American unions have tended to direct their contributions primarily to the Democratic Party, Canadian unions have been even more captive to one party, the New Democratic Party (NDP). The NDP, formed by organized labor and officially constituted as a vehicle for unions' political goals, has typically received 20 to 30 percent of its contributions from labor unions (Stanbury 1989). In 2003, in anticipation of the new contribution limits, unions gave five million dollars to the NDP (more than half of the NDP's revenue that year) for construction of a new party headquarters in Ottawa that could then serve as collateral for NDP loans (Jansen and Young 2009). Unions, then, were affected far more by the CEA amendments than were corporations, and in contrast to the American case, unions had no alternate external vehicles for spending.

Issue advocacy, or electioneering, advertisements were ubiquitous in American elections of the late 1990s, to the point that their effects could be precisely analyzed by political scientists. Groups have made similar efforts in Canada but on a far smaller scale. Virtually all discussions of electioneering in Canada begin with the 1988 election, which was unusual in that conflict over a dominant national political issue, the Free Trade Agreement (FTA) with the United States, coincided with the election. Canada's two major parties took conflicting stands on the issue, with the Progressive Conservatives supporting the deal and the Liberals opposing it; the NDP also opposed it but did so much less vigorously than did the Liberals. The most commonly accepted estimate of group spending on issue advocacy in this election is $4.7 million, 75 percent of which was spent by pro-free-trade groups (Carty, Cross, and Young 2000, 95). Some estimates range substantially higher, noting that this figure does not include in-kind contributions, volunteer efforts, letters written by corporations (including many American corporations) to shareholders and employees, and other aspects of the campaign (Fraser 1989, 324). The standard recounting of the 1988 election is that the Pro-Canada Network (a coalition of groups including the Council of Canadians, the National Action Committee, the Canadian Labour Congress, and the Canadian Auto Workers) began the conflict by spending $650,000 on a newspaper insert and that the Canadian Alliance for Trade and Job Opportunities (whose members included the Business Council on National Issues, the National Citizens Coalition, and the Canadian Chamber of Commerce) responded with a vigorous campaign of newspaper, radio, and television advertisements (Ayres 1998; Fraser 1989; Salutin 1989; Whitehorn 1992, 228). The pro-FTA advertising included some ads directly targeting individual politicians or parties, but even in cases where parties or politicians were not mentioned, the vote choice encouraged by advocates or opponents of the FTA was clear.

The consequences of these advertising efforts are not clear, however; as Johnston et al. (1992) conclude, the pro- and anti-FTA groups may well have canceled out each other's spending. Thirty-one percent of voters reported being influenced by the advertisements, and an additional 14 percent said that while they had not been influenced, they believed the election outcome had been affected (Crete 1991). Yet the election outcome could have been accurately predicted from polls taken of voters before the advertising took place (Johnston et al. 1992). Some observers worried that the 1988 election foreshadowed things to come—that is, a more American style of electoral competition. In subsequent elections, however, the lack of an issue that galvanized the business community and that resonated nationally drove aggregate group spending on elections down to approximately half a million dollars in 2000 (Eagles 2004).

Apart from the 1988 election, the history of interest group activity in Canadian elections is far more episodic than in the United States. Pross (1992, 172) notes that groups engaged in electioneering activities at least as far back as 1977. Yet the volatility of the Canadian parties' fortunes makes it difficult to draw conclusions about the groups' effectiveness. For example, Jeffrey (1999, 411) summarizes the activities of the National Citizens Coalition in the 1993 elections: the group spent fifty thousand dollars on advertisements targeting two Progressive Conservative MPs in Alberta, including sitting prime minister Kim Campbell. Both members lost, but so did 167 of the 169 Progressive Conservative incumbents standing for re-election. Thus, it is hard to argue that the NCC ads mattered. Similarly, Tanguay and Kay (1991; see also Eagles 2004) analyzed the consequences of volunteer activity by Campaign Life, the major Canadian antiabortion group, in elections during the 1990s. Although Campaign Life claimed success in instances where pro-choice members of Parliament were defeated, a comparison of vote margins over multiple elections shows that Campaign Life's activities may have hurt more than helped the candidates they supported. The only study that shows a strong effect for group activity is Tanguay's (2002) examination of the 1999 Ontario provincial election. In that case, the Ontario Election Network, a coalition of labor unions and advocacy groups, used newsletters, radio and television advertisements, yard signs, and pamphlets to advocate the election of twenty-six different candidates; while the coalition did not reach its stated goal of defeating the Progressive Conservative government of Premier Mike Harris, it reduced the number of seats held by the party and the vote share of PC incumbents in the targeted ridings.

This rather haphazard history of group involvement in Canadian elections shows the difficulties of comparing the consequences of campaign finance reform in Canada and the United States. There is no concerted strategy for different group sectors. Canadian groups clearly had the ability to engage in election activity during the 1980s and 1990s, but they did not always use this ability. When they did so, they often spent quite small amounts of money, leading some observers to argue that group advertising was geared more toward generating media coverage than toward swaying election results (see Carty and Eagles 2005), and the strategies used by groups that advertised were not necessarily representative of the approaches of other groups of the same "type." Some scholars have argued that Canadian politics has provided its most consequential moments of political deliberation outside of elections—for example, many groups engaged in extensive advocacy during the debates over ratification of the Charlottetown and Meech Lake accords (Jeffrey 1993), and more recently, labor unions aired advertisements discussing the late 2008 threat by the Liberal Party, the NDP, and the Bloc Québécois to bring down the Conservative government and form a coalition government.

In a broad sense, however, different sectors of the Canadian interest group community share the basic traits of their American counterparts. Business groups have largely been access-oriented in both countries, preferring not to engage in electoral politics unless provoked. Organized labor in both countries has been more electorally assertive and more inclined to engage in political communications with its members, although the existence of the NDP and the controversy over strategic voting in Canada have brought about some divergence in strategies. Advocacy groups on the right are similarly decentralized in both countries, although they are less powerful in Canada. Groups on the left in both countries have been more inclined to make public appeals, but Canadian groups have been less involved in elections than their American counterparts, perhaps in part because the two major parties are less polarized on many issues.

Conclusions

These summaries include three types of comparisons. The first is a comparison of groups across time. In both the United States and Canada, a substantial diffusion of information about political strategy occurred across all group types. Techniques pioneered by some group types were adopted by groups with conflicting goals, with group advocacy thereby pulling politicians in numerous, opposing directions. Canadian groups were more uneven in their efforts than were Americans, but changes in both nations—polarization between the political Left and Right, the enactment of landmark laws such as the nations' free trade bills, and the increasing salience of postmaterialist concerns—ensured an overall increase in the role of groups in the political process.

The second relevant comparison is of group types. Groups vary in financial and other types of resources—membership, information, and so forth. While a steady increase in political activity took place among all types of American groups, and episodic increases occurred among Canadian groups of all types, substantial variations existed in groups' abilities and incentives to become more active. Organized labor in both countries increasingly focused on mobilizing its members, with occasional efforts to mobilize nonmembers as well. Advocacy groups' efforts waxed and waned according to the political importance of their issues of concern, but those American groups with substantial financial resources increasingly relied on advertising to communicate with the public. Canadian groups had less success in doing so but had some bursts of activity. And business groups became substantially more politicized when threatened by labor or advocacy groups, often eschewing their traditional role as low-key funders of politicians or parties to communicate with the public. Cumulatively, these developments prioritized independent spending over political contributions, threatening candidates' and parties' role in establishing the issues in play during the election.

The third comparison is between nations—or, rather, between political systems. Institutional features determined the choices groups in the two countries could make about how to spend their money. In the United States, PACs provided one alternative throughout this period, but the rise of soft money spending and the loose regulation of independent expenditures ensured that groups could allocate money depending on their needs in any given election. Changes in Democratic and Republican fortunes, coupled with the tighter discipline of the congressional Republican Party in the 1990s, also influenced groups' choices about whether to contribute money or spend it independently. In Canada, groups could give directly to the parties throughout this time, and independent expenditures were even less restricted. Groups' inability to expect either clear returns on contributions or policy effects from independent advocacy (given the fact that advocacy could yield electoral results only if it changed the governing party's policies) meant that Canadian groups could not hope to compete with the parties in setting policy.

These comparisons are important for understanding the development of reform proposals in the United States and Canada. The two nations' reforms addressed clear trends in group activity but also ensured that the effect on groups would not be precisely the same in the two systems—both because the two nations' groups played different roles as of the early 2000s and because groups' options were influenced by different institutional arrangements. The similarity between the two packages indicates that the problems perceived by politicians had important shared themes but that the groups affected and the consequences for groups would not be identical. The next chapter considers commonalities in the American and Canadian reform packages with an eye toward establishing that the trends in this chapter shaped reformers' actions.

3 | Campaign Finance Reform

The U.S. and Canadian campaign finance reforms of the 1970s and 2000s have much in common, but the political circumstances under which reforms were made differ somewhat. As a result, in the United States, politicians sought to exert control over the demonstrated behavior of groups, while in Canada, politicians sought to ward off potential group activities. American groups were much more active in expanding the scope of what groups can do in campaigns than were Canadian groups, but as of the 1990s there was little in Canadian law that prohibited groups from following the American example. Although reform proposals in both countries were developed before the types of group activities that eventually precipitated votes for reform had spiraled out of control, Canadians had the benefit of observing group responses in the United States and of acting to close off some of the immediate avenues by which American groups adapted to the law.

In the United States, the original McCain-Feingold proposals of the 1990s offered a wide range of reforms to the campaign finance system, including a system of voluntary spending limits for congressional candidates and a tax on broadcast television networks that would fund television advertising for candidates. These components were eventually dropped as John McCain and Russell Feingold shifted their focus to the soft money abuses of the 1996 election and the rise in group electioneering (Dwyre and Farrar-Myers 2000). In Canada in 1991, the Royal Commission on Electoral Reform and Party Financing, also known as the Lortie Commission, issued a series of wide-ranging studies of all aspects of party finance and ultimately recommended many of the reforms that were enacted in the 2000s (Lortie 1991). In both cases, the decade between proposal and legislation allowed legislators to narrow the focus of the proposed reforms to demonstrated instances where politicians or parties had sacrificed or were in danger of sacrificing control of the electoral process to groups that they had initially empowered through the 1970s reforms.

This chapter summarizes the content of the two nations' reform packages of the 2000s. As theories of campaign finance predict, the passage of time between the 1970s reforms and the activities of groups in the 1990s ensured that group activities had gone far beyond those that legislators of the 1970s might have foreseen or sanctioned. These developments had their roots in political issues that arose in the 1980s, developments in the technologies used by groups to identify and communicate with supporters, and groups' efforts to learn from the tactics adopted by their allies and competitors. In some cases, these allies and competitors were other groups, while in other instances, they were politicians seeking to use groups to advance other electoral goals. The two nations' reforms addressed legitimate concerns about group influence on elections but were not solely precipitated by groups, solely about groups, or solely responsible for changes in interest group politics that followed.

Campaign Finance Reform in the United States and Canada

The reforms of the 2000s were not the first instance when the two countries shared a path toward regulating campaigns. Both the United States and Canada enacted major reforms during the early 1970s. In the United States, the amendments to the 1974 Federal Election Campaign Act (FECA) established limits on the amount of money individuals could contribute to politicians (one thousand dollars per election cycle), political parties (twenty thousand dollars per cycle), registered nonparty political groups (PACs, five thousand dollars), and in total (twenty-five thousand dollars) and established limits on the amount of money a PAC could contribute to a candidate (five thousand dollars) or a party (fifteen thousand dollars), although there is no aggregate limit on what PACs can contribute. The original version of FECA (passed in 1971) also enhanced disclosure laws and established limits on candidate spending and on contributions by candidates to their campaigns. These spending limits were subsequently overruled by the Supreme Court in *Buckley v. Valeo* (424 U.S. 1 [1976]), which established candidate spending as a freedom-of-speech issue. In addition, the Revenue Act of 1971 established a public funding system for presidential candidates and a small tax credit for political contributions (repealed in 1986). FECA clearly increased scrutiny of contributions, but some observers have argued that it accelerated the development of PACs and helped incumbents far more than it helped challengers.

FECA was subsequently amended and clarified in several noteworthy ways. In 1979, Congress exempted money raised for the purpose of "party-building" activities, such as voter registration and turnout efforts (Corrado 2005, 29). These funds, which were exempt because they were not to be spent in direct support of a candidate, later became known as "soft money" and would become a major source of party funds by the 1990s and the subject of later reforms. Three Supreme Court decisions also widened the permissible scope of noncandidate expenditures. In its 1986 *FEC v. Massachusetts Citizens for Life* decision, the Court ruled that nonprofit corporations that did not have shareholders or engage in other business activities beyond the expression of political views could make unlimited independent expenditures in connection with elections (Potter 2005, 57). And in two related decisions, 1996's *Colorado Republican Federal Campaign Committee v. FEC* (Colorado I) and a second decision of the same name decided in 2001 (Colorado II), the Court allowed parties to make independent expenditures in elections but restricted the amount that could be spent in a coordinated fashion (Potter 2005, 54–55). Collectively, these amendments and decisions ensured that groups and parties could make a variety of restricted and unrestricted expenditures to influence elections. Just in terms of federal law, FECA had sprung several leaks by the 1990s.

In Canada, the Election Expenses Act (EEA) of 1974 did not create contribution limits but established spending limits, increased disclosure, and created a system of tax credits to encourage individuals to donate (see Stanbury 1989, 355–56). One of the EEA's stated goals was to reduce parties' dependence on corporations, and the measure appears to have had that effect. Corporate and union contributions comprised more than 75 percent of the money raised by the Liberals, the PCs, and the NDP prior to the act's passage, a figure that dropped to between 40 and 50 percent during the elections of the 1980s (Stanbury 1989). By the 1990s, however, some scholars contended that corporate and labor groups still played too large a role in party politics; in particular, businesses were seen as insulating the party system in general—the dominance of the Liberals and the PCs—by giving to both parties. The EEA sought to limit the nonparty groups' activities in elections, prohibiting such groups from directly advocating the election or defeat of a candidate or party, but they could discuss issues if they did so "in good faith," a provision that proved vague enough to allow virtually any advocacy advertising.

The next major set of campaign finance reforms in the United States was the Bipartisan Campaign Reform Act (BCRA) of 2002. BCRA was written in response to the perception that the original FECA was being subverted in two major areas. First, beginning in the early 1990s, both major parties began aggressively to solicit soft money contributions from individuals, corporations, and unions. By 2000, 46 percent of the money raised by the party committees was soft money (Corrado 2006b, 26). Soft money could not be used directly to advocate the election of a particular candidate but could be used to air advertisements that discussed issues of concern to the parties and for get-out-the-vote drives and other campaign expenses that stopped short of direct advocacy (Malbin 2003, 5–6). Second, organized interests also began to undertake extensive issue advocacy campaigns. Issue advocacy advertisements did not explicitly direct viewers to vote for or against a candidate (and were thus not limited by FECA) but often described representatives' voting records in harsh terms and closed by exhorting listeners to telephone representatives and tell them how they felt about their voting records. Issue advocacy ads by groups were functionally similar to the parties' soft money ads, since both relied on unrestricted contributions and both helped candidates while stopping short of providing direct endorsements.

BCRA entirely prohibits soft money contributions at the federal level. It also prohibits groups that accept corporate or labor funds (a category that also includes most advocacy groups) from airing radio or television advertisements that name a candidate during the thirty days preceding a primary election or the sixty days preceding a general election. BCRA doubled the amount of money individuals can give to candidates in any election cycle (from $1,000 to $2,000) and parties (from $5,000 to $10,000) as well as the aggregate amount individuals can give (from $50,000 to $97,500) and indexed those amounts to inflation. The legislation contained a complex formula for raising contribution limits for candidates whose opponents self-financed large portions of their campaigns.

BCRA did not entirely prevent groups from making contributions but diminished the relative value of their contributions. Prior to BCRA, corporations, labor unions, or advocacy groups could solicit money from individuals for political action committees (PACs) and could then use PAC money to make direct contributions, in amounts of no more than five thousand dollars, to candidates or parties or to air advertisements discussing the candidates. PACs are a major source of funds in House races (providing an average of more than 35 percent of successful candidates' funds in the past several elections) but are less important in senatorial and presidential elections (Jacobson 2008, 66). Contributions to PACs can be made only by individuals and are subject to a five-thousand-dollar limit. Although it increased individual limits and indexed them to inflation, BCRA did not change the limits on contributions from PACs, thereby increasing the importance of individual contributions and ensuring that they would continue to gain in value relative to group contributions.

The Canada Elections Act (CEA), which took effect in September 2000, prohibited nonparty groups from spending more than $150,000 total and no more than $3,000 in any riding on election-related advertising after a writ of election had been issued. These groups were also required to register with Elections Canada and to identify themselves in any advertisements. A similar bill establishing a $1,000-per-riding limit was passed in 1993 but was struck down by the Alberta Court of Appeals in 1996. The Canadian Supreme Court's 1997 *Libman v. Quebec* decision indicated, however, that the Supreme Court would accept limitations on advertising expenditures, setting up the CEA's eventual passage.[1] This bill was challenged in court by the National Citizens' Coalition, was struck down by the Alberta Court of Appeals, and was subsequently upheld, in *Harper v. Attorney General (Canada)*, by the Canadian Supreme Court in May 2004.

While the *Harper* challenge was playing out in the courts, the Chrétien government passed the 2003 CEA amendments, which took effect at the beginning of 2004. These amendments limited contributions to candidates by corporations or labor unions to no more than one thousand dollars per year, limited individual contributions to no more than five thousand dollars, expanded the availability of the political contribution tax credit, and created a public funding system for parties to offset their losses from the new contribution limits. Four years later, the Federal Accountability Act further tightened these limits. The Accountability Act, which took effect in January 2007, completely prohibits contributions by unions or corporations and restricts individuals to contributing no more than eleven hundred dollars (indexed to inflation) per year to any party, party association, leadership contestant, or candidate. The bill's restrictions on contributions in leadership contests addressed the one major area of party finance not addressed by the 2003 CEA amendments.

Some parallels are evident between these three major pieces of Canadian reform legislation and the two major components of BCRA. The prohibition on corporate and labor contributions in the 2003 CEA amendments roughly parallels the soft money ban in that they affect the same types of groups, rein in the same sort of unrestricted spending, and had a comparable financial effect—in 2000, for example, corporate and labor contributions comprised 51 percent of party fund-raising in Canada (Cross 2004, 147), only a slightly larger percentage than the American soft money and PAC contributions. Likewise, the third-party spending ban in Canada bears some resemblance to the issue advocacy restrictions in the

United States, although the Canadian law is stricter and arguably addresses a less consequential group activity.

Three components of Canadian campaign finance law that clearly have no parallel in the American case—spending limits, the tax credit, and the public funding system—have had noteworthy consequences for groups and for parties.[2] The party spending limits established in the EEA have generally been high enough that most parties do not reach the limits (Cross 2004, 161). These provisions have tended to restrain the major parties (particularly the Liberal Party) but have also encouraged the parties to spend money before elections are called or to spend it in ways not subject to the expense limits. The candidate spending limits, which are set by riding, rarely exceeded one hundred thousand dollars in the 2006 general election.[3] These limits enhance the role of parties while equalizing candidate spending somewhat. Overall, most Canadian analysts have argued that the spending limits have led to more balanced competition than in the United States, albeit only in parts of the country where two or more parties are competitive (see Young 2004).

Canada has had a tax credit since the passage of the EEA; under the contribution limits imposed in the FAA, individuals receive a credit of 75 percent for the first $400 that they give to a party, 50 percent of the next $350, and 33 percent for any additional money contributed. The fact that these limits are for contributions to parties, not to groups (under American law, contributions to parties, candidates, and PACs are treated similarly), may direct money away from nonparty organizations. And the public funding system established under the 2003 CEA amendments, which provides a quarterly allowance of approximately 44 cents (or $1.75 per year) per vote in the previous election to parties that receive at least 2 percent of the vote nationally, has three direct consequences: it reduces the need for parties to solicit funds, it closely ties parties to their prior vote totals (thus potentially benefiting the ruling party), and it rewards parties for the number of votes rather than seats that they receive. Tax credits and some aspects of public funding are limited to registered political parties; Bill C-3 (2004), passed after the Supreme Court's *Figueroa v. Canada (Attorney General)* decision, established that a party needs to run only one candidate to be registered. As chapter 6 shows, these benefits can encourage activists to form political parties even when these parties have no realistic chance of winning elections.

The two countries differ in the courts' role in interpreting campaign finance law. The *Buckley v. Valeo* decision, which invalidated much of the original FECA, clearly prompted BCRA's authors to modify their goals to accommodate the Supreme Court's equation of campaign spending with speech. Even so, substantial uncertainty arose following BCRA's passage about whether the Court would uphold the new law. A diverse array of plaintiffs, including the Chamber of Commerce, the AFL-CIO, the American Civil Liberties Union, and the National Rifle Association, filed suit immediately after the law's passage. The plaintiffs challenged all of the law's major provisions. In *McConnell v. FEC*, the court upheld all of the major components of the law. Writing for the majority, justices John Paul Stevens and Sandra Day O'Connor noted that the law had been crafted to satisfy the constraints placed on Congress by *Buckley* and that the regulations and the rationale for them were areas in which the Court should properly defer to Congress.

Subsequent Supreme Court decisions following the retirements of O'Connor and justice William Rehnquist and the appointment of justices John Roberts and Samuel Alito steadily chipped away at BCRA. The Court struck down one smaller component of BCRA (the millionaire's amendment) in its 2008 *Davis v. FEC* decision and diluted the effect of the electioneering restrictions in 2007's *Wisconsin Right to Life v. FEC*. In January 2010, the Court went even further. In *Citizens United v. FEC,* the justices struck down not only the electioneering restrictions in their entirety but also the 1990 *Austin v. Michigan Chamber of Commerce* decision, which prohibited corporations from engaging in direct advocacy on behalf of candidates. In the aftermath of BCRA, legislators and groups, then, had reason to be uncertain about the Court's immediate reaction, but the Court ultimately went far beyond what McCain and Feingold could have expected when it began dismantling BCRA.

Just as Canada's reform package comprised several different laws, so the judicial response to reform in Canada took the form of several individual cases rather than one omnibus challenge to the law. The *Harper* decision was just one of several narrower campaign finance decisions; others include *Figueroa v. Canada* (2003), which invalidated the 2003 amendments' threshold for parties to receive public financing; *R. v. Bryan* (2005), which concerned citizens' ability to publish election results before the polls had closed; and *Libman v. Quebec* (1997), which found that the province could not limit the number of recognized fund-raising committees in its secession referendum (see Manfredi and Rush 2008). The absence of direct challenges to the law's main provisions ensured that there was little question about whether the reform legislation's major provisions would stand up as Canadians looked toward their next federal elections following the enactment of the 2003 amendments. The fact that

Canadian elections do not take place according to a predictable calendar already hampers any sort of election planning, but to the extent that groups could make plans, uncertainty about the law was less of a hindrance to planning than was the case in the United States following BCRA's passage.

Table 3.1 summarizes the provisions of BCRA and of the various Canadian party finance reforms of the 2000s relevant to interest groups, corporations, and labor unions.

The Causes of Reform

As these summaries show, campaign finance reform is not entirely unrelated to group politics and has serious implications for groups' options. It is somewhat easier to argue that group activities during the 1990s "caused" reform in the United States than in Canada. Few reformers would have argued that group activities were the most serious abuses of the old finance system; much of the testimony in the American court challenges to BCRA focused on party fund-raising practices or wealthy individual donors. This chapter has thus sought to show not only how group activities led to reform but also the extent to which reform prohibited some widely practiced group activities while remaining silent on others.

In the introduction, I argued that the basic contours of campaign finance reform in the United States and Canada provide a sort of natural experiment in the effects of political institutions on interest group behavior. As this chapter makes clear, the stimulus in this experiment—the reform packages—is not exactly the same in both cases. The United States and Canada enacted similar laws, but the differences are somewhat consequential. Likewise, the status quo ante—the state of interest group politics in both countries—also was not identical. Canadian groups arguably resemble American groups more than do the groups of any other nation (and vice versa), in part for reasons of geography and in part because the two nations' political systems and cultures have some similarities. But the basic institutional differences between the countries had already set their respective groups on different paths. Reformers had the same basic concerns: Depending on the level of cynicism about legislators, the overriding concern was either that groups not corrupt the democratic process or that groups not threaten legislators' ability to control campaign discourse. Yet the degree to which groups posed a real threat to incumbent legislators or

TABLE 3.1. Major Provisions of Recent American and Canadian Campaign Finance Reforms Relevant to Groups

	United States	Canada
Legislation (year of passage):	Bipartisan Campaign Reform Act (2002)	Canada Elections Act (CEA, 2000) CEA Amendments (2003) Federal Accountability Act (2006)
Contributions	Soft money contributions by business, labor, and individuals prohibited	Business and labor contributions limited to $1,000 per year in total (CEA Amendments); business and labor contributions subsequently prohibited (Accountability Act)
	Individual contribution limits (by source and in the aggregate) raised and adjusted for inflation; PAC limits not raised. No limits on total amount of money raised by candidates or parties.	Individual contributions limited to $5,000 per year (CEA Amendments); individual contributions subsequently limited to $1,100 and adjusted for inflation (Federal Accountability Act). Contribution limits based on size of riding.
Issue advocacy	Radio and television advertising that names a candidate for federal office prohibited in the 30 days before a primary election and 60 days before a general election unless paid for with PAC funds	All advertising that addresses election issues limited to $150,000 per group in total and $3,000 in group advertising pertaining to any candidate or party leader (CEA)
Tax credits	None	Individuals receive a 75 percent tax credit for the first $400 given to a party, 50 percent of the next $350, and 33 percent thereafter (Federal Accountability Act).
Public funding	None	$1.75 per vote annually to parties that receive more than 2 percent of federal vote; reimbursement of 60 percent of campaign expenses (CEA Amendments)
Court challenges	McConnell v. FEC upholds major provisions of BCRA Wisconsin Right to Life v. FEC creates exception for some issue advocacy advertising. Citizens United v. FEC overturns electioneering restrictions, removes limits on corporate express advocacy	Harper v. Canada (Attorney General) upholds issue advocacy restrictions of Canada Elections Act. Figueroa v. Canada (Attorney General) strikes down provision of Canada Elections Act setting threshold for number of candidates party must run to qualify for registered party status.

to political parties differed; American groups had demonstrated their ability to shape campaign discourse during the 1990s, while in Canada, apart from the 1988 election, groups merely had the potential to shape the terms of debate in campaigns.

Legislators' stated motives in passing reforms in these two countries also differed, but such stated rationales do not necessarily reflect the true reasons for these reforms. Because the *Buckley* court claimed that reducing corruption or the appearance of corruption is a valid reason for limiting spending in elections, reformers have subsequently made arguments based on corruption. Likewise, the *Buckley* court clearly stated that some other concerns—such as leveling the playing field—are not constitutionally legitimate reasons for limiting campaign spending or speech. Ergo, few reformers have explicitly made arguments in this vein, although some interpreters of reform proposals have suggested this goal and have analyzed reform proposals with it in mind. The Canadian courts have permitted more justifications for reform than have the American courts. The paper trail of Canadian reformers—most notably in the multivolume collection of analyses left behind by the Lortie Commission—provides so many different rationales for all sorts of party finance reforms that it is difficult to isolate one individual argument on behalf of reform. In both cases, whatever the underlying logic and whatever the expected consequences for groups, appearance is not necessarily reality.

Reformers would have been politically imprudent to contend that they sought to reassert the control over groups that existed immediately after the passage of the FECA and the EEA. While the public in both countries remains suspicious of groups' role in the political process, the public does not necessarily hold much more favorable views of its elected legislators or of political parties, so an argument about who should wield power would seem a political nonstarter. Because BCRA and the various Canadian reforms had major consequences for actors other than interest groups, seeing these reforms as solely seeking to rein in interest groups would no doubt be too narrow a reading. Nonetheless, the histories provided in chapter 2 demonstrate that the activities in which groups in both countries engaged during the 1990s went far beyond what the authors of FECA and the EEA could have envisioned and that these activities were significantly curtailed by BCRA, the CEA, and the CEA amendments. Following the passage of these laws, groups were in many ways returned to their 1970s footing, and the major ongoing groups lost some of their ability to shape election politics. It seems reasonable to assume that this result was intended.

Even though legislators may seek, in a cartel-like fashion, to control the issues raised in campaigns, they do not have perfect foresight. Many analysts of campaign finance have contended that reforms always have unintended consequences; some observers have argued that these unintended consequences will inevitably subvert reformers' intentions and that the only way to avoid these consequences is to deregulate campaign finance entirely (see, e.g., Samples 2006; Smith 2001). The next four chapters explore American and Canadian groups' responses to reform. In some cases, legislators may have easily predicted these responses; in others, however, the results may have been surprising. Just as the behavior of groups in the 1990s was strongly shaped by immediate political events and changes in campaign technology, so many of the changes in the years following BCRA and the Canadian reforms represent a combination of responses to the law, responses to political events, and the development of new technologies. These factors blend in ways that are often difficult to parse but that can also evade the central question here. To take one obvious American example, have the high-spending, Internet-based presidential campaigns of 2004 and 2008 been influenced by BCRA, are they a response to the politics of the George W. Bush administration, or are they a means of harnessing new technology? The answer is certainly that they are a combination of the three, but the consequences of each of these factors cannot necessarily be isolated. In Canada, why has third-party advertising not been a factor in post-1988 elections, particularly for businesses or labor? Have the characteristics of individual elections and the platforms of the parties muted combat between groups? In both instances, we have at least a partial justification for the cross-national comparison. Holding constant the nature of the legal change enables us to be more certain that shared changes in group behavior have something to do with the law, not with political events. And we can develop a means of substituting institutions for people—that is, we can look beyond the decisions of, for example, George W. Bush or Stephen Harper to the institutional roles that they play and the ways in which their incentives are shaped by the political systems in which they reside. This is a tall order, but the similarities in pre- and postreform group behavior are significant enough that they can provide some insight into the ways in which institutions create different types of group behavior.

Part II | Consequences of Reform

4 | Measuring the Effects of Reform

Campaign finance reform in both the United States and Canada had several immediate effects. As the two nations' laws intended, corporate and labor spending played less of a role in the immediate postreform elections than had previously been the case. Changes in individual contribution limits also ensured that individuals played a much larger role in funding campaigns than they had in earlier times. It is difficult to argue that harm was done to the parties, however. American parties raised enough hard money to alleviate any harmful consequences of BCRA. Canadian party spending did not increase, but it is difficult to argue that it failed to do so as a consequence of the CEA amendments. In both nations, changes in the political context complicate our efforts to understand the role of reform in campaign fund-raising and spending.

Many spending decisions are difficult to measure. In particular, interest groups' choices about how to reallocate their money are difficult to track. In this chapter, I first present what can be easily observed through analysis of pre- and postreform fund-raising by parties and candidates in the United States and Canada, and I then discuss the limitations of what we can infer from aggregate data. Both nations' governments provide summary data on a variety of different types of campaign contributions and expenditures, but the data differ enough that direct comparisons are problematic. This situation brings up a major concern for advocates and opponents of reform—the transparency of the political system and our changing ability to measure the role of money in political campaigns.

After considering what types of group activities we can and cannot measure, I explore the consequences of variations in group characteristics and institutional characteristics in the two systems. Again, three types of comparisons appear here. First, there is a common trend over time and a common stimulus, in the form of reform legislation, at the same point in time. Although throughout I treat the two nations' reforms as similar pieces of legislation, the two laws are not identical, and the group responses in each country call attention to some of the differences between the bills. Second, within each country, labor unions, business groups, and advocacy groups were affected because of their characteristics—the nature of their memberships, their resources, and their goals—but these characteristics are shared across borders within group types. Third, the incentives and constraints provided by the political system differ in the two countries, so that groups that are functionally similar in each country receive different types of opportunities as a consequence of the law and the organization of political institutions.

This chapter, then, demonstrates the theoretical importance of the natural experiment described in the previous chapters, shows the immediate consequences of reform, and identifies some of the less quantifiable interest group adaptations, which will be considered in subsequent chapters.

Change We Can Measure, Change We Cannot Measure

A common starting point for analyses of campaign finance reform has been to look at aggregated contribution or expenditure data for different group types. Direct comparisons here are difficult and would arguably be misleading were they to be presented here without the context provided in the previous chapters. Apart from the differences in prior laws regarding contributions, the fact that Canadian law now completely prohibits business and labor contributions makes using the financial numbers unilluminating in comparing the two countries, although it does confirm some of the trends evident in the preceding chapters. It also serves as a means of highlighting the types of changes that we cannot directly measure—that is, whether the removal of money from the system has resulted in a decline in campaign activity or merely in a shift to less quantifiable or measurable activities such as member communications, mobilization, and other less transparent spending vehicles.

Change We Can Measure: Campaign Contributions and Independent Expenditures

Tables 4.1 and 4.2 show general patterns of corporate, labor, and group funding for candidates and parties in the United States and Canada in 2000 and 2004 (the most easily comparable pre- and postreform elections). There are many ways to calculate total contributions from the various group sources: These tables are meant primarily to provide a sense of scale and of the relationship between group contributions and total fundraising by parties and candidates. In both tables, I have combined all contributions (in the Canadian case, contributions to parties and candidates; in the American case, contributions to the parties and to general election House, Senate, and presidential candidates).[1] Both tables exclude transfers to candidates to avoid double-counting, and the Canadian table excludes federal reimbursements to candidates. The U.S. table also excludes general election public funds for presidential candidates. These are, then, rather conservative estimates of election-related spending.

The scale of American elections is obviously much larger: Even accounting for the fact that the U.S. population is roughly nine times that of Canada, the greater number of seats being contested in the United States, and the presence of a U.S. presidential election, the American system still includes substantially more money. Canadian parties do, however, operate with spending limits and with public financing. The differences in the changes within the two systems, however, are obvious: The American reforms removed some money from the political system and likely redirected other funds, as PAC contributions and individual hard money contributions increased in 2004. The Canadian reforms replaced much of the corporate and labor money with public funding, thereby helping the Liberal Party, the NDP, and the BQ to remain financially competitive with the

TABLE 4.1. Contributions to Canadian Political Parties, 2000 and 2004

	2000				2004		
Party	Corporations	Unions	Individuals	Total	Individual and Group Contributions	Public Funds	Total[a]
Liberal	11.9	<0.1	7.0	19.0	4.7	9.1	13.8
Canadian Alliance	6.8	0	12.0	19.6	—	—	—
NDP	0.2	3.0	5.8	9.0	5.2	1.9	7.1
Progressive Conservative	2.8	0	2.8	5.6	—	—	—
Bloc Québécois	0.4	<0.1	1.7	2.1	0.9	2.4	2.8
Conservative	—	—	—	—	10.9	8.5	19.4
Total	22.1	3.1	29.3	55.3	21.7	21.9	43.6

Source: Adapted from Cross 2004, 147; Elections Canada 2005; Sayers and Young 2004.
Note: All numbers in millions of dollars. — = not applicable.
[a]Total for 2004 does not include transfers of funds from previous years or federal reimbursements to candidates.

Conservatives (and explaining Stephen Harper's desire to do away with public financing in 2008). Canadian candidates can raise money independently of the party, subject to spending limits; for 2000, Cross (2004, 147) estimates that approximately $25.4 million was raised by candidates, independent of party transfers and federal reimbursements. The proportions, both by party and by funding source, resemble the proportions for party fund-raising. Elections Canada's 2004 aggregate figures do not permit the removal of party transfers from candidate fund-raising amounts.

TABLE 4.2.   Contributions to U.S. Political Parties, 2000 and 2004

	2000			2004		
	Democrats	Republicans	Total	Democrats	Republicans	Total
Business PACs (corporate and trade associations)	67.9	123.4	191.6	81.3	158.8	240.3
Labor union PACs	54.2	4.6	59.0	52.4	7.7	60.1
Ideological PACs	16.6	18.8	35.6	21.1	31.0	52.2
Other PACs/ Unknown	0.4	0.5	0.9	0.8	0.7	1.5
PAC total	139.1	151.8	287.1	155.6	198.2	354.1
Individual hard money contributions	381.6	515.5	910.0	810.2	856.3	1,674.6
Business soft money	160.0	220.0	381.8	—	—	—
Labor union soft money	30.0	0.4	30.4	—	—	—
Ideological group soft money	6.0	4.0	10.2	—	—	—
Other soft money	5.8	8.0	14.0	—	—	—
Total soft money	201.8	232.4	436.4	—	—	—
Total	722.5	899.7	1,633.5	965.8	1,054.5	2,028.7

Source: Federal Election Commission, Center for Responsive Politics.
Note: All numbers in millions of dollars. Row totals include third-party candidates. — = not applicable.

These tables do not take into account independent spending by advocacy groups; in the Canadian case, it is possible to do so, but the amounts are relatively trivial. For example, the Canadian Auto Workers, by most accounts one of the country's more politically active groups, reported spending $7,500 on election-related advertising in 2004. Estimates of spending by political groups in the United States are difficult to measure precisely or to aggregate, but one can gain a general sense of their magnitude. Baker and Magleby (2003, 75) estimate that the thirteen major groups they studied in 2000 accounted for $200 million in advocacy spending. In 2004, 527 groups (which can raise money in unlimited sums from individuals, corporations, unions, or other groups) spent $442.5 million.[2] Independent spending, then, can be as important as or more important than group contributions in American elections; such is clearly not the case in Canada.

Tables 4.1 and 4.2 show some of the immediate consequences of reform. As one moves further away from the passage of these laws, it becomes more difficult to separate the consequences of reform from the influences of other factors on contributors' behavior. Tables 4.3 and 4.4 present data on the 2006 and 2008 elections in Canada and the 2008 election in the United States. These tables follow the same format as tables 4.1 and 4.2 (except for the omission of the spending categories prohibited by BCRA), but the changes in contributions may also be influenced by a variety of other factors—for example, in the United States, by the declining popularity of George W. Bush and the Republican Party and by Barack Obama's decision to decline primary matching funds and general election public funding, and in Canada by the sagging fortunes of the Liberal Party. Table 4.5 compares the 2002 and 2006 midterm elections in the United States, allowing the reader to gauge the consequences of reform on congressional elections; here again, the 2006 election was far enough removed from the passage of BCRA that one can be less confident in attributing any changes in contributions to the passage of reform laws.

Tables 4.1 and 4.3 show that funding for Canadian political parties remained relatively stable following the passage of the reform laws.[3] This finding is expected, given the creation of the public financing program. While the electoral fortunes of the parties are now a larger determinant of financing than was previously the case, the overall amount of money raised in the election rebounded to 2000 levels by 2006 and held steady in 2008; public funds more than compensated for the loss of corporate and labor contributions, and individual contributions increased slightly despite the imposition of the stricter contribution limit. If Conservative fund-raising is compared to combined Alliance and PC fund-raising in 2000, three of the four parties active in both 2000 and 2008 increased their fund-raising slightly, with only the Liberals facing a reduction in the amount of money raised—again, as many observers might have predicted, given the Liberals' reliance on corporate contributions in 2000 and their declining seat and vote share in the 2004 and 2006 elections. Spending by the larger parties was contained, not reduced, by the institution of public funding for the parties. To the extent that smaller parties such as the Bloc Québécois, the NDP, and the Greens have received a steady stream of funds from their annual subsidies, reform may have increased

TABLE 4.3.   Contributions to Canadian Political Parties, 2006 and 2008

	2006			2008		
Party	Individual Contributions	Public Funds	Total[a]	Individual Contributions	Public Funds	Total[a]
Liberal	9.0	8.6	17.6	5.9	8.7	14.6
NDP	4.0	4.6	8.6	5.5	5.0	10.5
Bloc Québécois	0.5	3.0	3.5	0.7	3.0	3.7
Green	0.8	1.2	2.0	1.6	1.3	2.9
Conservative	18.6	9.4	28.0	21.2	10.4	31.6
Total	32.9	26.8	59.7	34.9	28.4	63.3

Source: Elections Canada.
Note: All numbers in millions of dollars.
[a]Totals do not include transfers of funds from previous years or federal reimbursements to candidates.

TABLE 4.4.   Contributions to U.S. Political Parties, 2008

	Democrats	Republicans	Total
Business PACs (corporate and trade associations)	157.2	163.2	320.5
Labor union PACs	66.3	5.9	72.5
Ideological PACs	34.8	30.2	65.2
Other PACs/Unknown	1.6	0.8	2.4
PAC total	259.9	200.1	460.6
Individual hard money contributions	1,264.2	991.3	2,263.8
Total	1,524.1	1,191.4	2,724.4

Source: Federal Election Commission, Center for Responsive Politics.
Note: All numbers in millions of dollars. Row totals include third-party candidates.

overall spending by the parties (relative to what would have been spent in the absence of reform).

The data on American parties and candidates present a somewhat more complicated story. As table 4.2 shows, the loss of soft money was more than offset by the increase in individual hard money fund-raising; table 4.4 shows a continued increase in fund-raising from individuals, although this phenomenon was fueled largely by the large presidential primary fields in both parties, the protracted Democratic primary, and the

TABLE 4.5.   Contributions to U.S. Political Parties, 2002 and 2006

	2002			2006		
	Democrats	Republicans	Total	Democrats	Republicans	Total
Business PACs (corporate and trade associations)	73.8	126.3	200.2	98.0	181.9	281.7
Labor union PACs	54.1	5.9	60.3	57.3	8.2	66.0
Ideological PACs	21.9	22.0	44.0	27.4	40.5	68.5
Other PACs/ Unknown	0.7	0.6	1.3	1.4	1.1	2.6
PAC total	150.6	154.2	305.9	184.1	231.7	418.8
Individual hard money contributions	290.2	352.7	645.4	549.5	586.2	1,139.8
Business soft money	142.0	209.7	352.1	—	—	—
Labor union soft money	35.4	0.4	35.9	—	—	—
Ideological group soft money	11.0	6.6	17.6	—	—	—
Other soft money	8.5	10.5	19.1	—	—	—
Total soft money	196.9	227.2	424.7	—	—	—
Total	637.7	734.1	1,376.0	733.6	817.9	1,558.6

Source: Federal Election Commission, Center for Responsive Politics.

Note: All numbers in millions of dollars. Row totals include third-party candidates. — = not applicable (soft money contributions were illegal in 2006 under BCRA).

Obama campaign's fund-raising success in the primary and general elections. It is hard to make the case, however, that the parties or politicians missed group money. Just as PAC money did not increase from 2000 to 2004 at a rate much greater than the secular trend over the previous decade, so PAC contributions did not increase in a particularly marked manner between 2004 and 2008. Business groups began to tilt more toward the Democrats in 2008 than had previously been the case, but this development represents typical access-related giving, insofar as the Republicans were not expected to regain a majority in either chamber of Congress in 2008. In neither 2004 nor 2008 could one claim that corporate or labor soft money found its way back into the system in the form of direct contributions. However, the increased individual limits and the increased fund-raising efforts by both parties mitigated any harmful consequences of the soft money ban. Table 4.5, which compares the pre- and post-BCRA midterm elections, presents a similar story, removing from the equation the complicating factor of presidential fund-raising.

Although total PAC spending and PAC contributions did not show a marked increase that could be connected to BCRA, PACs' independent expenditures grew very rapidly, from $21 million in 2000 to $57 million in 2004 and $135 million in 2008. This surge accounts for most of the growth in total PAC expenditures. The increase between 2004 and 2008 in part reflects the decline in the spending of 527s after 2004. That is, there is some indication here that pushed money first found a post-BCRA outlet in 527s and then was shifted to PACs and 501(c) groups.

Finally, some analysts predicted going into the 2004 election that 527 groups would provide an alternate source for corporate and labor spending. Although 527 groups may have fulfilled this function in 2004, it is equally possible that the increase in 2004 indicates an aggressive (and possibly unnecessary) outreach strategy by Democratic Party supporters concerned with the possible consequences of the soft money ban. Spending by 527s declined from $442.5 million in 2004 to $206.4 million in 2006 and increased only slightly to $258.0 million in 2008. Many of the most prominent 527 groups in 2006 and 2008, such as the SEIU, also maintained other accounts—that is, many of the largest 527s were connected to PACs and 501(c)(4), (c)(5), or (c)(6) funds. The creation of new spending vehicles in 2004, then, was not replicated or carried forward in 2006 or 2008, whether because of tightened FEC oversight of 527s or because of a sense on the part of potential donors that 527s were neither needed nor effective.

The Campaign Finance Institute (2009) estimates that 501(c) groups spent approximately $200 million in 2008, with a majority of the money spent in support of Republican candidates. This spending represents a substantial increase over previous elections—the Institute estimates that 501(c) groups spent less than $60 million in 2004. It is possible to argue that some soft money first found its way back into the system in the form of 527 contributions in 2004 and was then redirected into 501(c) spending when 527 expenditures became legally problematic. However, it is difficult to argue that this process is necessarily a direct consequence of reform in part because 501(c) spending tends to be episodic and focused on particular events, and 2008 arguably had at least one such catalyst, the Employee Free Choice Act championed by labor unions. At a minimum, this increase indicates that U.S. reforms did not silence groups to the same extent as did the Canadian reforms.

As one moves further away from the implementation date of BCRA and the CEA amendments, it becomes more difficult to connect changes in campaign financing practices with the effects of the law. Such was also the case with the reforms of the 1970s; not until the 1990s could the full effects of the Federal Election Campaign Act and the Election Expenses Act be gauged. Of course, political circumstances and court decisions complicate our ability to draw direct connections over such a long period of time; the fact that by 2010, only one of BCRA's major provisions remained standing makes it particularly difficult to measure exactly what changes reform wrought on the political landscape. As the data presented here show, even linking financing practices of 2006 and 2008 to reform is problematic, and establishing such connections will remain difficult for future elections. Nevertheless, BCRA and the CEA amendments may well have unforeseen consequences.

Change We Cannot Measure

Many of the most important group expenditures, however, cannot be measured. Some opponents of BCRA argued that the law would divert group money into less transparent types of spending. While in some instances such may be the case, many types of group spending are by their nature difficult to quantify and were so before the passage of BCRA and the 2003 CEA amendments. In particular, three types of group spending are impossible to measure in either the pre- or postreform context.

Mobilization and Internal Communication. Group appeals that are not transmitted through radio or television are difficult to quantify for two reasons. First, groups are not required to report the expense of communications with members in either the United States or Canada if these communications are not candidate-specific. Even if data were available, it is not possible to separate political communications from other types of communications. Groups with large membership bases devote a greater amount of their resources to member communications, and groups with smaller membership bases may seek to expand their memberships to engage in this sort of communication.

Mobilization work is similarly difficult to measure. Some American analyses have considered independent expenditures by groups, which include not only the cost of advertising but also direct mail, face-to-face encounters, e-mail, and other forms of contact. Magleby's Center for the Study of Elections and Democracy project has provided regular analyses of such efforts in targeted races (see, e.g., Monson 2004), but these data have been gathered only in select areas by recipients of these messages. That is, groups are not required to report the amount of money spent specifically on mobilization; while groups file expenditure reports, they list the recipients of funds, not the purpose of the spending. Data on Canadian groups are similarly hard to interpret. Reform in both countries privileges these sorts of efforts, but it is not possible to gauge the extent to which groups replaced contributions with advocacy work.

Bundling. The fact that BCRA increased the individual contribution limit and indexed it to inflation while leaving unchanged the limit for PACs led many U.S. groups to talk about increasing their efforts to encourage individuals to contribute. The prohibition on corporate and labor contributions in Canada arguably could have the same effect, even though individual contribution limits were decreased. That is, if groups cannot contribute at all, individual contributions become more attractive whether or not individuals can give more than before.

Bundling, or collecting contributions from individuals and forwarding them to candidates, has been a standard practice for some interest groups since the technique was developed by the Council for a Livable World in the 1960s (Sabato 1984, 86; Sorauf 1992, 268). Although the amount of bundled contributions and the number of bundling groups appears to have increased during the 1990s, any change in individual contribution limits could increase the amount that any group specializing in bundling large contributions could raise. It is difficult to evaluate any groups' claims about bundling, however, because the practice has both a legal connotation and a more informal connotation. Groups that physically collect individual contributions and distribute them to politicians (or groups that use the Internet for the same purpose) must report the donors and recipients of these bundling efforts to the FEC. Many of the group efforts considered in chapter 5, however, do not meet the legal definition of bundling. A group can encourage members to contribute to endorsed candidates and can track member contributions, but as long as the contributions are sent from the individual to the candidate, the group is not technically bundling and thus does not need to disclose its role in the contribution. In addition, laws governing disclosure of bundling data have changed several times over the past decade, most recently with the passage of the Honest Leadership and Open Government Act in 2007, which required candidates to report individuals or groups that bundled contributions.

There is no official Canadian parallel to bundling, although informal bundling undoubtedly occurs. American organizations such as the Center for Responsive Politics can track patterns in giving by looking, for example, at contributors' employers to see if employees of a particular firm contributed to the same candidate at roughly the same time; such findings provide at least the suspicion that giving is coordinated. Because Canadian contributors are not required to list employers, however, even this sort of imprecise analysis cannot be conducted.

Coalition Work.   Finally, groups can coordinate electoral strategy, subject to some legal limitations, not so much to increase the amounts of money spent but to allocate money more efficiently. American groups have claimed to have increased such activities following BCRA, but these changes are hard to measure. We can note coalition or peak groups (organizations that receive funding from other groups or count other groups as members), but it is harder to measure how much collaboration really goes on within such groups or through less formal means. In Canada, the lack of official recognition of such group efforts makes even this sort of approach problematic, and the new Canadian regulations appear to provide less of an impetus for coalition work than do the American regulations.

Reform and Transparency

There is much, then, that we cannot know with precision about the role of money in American and Canadian elections, and much of what we can know is specific to particular candidates or groups. It is thus difficult to gauge the financial effects of reform laws in either country on the political system. Insofar as reforms in both countries prohibited certain types of contributions that were easily measurable and replaced them with other types of activities that are less quantifiable, the election system in both countries may be seen as less transparent than before.

While opponents of reform have often argued for greater transparency, they have not necessarily been interested in this particular notion of it. Spending by 527 groups and 501(c)(4) groups in the United States unquestionably increased following BCRA, but these changes have proven less difficult to observe than some analysts predicted. Laws governing 527 disclosure have been strengthened, and Internal Revenue Service data on (c)(4) groups enable some conclusions to be drawn about these groups' activities (see Campaign Finance Institute 2009). Serious obstacles would impede any efforts to increase the reporting of mobilization expenditures, bundling, or coalition efforts. The definitions of these activities are by their nature imprecise—it would be difficult to separate political and nonpolitical coalition work or communications or to affix a dollar amount to these efforts as well as to assess the intent of individual donors. Not all campaign activity can be quantified.

These measurement issues ensure that any study of changing group activities will by its nature be somewhat qualitative. The risk here is that such a study will be ad hoc or impressionistic, but the merit is that a broader notion of change will incorporate a wider variety of activities than would a definition that stuck to financial data.

Assessing the Effects of Reform on Groups

Campaign finance reforms in the United States and Canada have not been exclusively or even primarily about groups. Four different political actors are affected by reform. *Candidates,* as the recipients of political contributions, are affected in that the permissible sources of contributions or permissible means of soliciting contributions are changed. *Political parties,* in their role as recipients of contributions, as contributors to candidates, and as the organizers of Congress or Parliament, are perhaps the actors addressed most directly by the reform laws of both countries. *Nonparty groups* likewise are affected as both contributors and recipients of money. And individual *citizens* are affected insofar as the amounts that they can contribute and the permissible recipients of their contributions are altered by these laws. The nature of the laws and of the political institutions of these two countries directly affect these actors' ability to alter their behavior.

It is possible to speak, then, about direct and indirect effects of campaign finance reform for groups. For example, the limitations on groups' electioneering efforts have immediate effects on what groups do with their money. Other changes that do not address groups at all can also alter group strategy, however. In the United States, the fact that individual contribution limits were increased and indexed to inflation while PAC contribution limits remained unchanged can privilege individuals over groups and can encourage groups to bundle contributions, but the effect is indirect. Although many American groups argued against the increase in individual contribution limits, the architects of BCRA never framed this increase as a means of restricting group influence.

A particularly complicated relationship to untangle, however, is that between parties and groups. Copious literature in the United States (e.g., LaRaja 2008; Malbin 2003, 2006) and Canada (Jansen and Young 2009) has addressed the effects of reform on parties. Yet in both countries, groups are not clearly separable from parties. Among American political scientists, a growing literature has advanced the notion of political parties as extended networks of elite donors, party officials, activists, and interest groups (see, e.g. Skinner 2005). The partisanship of so many of the larger American groups has complicated the argument that groups behave independently of their preferred parties. In many instances, it is impossible to make a clear distinction; the Republican Governors Association, for example, is not officially a national party organization but clearly operates in close consultation with the national organizations. And in other cases, parties have worked to build nonparty organizations, as the Republican Party did in transferring money to the National Right to Life Committee (O'Steen 2002). Although less evidence exists of this sort of behavior in Canadian politics, difficult cases may be found there, too. The party caucuses, for example, share goals with related interest groups, have at times shared members, and can be expected to be involved in the same social networks. And to take the most obvious case, the NDP shares many connections with the CLC and other labor unions, to the point that it is difficult to draw the line between NDP policy and labor union policy.

Moreover, political candidates often come from a group background, and many groups depend entirely on a very small number of individual activists. The point of noting the difficulty in drawing out the differences between direct and indirect effects and between groups and other types of political actors, however, is that any theory of the effects of shifting campaign finance laws on groups must take into account these gray areas. One useful means of framing these shifts comes from literature on the consequences of reform for the parties. Both LaRaja (2008) and Parker (2008) contend that campaign finance reforms in the United States historically have shifted the balance of power within and between the parties, with prior changes advantaging or disadvantaging party activists, interest groups, and large donors. A similar argument can be made about groups: Different types of interest groups have different types of resources, and reform privileges groups with particular types of resources while penalizing others. Even if we cannot be certain what is a "group," we can distinguish among groups according to their resources.

Making Distinctions among Groups

Studies of American interest groups frequently classify them according to the types of benefits (solidary, purposive or expressive, or material) provided to members (Clark and Wilson 1961; Salisbury 1969). Other analyses go further, differentiating groups according to their partisanship or level of partisanship (Wilson 1973). Still other examinations distinguish between the types of members—groups that are comprised primarily of members, as is the case with most advocacy groups, or groups that are comprised of other organizations, as is the case with peak business associations (Walker 1991).[4] Finally, some studies distinguish between access-seeking groups, such as corporate groups, and groups that seek electoral advantage, often at the expense of access (Wright 1996). In most instances, groups concerned with access have relied more on contributions, while groups concerned with election outcomes have relied more on electioneering. Corporate groups have traditionally sought access and have relied primarily on contributions, while many advocacy groups have been more concerned with influencing election outcomes and have leaned heavily toward one party or the other, depending on the partisan alignment on their issue of concern. American organized labor has pursued both strategies but has overwhelmingly supported the Democratic Party. Most American groups fall into one of four clusters—business groups (corporate or peak), labor unions, and liberal and conservative advocacy groups—as evidenced by the common trend in the activities among these groups, which, in turn, is rooted in the group types' distinct resources and goals.

The nature of Canadian political parties alters this framework somewhat. The absence of enduring ideological polarization between the two major parties has ensured that both corporate and advocacy groups have avoided electioneering, in part because partisanship yields few gains for the group—there are few issues where one major party is vastly and consistently superior to another—and in part because party discipline ensures that groups can gain few benefits from support of the party out of power. Hence, corporate groups, women's groups, and environmental groups have often professed indifference between the two major parties. The major exception to this rule has been organized labor, which has traditionally focused its contribution and electioneering efforts on helping the NDP, a party that has rarely approached the level of support of the Liberals or Conservatives but that has at times held the balance of power in minority governments and has governed in several provinces. Although few studies of Canadian interest groups rigorously differentiate among the strategies of corporate, labor, and advocacy groups, the distinction does exist; many prominent Canadian studies have focused primarily on one of these three categories (on business groups, see Coleman and Grant 1985; Coleman and Jacek 1983; on labor, see Albo 1990; Archer and Whitehorn 1997; Kwavnick 1970, 1975; Yates 1993; on advocacy groups, see Smith 2005). Studies have also increasingly emphasized differentiating right-wing populist advocacy groups from traditional advocacy groups (see Harrison 1995; Jeffrey 1999; Laycock 2002). Thus, Canadian interest group politics comprises three or perhaps four clusters of groups that roughly parallel American group differences, with the important caveat that the Canadian case features far less partisan sorting, although such partisanship may be emerging or have emerged and then receded among the groups aligned with the Reform movement.

In selecting groups to study, then, it is important not only to consider the most active groups but to ensure representation from each of the different clusters. A secondary concern lies in drawing parallels between Canadian and American groups; in some cases, the same group exists in both countries, while in others, groups have obvious links across borders. Only a small number of important groups cannot be matched in this manner.

Chapters 5–7 focus on several such matched groups. In the summary of American interest group politics, I draw primarily on interview-based work conducted with more than twenty different groups and summarized in two earlier studies of responses to BCRA (see Boatright et al. 2003, 2006). These groups include peak business associations (the Chamber of Commerce, the National Association of Realtors, and the Business-Industry Political Action Committee), labor unions (primarily the AFL-CIO but also several affiliated unions), liberal advocacy groups (the Sierra Club, Planned Parenthood, MoveOn.org, the League of Conservation Voters, and the NAACP National Voter Fund), and conservative advocacy groups (the National Rifle Association and the Club for Growth). Canadian groups were chosen primarily with regard to their level of political activity, but most can be paired with the U.S. groups. The interview comments in the Canadian chapter are drawn from discussions with peak business groups (the Canadian Federation of Independent Businesses, parallel to but not formally affiliated with the U.S. National Federation of Independent Businesses; the Canadian Council of Chief Executives, which roughly parallels the U.S. Business Roundtable and BIPAC; Canadian Manufacturers and Exporters, a peak organization roughly equivalent to the U.S. National Association of Manufacturers, BIPAC's primary sponsor; and the Canadian Chamber of Commerce, formally associated with its American counterpart); labor unions (the Canadian Labour Congress, which parallels the AFL-CIO; two international unions that belong to the CLC, the United Food and Commercial Workers and the United Steelworkers; and one major Canadian union that is not an international, the Canadian Auto Workers); and advocacy groups (Sierra Club Canada; the Campaign Life Coalition, the major Canadian antiabortion group, paralleling the U.S. National Right to Life Committee; the Canadian Taxpayers Federation, which is similar in focus to the U.S. National Taxpayers Union and Americans for Tax Reform; the National Citizens Coalition; and Environment Voters). Together, these groups provide a fairly comprehensive overview of the different electoral strategies pursued by Canadian groups and their degree of correspondence with American strategies.

My semistructured interviews with these groups focused on four topics: how the groups viewed campaign finance reform and how they had been affected by it; how they behave during a typical election; how much issues of regionalism, federalism, recent political events, and institutions influenced electoral activities; and, in the case of Canadian groups, what sort of relationship the groups had with similar American groups. Unless otherwise attributed, the comments in these chapters on group activities are drawn from the interviews.

Group responses could be sorted in many plausible ways. Some analyses of interest groups, for example, have been based on the assumption that the relevant division is between group activities (such as contributions, independent expenditures, and issue advocacy) rather than between group types. Other studies have considered PACs and 501(c) groups separately. I have chosen to present first a summary of American groups' reactions, broken out into labor unions, corporations, and advocacy groups, and then to turn my attention to Canadian groups, broken out into similar categories. I selected this method because groups clearly forge alliances and gather information across group type and to a lesser extent across borders, and the adaptations speak for themselves. Labor unions, corporations, and advocacy groups took divergent approaches to reform in the United States because of their different resources and goals. Canadian groups, too, diverged in their responses to reform, but the systemwide consequences of Canadian reform differ enough from those in the United States to merit separate consideration. The patterns in group responses are sufficiently clear to justify my approach.

5 | The American Response

American interest groups had plenty of time to prepare for the implementation of the Bipartisan Campaign Reform Act (BCRA), which was signed into law on March 27, 2002, but did not take effect until the following November 6, the day after the 2002 elections. This delay ensured that groups would have a full election cycle to develop responses to the law. For any groups waiting on the Supreme Court, the *McConnell v. FEC* decision, which upheld almost all components of the law, was handed down December 10, 2003. The timing of this decision left groups with ample time to implement changes.

This sequence of events ensured that the period from 2000 to 2004 would be marked by a relatively orderly development of strategies. The 2000 elections thus represent the peak of groups' prereform behavior—decisions about campaign contributions and advertising are geared entirely to the election at hand and draw on lessons learned from elections during the 1990s. The 2002 elections can be seen, in Magleby and Monson's (2004) words, as "the last hurrah"—a chance for groups to engage either in one last round of soft money contributions or in unabashed electioneering, with the knowledge that they would be unable to do so in subsequent elections. And despite the dramatic events of George W. Bush's first term in office, the similarities between 2004 and 2000—a polarized electorate, a closely divided Congress, and the two parties' agreement that the states in play in the presidential election would be the same—allow one to come as close as the political world may allow to seeing the 2004 election as a replay of 2000 but with different rules. Not all changes in group activities between 2000 and 2004 resulted solely from changes in campaign finance law, but dramatic changes in the political landscape can be discarded as a potential cause for changing group strategies, permitting us to focus instead on gradual changes in communications technology, in group resources, or in the goals of political elites. As this chapter shows, campaign finance reform shaped groups' options, but the influence of BCRA was subtle, many of the more dramatic predictions of change were not borne out, and the end result was a gentle push for the largest interest groups in a direction that they might have pursued or sought to pursue even without changes in the law.

Table 5.1 summarizes the changes in interest group strategy between 2000 and 2004. Interest groups have, of course, subsequently continued to develop new strategies. This chapter is largely devoted to the events of 2000, 2002, and 2004, although I do briefly discuss the 2006 and 2008 elections, which brought sweeping change to the American political system and which also were shaped by BCRA, at least to some extent. Few analysts, however, have argued that BCRA caused the Democratic gains of 2006 or the election of Barack Obama in 2008. When comparing the effects of reform in the United States and Canada, hewing closer to groups' immediate pre- and postelection activities reduces the likelihood of confusing broader changes in the political environment with changes in groups' legal options. This chapter looks at labor, business, and advocacy

TABLE 5.1.   American Interest Group Activities before and after BCRA, by Group Type

Group Type	Pre-BCRA Activities	Post-BCRA Activities
Business/industry associations	PAC contributions, soft money contributions	PAC contributions do not increase dramatically. Overall decline in contributions.
Peak business associations	PAC contributions, grassroots work	Increased grassroots work
Labor unions	Grassroots work, PAC contributions, soft money contributions, TV and radio advertising	Increased member mobilization. Some early advertising. Contributions to 527 organizations.
Large membership issue advocacy groups	TV and radio advertising, endorsements, some grassroots work	Increased grassroots work; some early advertising. Development of multigroup coalitions and more complex organizations.

groups and draws some conclusions about the relationship between reform and group activities based on these organizations' differing objectives and resources.

Organized Labor

After the passage of BCRA, many observers expected that organized labor might have the most difficult time of any set of interest groups in responding to the law's new restrictions. Unions routinely were among the top soft money donors and the biggest purchasers of television advertisements in the weeks preceding Election Day, and unions appeared less able than other groups to increase their hard money fund-raising. When combined with the broader structural problems unions have faced for at least the past two decades, the new restrictions on election-related spending appeared to pose a substantial threat to organized labor's political clout. In the elections immediately following BCRA's implementation, however, labor adapted surprisingly well to the law. Labor arguably played a larger role in the 2004 election than it did in 2002, and the development of several new labor-supported organizations proceeded with somewhat less conflict among union leaders than might have been expected (see Francia 2006, 160; Roof 2008). Organized labor has not lost its ability to spend substantially on election-related activity, and several international unions spent more in 2004, 2006, and 2008 than had ever before been the case. Labor's adaptations have, however, done little to ameliorate its long-term decline, and the departure of several large unions from the AFL-CIO in 2005 is just one sign of many unions' frustration regarding organized labor's troubles in setting the agenda in Washington.

Election Strategy

The 2000 Elections. By 2000, the AFL-CIO was drawing on a more ongoing set of volunteers than had been the case during the 1990s, using individuals trained as organizers to do much of the personal contact. By 2000, the AFL-CIO also had a larger list of individuals from which to choose. Former AFL-CIO political director Steve Rosenthal estimates that the group had thirteen thousand full-time organizers and one hundred thousand volunteers active in the twelve states the group targeted in 2000.

This network was put to work in several House and Senate races as well as in the presidential race. The AFL-CIO targeted seventy-one House districts, more than in 1998 but fewer than in 1996. The organization sought to focus on competitive districts with at least twenty-five thousand union members. Several Senate seats also received substantial attention from the AFL-CIO. In Michigan, for example, the United Auto Workers had negotiated Election Day as a paid holiday, ensuring that thousands of union members would be available to serve as poll workers or to distribute last-minute fliers or leaflets. The AFL-CIO used its recently constructed computer database of members to cross-check union members against Michigan's voter registration lists.

Several AFL-CIO unions also undertook activities in 2000. The American Federation of Teachers (AFT) worked closely with the NAACP to turn out votes for Democratic presidential candidate Al Gore in several major urban areas and for Senate races, most notably Hillary Clinton's New York campaign. The Service Employees' International Union (SEIU) made its most coordinated national political effort ever, expanding its focus from the seven or eight states in which it had worked in previous elections to more than twenty states. The SEIU claims that between sixteen thousand and twenty thousand members volunteered in the 2000 election, and the organization's ubiquitous purple trucks served as mobile centers for get-out-the-vote calls. The SEIU conducted surveys and focus groups to find out how best to tailor its message to members.

The 2002 Elections.   In 2002, unions followed a similar agenda but had a sense that it would be difficult to top the efforts of 2000. It was apparent early in the election season that the 2002 elections would be difficult for labor; many of the competitive races were not in districts or states that had strong union presences, and even in locales that had such presences, some of the stronger candidates lacked union ties. The issue environment also did not favor unions, although some unions, such as the SEIU, took out advertisements that addressed national security concerns. In addition to these problems, some of the strongest labor efforts were also lost on weak Democratic candidates.

The AFL-CIO ultimately spent thirty-five million dollars on voter mobilization, assembled 750 paid staff members and 4,000 local coordinators, and expanded its efforts to match membership lists with voter registration files. According to internal data, the AFL-CIO improved on its numbers of 2000: 68 percent of union members voted for Democratic candidates in the House, and 70 percent voted for Democratic Senate candidates in battleground states; 93 percent of union members in these states reported being contacted by their unions.[1] After the election, Rosenthal

(2002) attributed Democratic losses in the Senate to the fact that most of the Republican gains came in states with low union density, including Georgia, New Hampshire, and the Carolinas.

One of the most notable aspects of 2002, however, was that the AFL-CIO ceased all television advertising as of October 7. Union leaders attributed this decision to the glut of issue advertisements in battleground states or districts and to the unfavorable issue environment, but Republicans trumpeted the change as evidence that Democrats were having a difficult time in these races. The AFL-CIO remained one of the major advertisers among Democratic-leaning groups, but its spending dropped substantially from previous elections (Magleby and Tanner 2004, 75). The SEIU and the National Education Association (NEA) also continued to run advertisements, but again, their advertising buys were much smaller than had been the case in 2000 or even 1998.

The 2004 Elections. The AFL-CIO followed the same personal-contact strategy in 2004, again increasing its sophistication. In addition to the spending by labor-supported 527s, the AFL-CIO spent forty-five million dollars on mobilizing members. The AFL-CIO reported that five thousand members were doing paid political work, a threefold increase from 2000, and that two hundred thousand members were doing volunteer work (Williams 2004). Other unions also increased their spending; the SEIU spent sixty-five million dollars on mobilization, including forty million dollars to cover the salaries of SEIU members on leave from their jobs. Because of the small number of battleground states, many larger unions paid to send members to other states to do mobilization work. Other unions, such as the United Mine Workers, often had the good fortune to have their members concentrated in battleground states and undertook mobilization work without the cost of sending members elsewhere.

The overall results of the 2004 election were disappointing for unions. The percentage of union members who supported the Democratic presidential ticket was comparable to 2000—one exit poll showed that two-thirds of union members voted for John Kerry (Strope 2004). But the percentage of voters who were union members dropped to 14 percent, and the percentage who came from union households fell to 24 percent. It is hard to know how to read these figures—it may simply be that in an election where mobilization is so important to both parties, labor's efforts become less important even if they are no less effective. Whatever the cause of this decline, however, the 2004 election results abetted factional conflicts that had been brewing within the AFL-CIO before the election.

External Context

Apart from the appearance of large 527 organizations, the changes in union strategy from 2000 through 2004, 2006, and 2008 appear to be more of a gradual development than a sudden reaction to changes in campaign finance law. Many contextual factors have influenced unions' development; BCRA is only one piece of this context.

Presidential Politics. In 2000, unions experienced little conflict about endorsing Gore. In 2004, however, unions initially split among Democratic contenders Howard Dean, John Kerry, and Richard Gephardt. Many analysts viewed this conflict as an episode in the ongoing battle over the AFL-CIO's direction and over who would succeed John Sweeney should Sweeney step down following the election. AFSCME and SEIU's joint endorsement of Dean was notable because some observers saw it as a resolution of the conflict over organizing and political tactics that pitted the AFL-CIO's two largest unions against each other. Other news reports, however, cast the joint endorsement as either a somewhat grudging concession to share the stage by the SEIU, which had already decided to endorse Dean, or an effort by AFSCME's Gerald McEntee to avoid being upstaged by the SEIU's Andrew Stern. Regardless of the reason, the fact that two of the AFL-CIO's most influential unions would be competing against the twenty-one-union Gephardt coalition in Iowa accentuated the visibility of the AFL-CIO's internal split.

Congressional Politics. At the congressional level, the AFL-CIO and its member unions spent 2000, 2002, and 2004 slowly adjusting to the Republican majorities and to the need to maintain some access to Republican members of Congress. The AFL-CIO did not pursue this strategy to the same degree as some of its member unions and parted ways with many of the liberal advocacy groups that at times support moderate Republicans. In 2002, Rosenthal had argued that the AFL-CIO needed to shepherd its limited resources and should not court Republicans simply because they were slightly better on labor issues than their colleagues: "We shouldn't be lowering the bar for our endorsement. Instead of endorsing more mediocre Republicans, we should be endorsing fewer mediocre Democrats" (Moberg 2002, 15). Francia (2000) has shown, however, that AFL-CIO contributions to all types of candidates—Republican or Democrat, conservative, moderate, or liberal—increased in raw dollar terms following the 1996 elections,[2] and Francia provides several instances of Sweeney's conciliatory 1998 statements about courting Republicans.

Further evidence that labor increased its access-seeking behavior comes from the appearance of Democratic House leader Nancy Pelosi and DCCC chair Robert Matsui at a March 2004 AFL-CIO retreat. Both Pelosi and Matsui urged the assembled union leaders not to contribute to House Republicans. According to one union leader who was present, the National Association of Letter Carriers' George Gould, Pelosi and Matsui were responding to an event benefiting Speaker Dennis Hastert's Keep Our Majority PAC that involved several more moderate unions. Several unions also supported incumbent Pennsylvania Republican senator Arlen Specter in his contested primary in 2004; Specter's coalition even included several of the more militant unions, such as the International Union of Painters and Allied Trades (IUPAT). Gould spoke about working to establish relationships with members of Congress against whom the union had previously campaigned; he mentioned an independent expenditure against Republican Robert Ney that ultimately led to greater dialogue between the union and Ney and the union's subsequent decision not to campaign against Ney in future elections.

Communications Technology. Because labor unions are not voluntary membership groups, they have less need than do advocacy groups to use communications technology to recruit members or to ensure that existing members know of their activities. However, union members are more likely than the average citizen to own computers—according to internal surveys conducted in 2002, 77 percent of union members used e-mail and were on union e-mail lists.[3] Studies from 2000, 2002, and 2004 showed that slightly more than 60 percent of the general public had Internet access at the time (Bimber 2004, 211). In 2000, the AFL-CIO introduced a program to provide free home computers to members who agreed to use the AFL-CIO Web site as their home page (Mattzie 2004). At the time, few unions used the splashy methods that some advocacy groups have used to rally their members— they did not, for example, distribute political videos on their Web sites, and most union Web sites did not contain the type of political rhetoric that advocacy groups' sites employ. The Change to Win Coalition began to add these strategies in the 2006 and 2008 elections. According to Tom Mattzie (2004), then of the AFL-CIO Public Affairs Department, the AFL-CIO increased its e-mail contact with members as a means of cementing the year-round contact that Rosenthal and others argue is important for establishing the trust that precedes election-related contacts.

One intriguing development in the AFL-CIO's use of the Internet has been the creation of Working America, a new type of "nonunion union" within the AFL-CIO that anyone can join free of charge. In early 2004, the AFL-CIO began canvassing neighborhoods with large union populations, looking for people who were not unionized but were in jobs similar to union members (or displayed attitudes similar to union members) and asking them to join Working America.[4] The AFL-CIO also added a section to its Web site allowing citizens to join Working America by sending the union their e-mail addresses. Membership in Working America does not confer voting rights within the union or any other benefits, but it does enable the AFL-CIO to broaden the number of individuals whom it can contact and to count these contacts as membership communications. And, perhaps particularly important, the AFL-CIO can solicit contributions to its PAC from these individuals, who will have no competing union allegiances for their money. As of June 2004, Working America director Karen Nussbaum (2004) claimed that the organization had registered three hundred thousand people and that the AFL-CIO had set targets for membership in battleground states such as Ohio, with a goal of recruiting one million members by the 2004 election.

BCRA

These contextual factors contributed to the evolution of labor's strategy in 2004; they were influenced or abetted by BCRA, but not entirely caused by BCRA. During the 1990s, organized labor began to recognize that it needed to establish a political program independent of the Democratic Party. Yet changes in campaign finance law were required to bring about many aspects of this new program, and although these changes may ultimately improve organized labor's ability to advocate on behalf of its members, many people within the AFL-CIO resisted these changes.

Hard and Soft Money. Despite the AFL-CIO's argument that it could not increase contributions to its PAC, some unions either increased PAC receipts or found that they had greater freedom for PAC spending under BCRA. The SEIU dramatically increased its PAC receipts in 2004, and both the AFT and the NEA found that they had much greater freedom to spend PAC dollars because their soft money contributions had previously come out of their PACs. The AFL-CIO did not contest BCRA's soft money ban to the extent that the organization contested other provisions of the law. AFL-CIO leaders claimed that despite organized labor's large contributions to the Democratic Party, contributions from businesses to both parties exceeded labor's total contributions by a factor of twelve to one in 2002 and nine to one in 2000. The AFL-CIO also redirected the money it had been giving to the parties into other venues for political activity, most notably toward member mobilization and toward new 527 organizations. The AFL-CIO has a large enough membership and a broad enough issue focus that it would not necessarily lose its leverage in seeking to communicate its immediate policy goals to party leaders. The same, however, cannot be said for many of its member unions.

Several leaders of individual unions reported that they felt they had lost a crucial means of communication with the parties with the abolition of soft money. Liz Smith of the AFT noted that her union had lost its ability to connect political contributions to its particular goals. Because 527s cannot be held directly accountable by their donors and because of the lack of a direct link between 527s and party leaders, the AFT could no longer combine contributions with advocacy. Despite these misgivings, however, the AFT contributed to six newly formed 527s, including America Votes and the Media Fund.

According to Sean McGarvey of the IUPAT, BCRA did not really affect what his union does best, which is to field volunteers to help candidates. IUPAT was not one of the larger unions in soft money contributions—it gave $940,000 in 2000 but only $200,000 in 2002—but saw soft money as a way to increase its visibility among Democratic and occasionally Republican leaders. IUPAT did not see contributions to the 527s as furthering its objectives.

These comments indicate that many labor leaders saw soft money contributions as a means of establishing a relationship with the parties as much as of advancing a broader ideological agenda. Groups for which it makes sense to turn this money into contributions to 527 organizations must first be large enough to possess a seat at the table with party leaders and must have an agenda that goes beyond the immediate economic concerns of group members. Second, they must have adequate funds to mobilize their members before donating to 527s, again ensuring that larger unions would be better candidates for funding 527s. And third, they must at times find it advantageous to do advocacy work that is not necessarily tied to the name or reputation of their individual union. Such 527s as the Media Fund also are venues for unions to fund advertising without the viewer knowing that these ads are supported in part by unions. For a union such as IUPAT, which has always sought to make its members visible in their political activities, or the International Association of Firefighters, which feels that its members have substantial credibility and a positive public image that they can use for political purposes, funding activities through other organizations does not necessarily make sense.

Electioneering. Table 5.2 shows union spending on television advertisements in 2000, 2002, and 2004. The table does not include spending in 2004 by 527 groups other than those that were entirely dependent on union funds. The table shows roughly what labor leaders had been saying—union spending on advertising decreased between 2000 and 2004; some of the change may be attributable to BCRA, but the dramatic drop in spending between 2000 and 2002 indicates that unions also had strategic reasons to decrease their spending. A shift in timing also occurred, partly because of the electioneering rules. In 2000, most of the AFL-CIO's advertising aired after September 1. In 2004, the AFL-CIO and Communities for Quality Education (a group funded by the NEA) concentrated their advertising in the period between Super Tuesday and the national party conventions, avoiding the sixty-day period during which unions may not use their treasury funds to pay for candidate-specific advertising. In contrast, unions with ample PAC money, such as the United Auto Workers and SEIU, ran their ads in the fall, meaning that they had to be paid for with hard money. A comparison of table 5.2 with subsequent tables in this chapter shows that union spending on television advertisements remained substantial, but by 2004, many nonunion groups were spending far more.

Labor-Funded 527s. By 2004, several newly formed 527 organizations received labor funding. Some of these groups were small and had been put together for relatively narrow purposes. By the 2002 elections, however, it seemed evident that unions would attempt to form one or more overarching 527 groups that would pool resources from several of the internationals and then use them to replicate the AFL-CIO's turnout strategy for nonmembers. What was not clear was whether conflict between union leaders would enable the AFL-CIO and its members to avoid establishing competing 527s, thereby potentially duplicating each other's efforts.

The initial labor foray into establishing a turnout-oriented 527 was the Partnership for America's Families, which announced its formation with Rosenthal as director in June 2003. The Partnership began voter registration and mobilization efforts in urban areas of Pennsylvania and Ohio, using the 2003 Philadelphia mayoral race as a test case of whether the AFL-CIO's contact strategy could work among minorities and nonmembers. Soon after its formation, however, most members of the Partnership's board resigned

TABLE 5.2. Number of Candidate-Specific Broadcast Television Spots Purchased by Labor Unions and Other Labor Organizations, 2000–2004

	2000			2002			2004			
Organization	Top 75 Markets	Top 75 within 60 Days	Organization	Top 75 Markets	Top 75 within 60 Days	Organization	Top 75 Markets	Top 75 within 60 Days	210 Markets[a]	210 Markets/ 60 Days
AFL-CIO	17,050	9,779	AFL-CIO	4,244	2,945	AFL-CIO	5,642	0	10,962	0
NEA	511	511	NEA	194	194	Communities for Quality Education (NEA)	3,783	63	5,238	63
American Family Voices	447	0	Others	405	397	UAW	1,754	1,754	2,664	2,664
Others	59	0				SEIU	1,206	979	2,213	1,731
						AFSCME	430	0	2,111	0
						Others	833	580	1,314	1,314
Total	18,067	10,290	Total	4,843	3,536	Total	13,648	3,376	24,502	5,772

Source: Campaign Finance Institute analysis of data supplied by the Wisconsin Advertising Project.
[a] All 210 markets available only for 2004.

amid conflict over mobilizing minority voters. With union leaders exchanging barbs, Sweeney brokered a compromise: a new board would be constituted, and AFSCME would form its own 527, Voices for Working Families (VWF), with the AFL-CIO's Arlene Holt-Baker as director.

In August, Ellen Malcolm of EMILY's List announced the formation of America Coming Together (ACT), dedicated to canvassing, with Rosenthal as the group's CEO. ACT had less of a focus on civil rights issues than did VWF, and the two organizations would divide responsibilities. ACT would also work closely with a number of other organizations—the board included leaders of established organizations such as the Sierra Club as well as EMILY's List. In addition, ACT would collaborate with several recently formed groups, among them America Votes and several organizations targeting younger voters. The Partnership was essentially absorbed by ACT; Rosenthal brought most of the staff from the Partnership with him to ACT, and the group began canvassing efforts in the same areas where the Partnership had announced that it would work. ACT received a relatively small percentage of its $79.8 million budget from unions; the SEIU, at $4 million, and the Teamsters, at $1 million, were the only unions to give over $1 million. Yet ACT's strategy nonetheless represented a natural extension of the AFL-CIO's canvassing strategy in the previous several elections. The existence of ACT also enabled labor unions to focus their resources more directly on their members.

ACT's contact strategy closely resembled that used by the AFL-CIO but moved ahead technologically. At the 2004 Take Back America Conference, ACT's JoDee Winterhof (2004) explained that for each state in which ACT was active, voting, canvassing, and registration targets were set. Both paid and volunteer canvassers used Palm Pilots in their initial contacts with voters, acquiring information about issues of concern. This information was then linked to the individual's name, so that subsequent canvassers could provide information about the Bush administration's policies on these issues. The Palm Pilots were equipped with brief videos of local citizens discussing their views on the economy, job loss, and other issues.

After the 2004 election, Rosenthal (2004) argued that despite the outcome, ACT had met its target goals in the battleground states. The problem for ACT, he argued, was the Bush campaign's success in framing issues and Kerry's failure to position himself as a viable alternative.

Much of ACT's funding was funneled through another organization, the Joint Victory Campaign 2004, that collected donations for ACT and its sister organization, the Media Fund. As its name suggests, the Media Fund focused primarily on advertising, while ACT did no advertising on television or radio. According to CRP data, the Media Fund also received donations from several unions, including the SEIU, AFSCME, the AFT, the Laborers' Union, the Communications Workers of America, the Union of Needletrades, Industrial, and Textile Employees, the International Brotherhood of Electrical Workers, the Plumbers and Pipefitters Union, and the AFL-CIO. The Media Fund's primary purpose was to run advertisements critical of Bush in targeted states, but Kerry's substantial fund-raising before the Democratic Convention may have reduced the Media Fund's advertising. By March 2004, the Media Fund had focused its advertising on states where Bush was making appearances, seeking to bird-dog Bush by bringing up local issues. While ACT remained visible and in fact increased its profile as the election approached by organizing a series of high-profile rock concerts in targeted states, the Media Fund disbanded in the fall of 2004. The Media Fund's Harold Ickes became president of ACT in early 2005, but the group disbanded later that year.

These 527 groups served as a vehicle for union spending but were not run by union leaders. Contributions to ACT or the Media Fund certainly could not be leveraged on issue positions or campaigning strategies in the way that contributions to the parties might be. It would be hard to say that the issues these groups chose were not issues of importance to unions—all of the Media Fund's ads, for example, either discussed jobs and the economy or highlighted the relationship between the Bush administration and energy interests. ACT and the Media Fund attempted to keep unions abreast of their activities; during the spring Bal Harbour conference, leaders of both groups gave detailed presentations about their activities to the assembled union leaders, but the communication went only one way.

While ACT and VWF represent a natural expansion of the AFL-CIO's contact strategy, the Media Fund's advertising represents a slightly less obvious evolution. The AFL-CIO had been growing increasingly skeptical about large advertising campaigns, and the Media Fund enabled labor to speak to nonunion voters but covered the fact that the message was coming from a union. Despite statements opposing the use of "shell groups" or blandly named 527s, labor used this approach in the past and continued to do so after BCRA. Rosenthal referred to one ad purchase made in 1998 under a coalition name rather straightforwardly: "Frankly, we've taken a page out of [business's] book because in some places it's more effective to run an ad by the 'Coalition to Make Our Voices Heard' than it is to say 'paid for by the men and women of the AFL-CIO'" (Magleby 2000, 54). In 1996, the AFL-CIO may have wanted to attach its name to ads because of its desire to announce its expanded political program; by 2004, doing so was no longer necessary.

Summary

More than most other groups, labor has had political success in mobilizing its membership, but it has struggled with the desire or need to shape how others view labor. Labor's partisanship makes identifying the consequences of campaign finance reform particularly difficult. Unions were certainly willing to spend whatever it took to defeat George W. Bush and congressional Republicans, and these groups consequently improved on successful pre-BCRA strategies while pushing the limits of the law in regard to electioneering and communication with nonmembers. During the 2004 elections, the changes in labor's mobilization and electioneering efforts seemed a natural response to reform, but developments during Democratic administrations may be more difficult to link to changes in campaign finance law.

Business and Trade Associations

Although businesses and trade groups have a long history of lobbying Congress, they have not always been major forces in elections. This pattern changed in the late 1990s, when business leaders framed a joint venture, the Coalition: Americans Working for Real Change, almost entirely in reactive terms. In 1998 and 2000, according to many in the business community, labor outmobilized business, and in those elections, business groups' strategies of issue advocacy and soft money contributions did not provide an adequate counterweight to labor's efforts. As a result, the more politically prominent lead PACs, peak associations, and trade groups, including the Business-Industry Political Action Committee (BIPAC), the Chamber of Commerce, and the National Federation of Independent Businesses (NFIB), sought to expand their grassroots efforts. These groups used the Internet to provide customized candidate information to businesses and taught business owners how to encourage workers to vote and to provide information to workers without expressly advocating on behalf of any candidate. This development was not entirely unprecedented for business (see Phillips-Fein 2008), but BCRA enabled (or forced) businesses to refocus their efforts on this sort of communication.

For peak business groups, the money business PACs can provide to candidates is secondary to the mobilization efforts. One consequence of BCRA is that while business may still play as large a role as ever in elections, peak organizations, or the voice of the business community, rather than individual businesses are strongest.

Election Strategy

The 2000 Elections. The elections of 2000 marked two departures for business groups. First, several new front organizations debuted, spending vast amounts of money on television advertising. Citizens for Better Medicare (CBM), an organization funded by the pharmaceutical industry, spent $6.8 million on television ads favoring House Republicans (Baker and Magleby 2002). A similar organization, Americans for Job Security (AJS), also advertised heavily in several races, spending a total of $3.5 million for Republican Senate candidates and for George W. Bush's campaign. Although AJS has been described as a front group for the insurance industry, its funding base included the Chamber of Commerce and other business interests.

Second, 2000 marked the beginning of BIPAC's Web-based political communication program, then called Project 2000 and now known as the Prosperity Project (P2). Project 2000 sought to help companies expand their communications with employees; it consisted of candidate biographies and voting summaries tailored to the legislative interests of member companies. The materials were customized for individual businesses, so that the information provided appeared to come from the company rather than from a national trade association about which rank-and-file employees would be expected to know little. BIPAC also conducted research that showed that workers are likely to be receptive to and even welcoming of political information provided by their employers and that workers found employers to be more credible sources of political information than were labor unions. In its first year, the project had fifty companies as subscribers and delivered messages about the election to 1.5 million employees. BIPAC touted the program's efficiency—the project's reported cost of $450,000 translates to thirty cents per voter contacted, a rate that would be far superior to that of labor. Corporations cannot explicitly endorse candidates in communications that will reach beyond their restricted class (Potter 1997). Hence, to benefit from participation in P2, companies must be reasonably confident that if they provide employees with information about where candidates stand on issues of importance to the companies, employees will vote in the company's interests.

The 2002 Elections. In 2002, CBM disappeared but was replaced by the United Seniors Association, a similar group in the sense that while it claimed a grassroots following, the bulk of its advertisements were funded by the same large pharmaceutical corporations. United Seniors was the biggest nonparty spender on ads, with its $8.1 million expenditure more than doubling that of the second-largest spender, the AFL-CIO. AJS spent $1.6 million on advertisements. These groups ran many of their advertisements late in the campaign, to the point that some targeted candidates apparently were taken by surprise. The two Democratic House members defeated in 2002 had large advertising buys made in their districts by AJS or United Seniors in the closing weeks of the campaign, and neither of these candidates had been featured on lists of the most endangered House members in preelection analyses.

BIPAC's Web-based P2 program was expanded from 50 to 184 companies, and state-level Prosperity Projects were introduced in thirty-one states. The perceived success of business's get-out-the-vote strategy, however, created a rift between business groups and the Republican Party. BIPAC's chief executive officer, Greg Casey; Chamber of Commerce vice president Bruce Josten; the National Association of Wholesaler-Distributors's president, Dirk Van Dongen; and others saw the 2002 election as a vindication of business's new mobilization strategy and viewed this strategy as an effective response to BCRA. Many business groups welcomed the soft money ban as an opportunity to redirect money that would otherwise have gone to the parties into internal communications or into nonpolitical purposes, and they viewed programs such as the P2 as a means of helping to elect probusiness candidates for a fraction of the cost of soft money donations and of maintaining control over the political messages they sent. Thus, when Republican strategists sought to encourage businesses to help fund Republican 527s, they met opposition. Van Dongen told *Roll Call* that "business leaders have concluded that the better use of their resources is to mobilize their own kind," and another business leader noted that businesses were now better positioned to rebuff Republican pressure to donate to Republican candidates who were running against probusiness Democrats (Mullins 2003).

The 2004 Elections. The small number of closely contested states in the presidential race and the small number of competitive House and Senate races ensured that in 2004 business groups could narrowly target their resources. The shell groups that were a feature of the 2000 and 2002 elections were nowhere to be found in 2004, in part because their late advertising was now prohibited (although 527 groups could have taken on some of this work). Targeted mobilization work consequently became all the more important. BIPAC, for example, reduced the number of states in which it ran Prosperity Projects. In addition, although businesses did not move early to organize 527 organizations to counter the groups set up by liberal donors and labor unions, businesses had the benefit, as in 1996, of observing where these groups were active and evaluating these groups' activities before moving to counter them.

In 2004, business PACs leaned strongly toward the Republicans. A postelection analysis by the Associated Press (2004) indicated that 245 of the 268 largest corporate PACs gave a majority of their contributions to Republicans and that overall, corporate PACs favored Republicans by a ten-to-one margin. And business PACs grew between the 2002 and 2004 elections, though not as much as many analysts had expected. Long before the election, business association leaders were arguing that PACs would need to grow to replace the soft money businesses had given in the past, and some business associations worked extensively with individual companies to help companies grow their PACs. BIPAC, for example, conducted a series of training sessions and briefings for PAC directors and worked with the Graduate School of Political Management at George Washington University to develop a graduate program in PAC management (Tennille 2002).

The outcomes of the 2004 presidential and congressional elections gave peak business associations even more of a sense that their mobilization strategy was yielding results. According to BIPAC's Darrell Shull, internal studies estimated that the Prosperity Project yields one extra vote per ten people contacted, a fraction that he claimed equals the Bush margin of victory in four of the states where BIPAC was active (Shull 2004). And, he argued, BIPAC spent less than ten million dollars on the Prosperity Project, less than one-tenth what the SEIU, AFSCME, and ACT spent. BIPAC leaders were more sanguine, however, about the results of congressional campaigns; while Republicans made gains in both the House and the Senate, very few of the Democratic incumbents targeted by BIPAC were defeated, and in many of these races, the margins were not even close (Budde 2004). Thus, while business groups were content with their mobilization strategy, they felt that its effects were limited to open-seat congressional races and to the presidential race.

External Context

Presidential Politics. Business groups were early contributors to George W. Bush's 2004 presidential campaign. According to the Center for Responsive Politics, Bush received $2,000,000 in contributions from business PACs, while Kerry received only $141,918 from all PACs. This figure leaves aside, of course, contributions by individuals allied with these businesses, and it is also dwarfed by both candidates' overall fund-raising totals, but it indicates business groups' preference for Bush. Bush's domestic agenda was broad enough that most of the larger trade associations rallied around pieces of it. In some ways, most business groups' ability to support across-the-board tax cuts, for example, may have facilitated the ability of BIPAC and the Chamber of Commerce to provide nearly uniform issue content to their members.

However, the Bush campaign's financial resources may have limited business groups' active involvement in both of his campaigns. Although Edison Electric CEO Thomas Kuhn organized a group, CEOs for Bush, in 2003 (see Stone 2003), business groups did not appear to be as involved in the presidential race (or rather, involved in the presidential race to the exclusion of other campaigns) as did groups on the left. The fact that the Republican National Committee had a mobilization operation and was at the least not expected, in the months following the enactment of BCRA, to be as needy as the Democratic National Committee meant that business groups were not as vital a cog in the Bush campaign as liberal interest groups were for Kerry.

In addition, much of the rhetoric of business groups in 2003 and 2004 revolved around congressional politics. The Associated Builders and Contractors (ABC), for example, spoke frequently of being "twenty votes down in the House" and three or four votes down in the Senate but was less involved in the closing months of the Bush campaign. ABC had made an effort to endorse Bush particularly early, but as the campaign wore on, it expended resources in states such as Oklahoma and Alaska that were not important in the presidential race.

Congressional Politics. Differences in the strategies of corporate PACs and larger business trade associations are particularly notable in congressional races. Many larger corporate PACs tend to give most of their support to incumbents and to limit their activities primarily to making campaign donations. In part, such behavior results from a reluctance to alienate legislators whom these corporations might need to lobby. Trade associations, conversely, have greater freedom to choose candidates based on their ideology. In 2004, for example, twenty-seven of the twenty-nine candidates BIPAC supported were Republicans, while only nine were challengers. Trade associations are more ideological in their giving, albeit at a cost of struggling a bit more to reach consensus about which issues to promote and which candidates to support. Peak business groups also expressed a greater willingness to become involved in Democratic and Republican primaries between 2000 and 2004, in part as a consequence of redistricting and of a handful of races featuring two incumbents in 2002 and 2004 but also because this strategy enabled groups to become active in heavily partisan districts. In many of these cases, such involvement was limited to PAC contributions, but large trade associations' endorsements can frequently prompt contributions from many other groups.

Such activities were not always greeted warmly by the National Republican Senatorial Committee (NRSC) and the National Republican Congressional Committee (NRCC). During 2000, the NRCC maintained a 75 Percent Club, open to PACs that gave at least that percentage of their money to Republicans (Willis 2000). While NRCC chair Tom Reynolds referred to this effort merely as a means of recognizing Republican backers, the 75 percent figure can also be seen as a way of pressuring PACs to meet this threshold. One problem with establishing such a figure was that it diminished Republicans' leverage over businesses that had already given more than 75 percent of their money to party candidates. Casey, for example, noted that he told Republican leaders that he still could add 15 percent to his contributions to Democrats.

Another major development that affected business groups was the proliferation of leadership PACs. The amount of money contributed to candidates by these PACs, which are run by members of Congress or holders of other prominent political offices, grew from $11 million in 1998 to $27.5 million in 2004, and the number of member PACs grew from 119 to 222 over this period (Bedlington and Malbin 2003). Many observers believed that the passage of BCRA would increase the number and size of these PACs, and many business groups anticipated devoting a larger share of their resources to these PACs. PACs with stringent criteria for contributions have sought to develop criteria for contributions to leadership PACs; for example, ABC's PAC has relatively inflexible criteria for contributions to members, requiring not only that the sponsors of leadership PACs to which it donates must vote with ABC 70 percent of the time but that 85 percent of the contributions from the leadership PAC must go to members who also vote with ABC 70 percent of the time. Other companies, however, found that they needed to expand their PACs dramatically to keep up with increasing demand from members of Congress (see Alden and Buckley 2004).

Corporate PACs and business associations legally cannot bundle, but many larger business associations sought to come close by encouraging their restricted class to contribute in particular races and by seeking to keep track, either before or after the election, of contributions from their members. In 2002, ABC placed a video on its Web site describing the Senate races about which it was most concerned and encouraging members to become involved in these races. The National Association of Realtors inaugurated its Direct Giver program in 2004, enabling members to pledge a certain amount of money to Realtor-supported candidates and then report back about whether these donations had been made. The Realtors estimated that in 2004, two hundred members made pledges totaling about four hundred thousand dollars. Both of these groups also analyzed FEC data after the election to measure how much their members had contributed, a practice common among all types of interest groups.

Communications Technology. With the development of the Internet, business groups clearly were able to change their strategies. Numerous business organizations began to provide candidate information on their Web sites during the late 1990s, but the systematic presentation of candidate information by BIPAC merits particular notice. The Prosperity Project did not present features that have not been used by issue advocacy organizations but allowed companies to frame the information as they best saw fit, making themselves essentially on par with these organizations. A crucial difference was that citizens must seek out an advocacy group's political information, while the Prosperity Project materials were available to workers at their company sites, which employees likely check frequently for nonpolitical reasons, and thus came from a source employees were likely to know and perhaps to trust.

According to Casey, in 2000, BIPAC "relied on the site being pushed by national associations and national companies." Several companies, including Halliburton, Procter and Gamble, and Exxon-Mobil, initially signed on to use the site, albeit with skepticism, but later became advocates and encouraged other companies to use it. Business groups' general acceptance of the P2 and similar Internet-based mobilization efforts was clearly evident by 2004. According to Birnbaum and Edsall (2004), 91 of the 160 Business Roundtable members used the Prosperity Project. The Chamber of Commerce, using a similar system, enlisted 75 companies, 230 local chambers, and 95 trade associations in its mobilization effort. In addition to BIPAC's efforts, the Chamber sent thirty million e-mails and drew on its 215 political staff members in thirty-one states to send out direct mail and make phone calls (Morgenson and Justice 2005).

Many other trade associations either adapted the Prosperity Project (with the encouragement and support of BIPAC) or developed other Web-based techniques. ABC provided downloadable "Toolbox Talks" that employers could read to their employees. Each weekly talk had a different theme, but all were political in nature and sought to present the association's views on the issues of importance in elections. The Chamber of Commerce and the NFIB also substantially increased the amount of political information disseminated to and collected from members via the Internet. The biggest obstacle for each of these groups, as both the Chamber's Josten and BIPAC's Casey admit, has been employers' reluctance actively to engage in politics. Casey noted that businesses using the P2 often did not do as much as they could to publicize it, and he claimed that a wide range existed in the degree to which companies promoted the site, with those that aggressively pushed it having a track record of political engagement. Both BIPAC and the Chamber have sought to emphasize their ability to take political stances that their member companies may not be willing to take (Morgenson and Justice 2005), but for some companies, employee mobilization, even under the auspices of peak associations or without explicit political advocacy, may have a downside.

BCRA

From the beginning of the debate on the McCain-Feingold campaign finance reform proposals, corporations and labor unions were referred to as the two major groups whose political activity ought to be restricted. The judges' opinions in both the *McConnell* district court case and the Supreme Court case frequently cite organizations such as CBM and AJS. Many of the larger trade associations testified during the BCRA case, and most opposed the bill. But degrees of opposition existed, and groups differed in their grounds for opposing the bill. These differences correspond to groups' responses to the new law.

Soft and Hard Money. Well before the passage of BCRA, several large corporations had either stopped giving soft money to the parties entirely or had dramatically decreased their soft money giving (for a full list, see

Mullins and Mitchell 2001). In addition, many other companies had announced their support for a soft money ban but continued to make soft money donations. Because so many business groups felt that their soft money contributions were pulled rather than pushed into the system, it is unsurprising that following the enactment of BCRA, many businesses reported no adverse effects.

Although PAC giving did not increase substantially in 2004, businesses clearly expected it to do so. ABC expanded its PAC governing board in anticipation of doing more political work; the group expanded not only its giving to candidates but also its contributions to leadership PACs to approximately two hundred thousand dollars and expanded its PAC funding of independent expenditures to close to three hundred thousand dollars. Many groups worked to expand the number of contributors to their PACs; the Chamber of Commerce had lobbied Congress in 2001 to relax rules on soliciting employees for PAC contributions, claiming that up to 30 percent of contributions to the Chamber had been diverted into soft money accounts in the past but were in amounts small enough that they could have been used as hard money contributions. Although this language was not included in the bill, PACs sought to expand their solicitations to employees, and larger business associations worked to train their members in growing their PACs. One feature of the Prosperity Project, for example, is training for businesses in PAC solicitations and PAC management. BIPAC supplements its training with surveys of business PACs, monthly briefings for PAC directors on different subjects, and individualized evaluation of member companies' PACs.

For many larger PACs, however, matters continued very much as they had before. The National Association of Realtors maintained a similar contribution strategy throughout the elections of the 2000s, has continued to fund similar independent expenditure programs through these election cycles, and, perhaps because of the size of its PAC, found little cause to reevaluate its strategy. The Realtors' director of political programs, Greg Knopp, noted that his group's political efforts were largely synonymous with its PAC and that any experimentation with different strategies tended to be conducted by the Realtors' state-level PACs. The Realtors' PAC grew in terms of both money (from $2.5 million in 1998 to $7.5 million in 2005) and the number of members participating (from 28 percent during the 1990s to 44 percent by 2004), but Knopp and PAC director Scott Reiter attributed these increases to efforts the Realtors would have made regardless of BCRA and to Realtors' growing interest in being politically active.

Electioneering. Relatively few business groups advertise on television, although some business groups of course spend millions of dollars on election-related ads. Many groups that advertise heavily complained bitterly about allegations that their advertisements were geared toward the election. CBM, for example, claimed that 85 percent of its advertisements during the 1999–2000 election cycle were about pending legislation and that the only politician named in these ads was President Bill Clinton, who was not standing for election in 2000. Throughout the election cycle, CBM claimed that it was a temporary coalition devoted to injecting an issue into the political debate and that it would disband if Congress acted on that issue. AJS tended to be more open about admitting the electoral component of its advertisements, but AJS president Michael Dubke defended the ads on First Amendment grounds and defended the group's name by noting that it was not an attempt to mislead; moreover, he contended, if it had been an attempt to mislead, it would have failed, since the media almost always reported on the link between AJS and the insurance industry when covering the group. Dubke also argued that disclosure of donors diverted the public from the issues the group sought to emphasize: "We don't discuss our members. The reason is we find that in other groups that have attempted to do what we're doing, that their membership becomes the issue rather than the issue they're trying to advocate. We find that sticking to a strict mantra of not discussing our members allows our issues to come to the forefront" (Kotok and Thompson 2000, 31).

Business groups' opposition to BCRA's electioneering provisions falls into two categories. First, businesses defended the use of relatively vague names, like the Coalition or Americans for Job Security, by arguing that information on the members of these groups is generally available, that in many cases these names are accurate (e.g., the Coalition was, in fact, a coalition of several organizations), and that some corporations that are reluctant to speak out on political matters under their own names for fear of reprisals from unions or employees or out of concern for sales of their products will be more likely to contribute when they are part of a coalition (for anecdotal support, see Monroe 2002; Sandherr 2002).

Second, many business groups objected in accordance with broader principles. The electioneering ban, these groups argued, would lead Congress to pass legislation during the sixty-day window without the fear of groups taking to the airwaves in opposition. Groups across the political spectrum brought up this idea, but insofar as Congress has had to convene during this period to consider appropriations bills several times in the past decade, the objection by business groups may be rooted in legitimate concerns about legislation. This concern was voiced, in fact, by several groups that have done only limited advertising. ABC, for example, has run some radio ads, but political director Ned Monroe argued that ABC's advertising was such a small percentage of its overall budget that ABC's opposition was not grounded in its own advertising strategy.[5] Instead, he claimed that "because of the controversial nature of legislation, it takes a long time to get through both chambers and through conference, it comes in the final days, and we would not be able to communicate at all in those areas to educate constituents to communicate with their elected officials about these votes." Despite ABC's limited advertising, Monroe emphasized the importance of having the option to air advertisements.

Table 5.3 shows overall trends in advertising by business groups from 2000 through 2004. Business advertising in 2004 closely resembled business advertising in 2002 with the exception of the fact that the two large "shell" organizations, United Seniors and AJS, did virtually all of their advertising within the sixty-day window in 2002 but ran their ads earlier in 2004. News accounts from the fall indicate that these two groups moved toward mobilization, direct mail, and newspaper ads by September 2004 (Edsall and Grimaldi 2004). Campaign Media Analysis Group data compiled by Magleby, Monson, and Patterson (2005, 50–51, 57) show that United Seniors spent $6.3 million on advertisements aimed at the presidential race and congressional races, and AJS spent $1.1 million on advertisements aimed at congressional races in 2004. The two trade associations that purchased large numbers of advertisements, the National Association of Realtors and the American Medical Association, paid for these advertisements with PAC funds.

Most noteworthy in this table is the degree to which trade associations turned away from television advertising after the 2000 election. Both the Chamber of Commerce and the Business Roundtable abandoned their advertising campaigns by 2002, indicating that the change in strategy resulted more from these organizations' analyses than from changes in campaign finance law.

527 Groups. Going into the 2004 election, the open question about business activity was how much of the money that had formerly been given as soft money contributions to the parties would be directed into other political activities—either donated to other organizations or used internally. While it is difficult to measure money that is used internally, contributions to 527 organizations from businesses appeared to be scarce; the larger conservative 527s, Progress for America and the 2004 Club for

TABLE 5.3. Number of Candidate-Specific Broadcast Television Spots Purchased by Business Organizations, 2000–2004

	2000			2002			2004			
Organization	Top 75 Markets	Top 75 within 60 Days	Organization	Top 75 Markets	Top 75 within 60 Days	Organization	Top 75 Markets	Top 75 within 60 Days	210 Markets[a]	210 Markets/ 60 Days
Citizens for Better Medicare	10,876	10,753	United Seniors Association	10,915	9,055	Americans for Job Security	2,290	133	5,279	134
Americans for Job Security	6,069	5,007	Americans for Job Security	1,615	1,615	United Seniors Association	1,470	6	2,291	6
Chamber of Commerce	7,574	7,574	American Medical Association	915	725	National Association of Realtors	922	922	1,701	922
Business Roundtable	4,884	4,571	National Association of Realtors	200	200	American Medical Association	442	442	1,109	1,109
American Medical Association	577	543	Others	400	131	Others	297	191	734	455
Others	857	497								
Total	30,837	28,945	Total	14,045	11,726	Total	5,421	1,694	11,114	2,626

Source: Campaign Finance Institute analysis of data supplied by the Wisconsin Advertising Project.
[a]All 210 markets available only for 2004.

Growth, received few large donations from businesses; the largest Republican 527 donors were individuals (Weissman and Hassan 2005). Many of the same companies that expressed their willingness to do away with soft money in 2001 were conspicuous among the businesses that declined to donate to 527s (Cummings 2004). Some of these companies adopted formal policies against giving to 527s, while others simply did not contribute. Some groups continued to maintain their own 527 accounts; for example, the National Association of Realtors raised almost three million dollars for its 527 in 2004. But apart from this effort and the Chamber of Commerce's November Fund 527, few business groups contributed to 527s.

Summary

Business groups reacted to shifts in the context of their activities largely by expanding programs that had worked well in the past. Of the major changes in business group activities, the increasing focus on grassroots mobilization derived from a reaction to the activities of organized labor and the growing feasibility of using the Internet as a communication tool. These adaptations limited the damage BCRA might have done to businesses' ability to affect elections. The other major changes imposed on businesses—BCRA's restrictions on electioneering and soft money contributions—were mitigated somewhat by this strategy and by the business community's emphasis on PAC growth. The removal of soft money from the system certainly raised the possibility that individual companies would become less involved in party decision making, but business leaders' growing disenchantment with the leverage soft money provided them meant that not all businesses viewed this development as a loss. In the context of aggressive efforts of large trade associations and peak organizations and the probusiness outlook of the Bush administration and a Republican Congress, then, BCRA appears to have limited the political clout of individual corporations or interests while strengthening broader and less industry-specific business associations.

Advocacy Groups

The literature on American interest groups has frequently noted that the political Left boasts a much wider array of established advocacy groups than does the Right (see, e.g., La Raja 2008, 5). Although groups representing evangelicals or social conservatives flourished during the 1980s and early 1990s, few were major contributors to the parties or advertisers by the late 1990s. Thus, the advocacy groups most affected by BCRA were established, left-leaning organizations such as the Sierra Club, Planned Parenthood, and the Human Rights Campaign (HRC). These groups were also the most inclined to be part of the extended party network, which included politicians, labor leaders, and veteran political activists, and were also most likely to engage in a coordinated response to the new laws.

Many of the larger liberal advocacy groups were rather ambivalent supporters of BCRA as it worked its way through Congress. Representative among these groups is the Sierra Club, which announced its support for BCRA in a statement claiming that "the less money that has to be raised, the more likely it is that politicians will listen to regular people, not just big-money contributors."[6] Many leaders of membership-based liberal groups believed that campaign finance reform would strengthen small donors and hurt corporate donors or wealthy, conservative interests. Speaking after the passage of BCRA, however, Gloria Totten (2003), a former political director of NARAL, contended that many of these groups had not fully understood the consequences of BCRA and speculated that had they understood, more advocacy groups might have joined labor unions in opposing the bill. Totten's comments seem directed more toward the harm BCRA could do to the Democratic Party and to the candidates these groups support than toward the groups' activities. Campaign finance reform changed what many of these groups did in 2004, but the changes were subtle, indirect, and not always negative.

Well before 2004, most of these groups recognized a need for greater collaboration in election-related activities and had begun to work together more closely. Some of the newer 527s (particularly America Votes) served as a vehicle for such collaboration, but it would likely have increased even without BCRA. As the Sierra Club's Margaret Conway (2004) noted, organizations such as America Coming Together and America Votes had been in the planning stages before BCRA and in many cases merely solidified informal relationships among groups. This coordination may have led to a greater focus on the presidential election because all groups shared a preference for any Democratic nominee and because all felt they could use their issue stances against President Bush. This coordination also led to a more targeted approach regarding the expenditure of resources in particular states and even particular cities.

Few of these groups were major soft money donors, so BCRA's soft money restrictions did not affect them directly. Many groups had hoped that the restrictions would have the indirect effect of bringing in large individual donations that had previously gone to the parties, but there is little evidence that this shift took place. In fact, the opposite may have happened—some groups' 2000 activities were fueled by large individual donations, but the beneficiaries of high-profile individual donations in 2004 were new 527 organizations. To the extent that ongoing organizations benefited financially in 2004 for reasons other than anti-Bush sentiment, they did so because of increased hard money limits. Groups that bundle contributions—veteran groups such as EMILY's List and groups that had just begun to bundle contributions, such as the HRC and Progressive Majority—increased their giving to candidates.

For the most part, however, the greatest asset of many of these groups is their reputation. The fact that the Sierra Club has long been associated with environmentalism and that Planned Parenthood has long been associated with reproductive issues makes issue-oriented communications from these groups more valuable than similar communications from a group such as the Media Fund. This asset, though, is most effectively exploited through advertising. Many smaller organizations use advertisements not solely to influence elections but also to get their issues in play early in campaigns. Such groups continued to advertise and followed up advertisements with targeted mail or telephone campaigns. A few of these groups also experimented with targeted Internet activities but were not enthusiastic about the results.

Election Strategy

The 2000 Elections.   While for many Americans the most noteworthy aspect of the 2000 election was Bush's narrow victory over Gore in the presidential race, for many interest groups on the left, the big stories were the dramatic increase in electioneering activity and the better-than-expected showing of Democrats in Senate races. The 2000 races featured an unprecedented level of activity for many liberal groups. For example, the League of Conservation Voters (LCV) spent $13,000,000 on the 2000 election, compared to only $4,000,000 in 1998 and $1,500,000 in 1996 (Birnbaum 1996). A total of $5,200,000 of this money was in television advertisements run after Super Tuesday, and as much as $700,000 was spent in the Michigan Senate race alone. The LCV also bundled contributions for candidates, held events in candidates' local media markets, engaged in independent expenditures, and employed a daily tracking system to evaluate campaigns and how LCV activity was being received.

LCV benefited in 2000 from several large individual donations, including $650,000 from members of the Rockefeller family. Other groups received even larger individual donations. Both Planned Parenthood and NARAL Pro-Choice America benefited from large grants from Pro-Choice Vote, a 527 organization established by Jane Fonda. Planned Parenthood spent $12,000,000 nationally on political activity in 2000, including $7,000,000 in the presidential race. Most of this money was spent on television, although Planned Parenthood did some radio and print advertising, e-mail, and recorded phone messages from celebrities. Throughout the election, Planned Parenthood conducted polls on the effectiveness of its advertising, and after the election it provided members with a district-by-district analysis of its activities. Most remarkable about Planned Parenthood's activities was the absence of a (c)(4) political operation before 1998 and the fact that it had set a goal of only $3,500,000 for spending in 2000. This new and overtly partisan strategy re-created the organization's political image while capitalizing on its reputation as a relatively apolitical group.

The NAACP also substantially increased its spending in 2000, establishing a new (c)(4) organization, the National Voter Fund (NVF), for issue advocacy, voter registration, and voter mobilization. The NVF was funded in part by a large anonymous grant. Although the NVF engaged in some television advertising—including a well-publicized and frequently criticized ad linking Bush's policies as Texas governor to the racially motivated murder of James Byrd Jr. in Texas—the NVF concentrated primarily on personal appeals. The organization selected nineteen states and forty House districts where it believed that African American voters could have an impact and built a 3.8 million person voter file in these areas, concentrating on "infrequent voters," which it defined as individuals who were registered to vote but had voted two or fewer times in the last four elections. These individuals received repeated contacts in different forms; the NVF's Heather Booth estimated that each of these individuals received seven mail contacts, seven phone calls, and five personal visits. The NVF hired statistical consultants to measure the effects of its activities (see Green and Gerber 2004) and supplemented them with less formal mobilization techniques—work with African American churches, volunteer training, and Election Day celebrations.

While Planned Parenthood and the NAACP were notable because they became far more visible politically in 2000 than in earlier years, other large liberal organizations followed a similar pattern. The Sierra Club had increased its spending on advertisements related to the environment in the 1990s, drawing heavily on large individual donations to do so. Like

LCV, the Sierra Club sought to improve its targeting in 2000, and it provided advice to the NAACP on its efforts. The Brady Campaign to Prevent Gun Violence (at the time still known as Handgun Control Inc.) benefited from a surge in contributions following the Columbine shootings; despite some Democratic candidates' reluctance to discuss gun-related issues, the Brady Campaign spent between $2,500,000 and $5,000,000 on television advertisements (up from $150,000 in 1998). And People for the American Way supplemented its voter mobilization efforts with television ads in swing states, discussing Supreme Court vacancies and warning voters not to vote for Ralph Nader.

As table 5.4 shows, advertising was a major component of each of these groups' strategies. Six liberal advocacy groups ran more than a thousand advertisements in 2000, and each of these groups aired more than three-quarters of its advertisements within two months of the election. Yet many organizations reported that they relied heavily on television because they had so much more money that they could indulge in this luxury.

The 2002 Elections.   The proximity of the 2002 elections to the 2001 terrorist attacks and the looming war in Iraq may have influenced the election more than did the activities of advocacy groups. These elections saw a decline in activity among several of the most active groups from 2000. Table 5.4 shows the decline in advertising; while three of 2000's five most prolific advertisers among liberal groups remained atop the list, the number of advertisements aired by these groups declined. Some of the decline may have resulted from the fact that no presidential election took place in 2002, but some of the decline also occurred because of the absence of the large donations that had stimulated groups' activities. While spending by these groups declined, however, overall spending in high-profile races increased. In South Dakota, fourteen different interest groups advertised in support of Democratic incumbent Tim Johnson (Bart and Meader 2004). In Missouri, the average voter saw thirteen advertisements per day and received four pieces of mail per day pertaining to the state's Senate race (Kropf et al. 2004).

Many of the organizations heavily involved in the 2000 elections saw cause to reevaluate their strategies in 2002. Some organizations sought to increase their use of e-mail and Internet communication, while others worked to develop closer relationships with their state and local affiliates to empower local organizers and activists. After lying dormant for several years, ProNet, an informal coordinating committee for various liberal groups, resumed operation. Planned Parenthood pared back its advertis-

TABLE 5.4. Number of Candidate-Specific Broadcast Television Spots Purchased by Liberal and Conservative Advocacy Groups, 2000–2004

2000

Organization	Top 75 Markets	Top 75 within 60 Days
Liberal Groups		
Planned Parenthood	5,916	5,916
EMILY's List	3,514	3,445
Handgun Control	2,867	2,443
Sierra Club	2,245	1,715
LCV	1,705	1,705
Campaign for a Progressive Future	1,262	979
NAACP	468	468
Others	692	98
Subtotal	**18,669**	**16,769**
Conservative Groups		
U.S. Term Limits	978	37
Americans for Limited Terms	535	195
NRA	395	358
Others	39	39
Subtotal	**1,947**	**629**
Total	**20,616**	**17,398**

2002

Organization	Top 75 Markets	Top 75 within 60 Days
Liberal Groups		
Sierra Club	1,611	1,078
EMILY's List	896	0
LCV	830	830
Reform Voter Project	665	419
NARAL	386	386
Others	478	478
Subtotal	**4,866**	**3,191**
Conservative Groups		
Club for Growth	1,574	817
Subtotal	**1,574**	**817**
Total	**6,440**	**4,008**

2004

Organization	Top 75 Markets	Top 75 within 60 Days	210 Markets[a]	210 Markets/ 60 Days
Liberal Groups				
Media Fund	40,430	5,000	74,915	9,442
MoveOn.org	24,257	3,944	43,143	7,314
New Democrat Network	5,755	5,546	10,609	10,196
Citizens for a Strong Senate	3,830	3,830	6,136	6,136
LCV	3,182	2,861	3,425	3,035
EMILY's List	2,399	851	3,955	851
Stronger America Now	742	742	1,289	1,289
Others	2,217	2,094	3,143	2,820
Subtotal	**82,812**	**24,868**	**146,615**	**41,083**
Conservative Groups				
Progress for America	8,960	7,433	23,354	19,498
Swift Boat Veterans	5,077	4,078	8,690	6,836
Club for Growth	4,760	1,602	8,151	2,934
Americans United to Preserve Marriage	549	549	705	705
NRA	538	484	1,083	1,029
Others	1,015	688	1,827	1,130
Subtotal	**20,899**	**14,834**	**43,810**	**32,132**
Total	**103,711**	**39,702**	**190,425**	**73,215**

Source: Campaign Finance Institute analysis of data supplied by the Wisconsin Advertising Project.

[a] All 210 markets available only for 2004.

ing budget, airing television ads that discussed the organization's history but did not name candidates; such ads were aimed, in part, at drawing viewers' attention to other types of communication from the group. The National Council of la Raza (NCLR) sought to emulate the NAACP's registration and mobilization strategy but did so with goals other than partisan change in mind—by focusing on states that have not traditionally been viewed as Latino strongholds, NCLR sought to raise the political profile of Latino communities in states North Carolina, Arkansas, and Iowa rather than to unseat officeholders. And the Brady Campaign decreased its spending, focusing on only two House races and one gubernatorial election.

The 2004 Elections.   In 2004, many of these groups continued in the trend begun in 2002. Planned Parenthood, HRC, the Sierra Club, and NARAL emphasized the training of activists, and in many cases these groups employed "microtargeting"—focusing on particular demographic groups within battleground states. Using survey data and voter files, these groups tailored appeals to, for example, single younger women, young mothers, Spanish speakers, or other groups. When these groups advertised, they employed similar strategies—purchasing time on cable networks whose viewers matched the demographic groups being pursued or running advertisements to coincide with visits from President Bush.

Although these organizations failed in their major 2004 goal, defeating President Bush, their narrow targeting ultimately may have been useful in evaluating their efforts; a group that focuses on one state, for example, will have less difficulty measuring its success or failure in that state than will a group that focuses its efforts more widely. The 2004 elections featured several House and Senate elections that involved liberal advocacy groups, but for most of the groups considered here, the presidential race overshadowed everything else.

External Context

Presidential Politics.   Long before it became apparent that Kerry would become the Democratic nominee, all of the groups discussed here were united in their preference for anyone but Bush. Environmental groups had criticized Bush in 2000, but not nearly to the degree that they did in the 2004 campaign. Many environmental groups reported that they felt their issues were drowned out in many 2002 races, but the membership of these groups grew rapidly under the Bush administration. LCV, for example, allocated a much larger percentage of its resources to the presidential race than it had in the past and began advertising in March 2004, far earlier than had ever before been the case.

Apart from sentiment regarding Bush, the controversial resolution of the 2000 election brought about shifts in group strategy. For example, in 1998 and 2000, People for the American Way had primarily used advertisements and traditional voter mobilization techniques. After the 2000 election, however, it developed an Election Protection program to concentrate on voter disenfranchisement. In states where disenfranchisement was expected to be widespread, the group distributed a Voter's Bill of Rights, trained volunteers to serve as poll monitors, and established a same-day legal assistance hotline for individuals who believed they had been denied their right to vote. People for the American Way spent $3 million on the program in 2002 and twice that amount in 2004. While the effort was nonpartisan, the states where disenfranchisement was expected to occur, noted the group's Kimberly Robison, would be those where the election was likely to be close, and the voters the group feared would be penalized would tend to be African Americans and other minorities, who would be likely Democratic voters. The new 527 organization America Votes also sought to emphasize voter protection in its mobilization efforts.

Another aspect of presidential politics that affected group decisions over this span of time was the fractured nature of the Democratic primary field. In 2000, many groups did not endorse in the Democratic primary, but with only two candidates and one clear favorite, it was less likely that any of these groups would play kingmaker. In 2004, many groups called attention to themselves by holding events at which the candidates spoke. The HRC, the LCV, EMILY's List, and the Campaign for America's Future held events at which most of the presidential candidates spoke. Some groups endorsed before the primary outcome was clear, but the plethora of candidates ensured that groups' messages throughout 2003 and early 2004 tended to emphasize opposition to Bush more than support for any of the Democratic alternatives.

Congressional Politics. Many organizations focused less on the House in 2002 and 2004 than they had in 2000 because they felt that Democrats were unlikely to win enough seats there to gain a majority. These perceptions also determined the level of partisanship in group activity. Groups' perceptions that Democrats had little chance at gaining control of the House led many groups to emphasize shoring up their Republican supporters. For example, in 2002, the Brady Campaign and the HRC supported Republican Connie Morella's reelection bid in Maryland's Eighth District, and the LCV took out ads on behalf of Iowa Republican Jim Leach. It may seem counterintuitive, but the HRC's Winnie Stachelberg argued that a group such as hers can help a Republican more than it can help a Democrat—the HRC's endorsement of a Republican can signal to independent voters that that candidate is a moderate, while an endorsement of a Democrat will merely second what voters already presume. As was the case for business groups, many liberal advocacy groups also become more involved in congressional primaries than had been the case in the past.

Campaign Issues. The dominant new issue in the 2002 and 2004 elections was national security. Just as this topic sidelined labor and business groups, it did not play to the strengths of very many of the liberal organizations. In the view of many group leaders, national security concerns pushed issues such as environmental protection, reproductive rights, and civil rights off the legislative agenda and out of the public spotlight for several months following the September 11 attacks. This change disadvantaged advocacy groups even more than it did other groups for several reasons. First, organizations refrained from making political appeals for several months during 2001 and 2002. Second, fund-raising became more difficult because of concerns that donors would not be receptive or that they would be thinking more about charitable contributions. And third, the changed roles of administration figures such as attorney general John Ashcroft (a convenient villain for many of these groups), the president, and the vice president rendered criticism of them more difficult.

Not all liberal groups were left without issues following the September 11 attacks, however. The Sierra Club's Margaret Conway noted that early in Bush's term, the group had sought to frame environmental issues as a matter of corporate responsibility, playing off of the Enron scandal and other instances of corporate malfeasance. After September 11 and the beginning of the Iraq War, the group shifted its focus to framing environmental issues as matters of national security, public health, and safety. And civil liberties groups such as the ACLU and, to a lesser extent, People for the American Way made opposition to the Patriot Act a centerpiece of their appeals in 2002, 2003, and 2004. For the most part, however, group leaders who may personally have opposed the war in Iraq struggled with ways to get across their views on issues unrelated to the war.

One liberal group that found itself gaining far more visibility than ever before was the HRC. Throughout the 1990s, HRC had spent much of its time focusing on antidiscrimination laws, targeting its appeals primarily to its members and to legislators. HRC had sought to demonstrate its financial clout to members of Congress, to train volunteers for activism on the local level, and to educate candidates on how to talk about gay and lesbian issues. With the 2003 *Lawrence v. Texas* Supreme Court ruling striking down state sodomy laws and the Massachusetts Supreme Court's 2003 *Goodridge v. Department of Public Health* decision allowing same-sex marriage, the HRC became more visible and shifted its legislative efforts. At the federal level, this strategy entailed seeking to block the Bush administration's proposal for a constitutional amendment barring same-sex marriage. The group also sought to block proposed constitutional amendments in fourteen states.

Some groups found that they had little to talk about, however. Congress considered virtually no gun legislation (one vote in the House and two in the Senate) during 2001 and 2002, leaving groups on both sides of the issue with few means of evaluating members of Congress. The National Rifle Association remained active, but the Brady Campaign struggled to find issues to discuss. In 2000, it had initiated a "Dangerous Dozen" list of members to target and had aired television advertisements in several major urban areas. When the House of Representatives declined to bring up legislation to extend the Clinton administration's assault weapons ban, the Brady Campaign was left in the difficult position of trying to criticize congressional inaction rather than pointing to specific policy outcomes of which it disapproved (Rich and Labbe 2004).

Communications Technology. Two important developments took place in how groups could communicate with their members or the public during this time frame—changes in the television market and changes in e-mail and other computerized communication. Both of these changes were gradual, but they exerted significant effects on what groups could do. First, consensus grew that television's effectiveness was declining. According to Nielsen estimates, by 2004, only 52 percent of television viewers were watching the major television networks at any given time, down from 71 percent in 1992 (Farhi 2004), although television remained better than other media for reaching people. Democratic media consultant Jim Margolis estimates that while people once needed five viewings of an advertisement to remember it, as many as twelve viewings are now required (Farhi 2004). Some groups responded to these trends by entirely withdrawing their advertisements, while others sought to use the increasing segmentation of the television audience to their advantage. Planned Parenthood, for example, purchased no advertisements on broadcast television but gathered research on women's cable television viewing habits and then purchased advertisements on stations such as the Food Channel, the Learning Channel, and Home and Garden immediately before it began its canvassing.

Second, beginning in the late 1990s, many organizations also began to explore how best to communicate through e-mail or through Web sites (see Bosso and Collins 2002). The fund-raising success of MoveOn.org and the Howard Dean campaign convinced many established groups that they could use the Internet to raise money, but using the Internet as a means of mobilizing group members for other activities proved more difficult. The Sierra Club had experimented in 2000 with video voter guides, available through the group's Web site, and banner advertising. Other groups did not invest as heavily in Internet use, judging that their resources were best used elsewhere.

However, the Internet provided groups with a means of distributing advertisements that either were too expensive to air on television or were too overtly partisan to succeed as television ads. Progressive Majority, a relatively new organization, used its Web site for video clips describing the organization and its goals. The HRC distributed animated cartoons criticizing the Bush administration's views on gay marriage. And People for the American Way developed an animated cartoon of Chief Justice William Rehnquist that illustrated the group's views on future Supreme Court nominations. Such advertisements likely had little effect on voting decisions, but the goal was to mobilize members. A successful advertisement would amuse viewers enough that they would encourage others to view it, and the video would be a means of generating word-of-mouth or media attention. Group Web sites also have proven useful in backing up claims made in other media. With the presumption that those who consulted a group's Web site would be more sympathetic to a group's aims than the average recipient of information from other sources, groups could use other media to steer citizens toward their Web sites.

BCRA

Because few advocacy groups were major soft money donors, few felt any direct effect from the law regarding these provisions. With advertising so important to many of these groups, however, the advertising restrictions forced them to reconsider the timing of their ads and the wisdom of continuing to rely on television and radio commercials. The reduced ability to use electioneering to draw attention to their issues meant that the most notable change in advocacy group activities that can be attributed to BCRA was an increasing involvement in multigroup coalitions.

Hard and Soft Money. The increased hard money limits encouraged groups to bundle contributions. Apart from groups such as EMILY's List, whose primary purpose is bundling and which bundled more than eight million dollars for candidates in both 2000 and 2002,[7] other established organizations had begun to bundle contributions prior to BCRA's implementation. The LCV bundled contributions for three Senate candidates in 2004, the HRC bundled for six congressional candidates, and several newer organizations, including MoveOn.org and Progressive Majority, cultivated small donors for bundling.

Electioneering. The electioneering restrictions generated three obvious responses—earlier advertising, advertising using other media, or changes in the content of late advertisements so that candidates were not named. Liberal groups explored all three of these responses. The Sierra Club has traditionally begun to roll out advertisements very early in the electoral season. In 2002, it began running advertisements in eight Senate races in April, to coincide with Earth Day. In both 2000 and 2002, the Sierra Club ran rather broad ads (that is, ads without district-specific or state-specific references other than the names of the candidates) early and followed with ads more narrowly targeted to local issues later in the cycle. Early advertising can also reach the public before it becomes overwhelmed by advertisements; many group leaders noted that they felt that late advertisements in battleground Senate races in 2002 were wasted because they were swamped by the sheer volume of advertising.

Other groups also experimented with using ads that did not name candidates but steered viewers toward other media that did. In 2002, Planned Parenthood aired an advertisement in Missouri and Minnesota (which had competitive Senate races) that discussed Planned Parenthood's history and some of the issues of current concern to the organization but did not mention candidates. Although Planned Parenthood lacked the resources to air more political advertisements later in the cycle, the ad was intended to improve the group's visibility so that future political communication would be better received. Such advertisements could, for example, direct viewers to group Web sites or introduce issues into the campaign.

As the discussion of individual election cycles and the data in table 5.4

indicate, much of the change in electioneering may be unrelated to BCRA. That is, BCRA may have penalized some electioneering groups but does not explain the decline in advertising by groups such as LCV or Planned Parenthood that were exempt from the restrictions.

The New 527 Organizations. The majority of the funding for Democratic 527 groups came from wealthy individuals and labor unions (Weissman and Hassan 2005). While these organizations had been expected to attract much of the soft money that had formerly gone to the Democratic Party, they may also have siphoned off some of the larger contributions that would have gone to interest groups. In 2002 and 2003, many groups were optimistic about receiving large contributions from former soft money donors. Yet of the ongoing advocacy groups discussed in this chapter, only the LCV reported a contribution to its 527 group of more than one million dollars in 2004, while fifty-one individuals contributed one million dollars or more to newly established 527 organizations (Weissman and Hassan 2005). Restrictions on electioneering led to a movement toward a broader political strategy for ongoing groups in the 2004 elections, and the new 527 organizations formalized some of this activity. These organizations also separately addressed election-related activities that advocacy groups may have been prepared to address but for which they were not necessarily well suited.

The most noteworthy 527 for the purposes of analyzing liberal advocacy groups is America Votes. According to CRP data, apart from five hundred thousand dollars in seed money from two individual donors, America Votes was funded through fifty-thousand-dollar contributions from seventeen labor unions and advocacy groups. This coalition was active in seventeen states; member groups shared polling, targeting, and candidate training sessions. America Votes divided states into geographic regions for voter contact and coordinated member groups' rapid response efforts. It also sought to integrate groups dedicated to mobilizing younger voters— for example, Twenty-first Century Democrats and ClickBackAmerica (the component of MoveOn.org dedicated to younger voters)—with traditional, older interest groups. Part of the long-term goal of this effort was to expand the voter files of these groups and fill in information on younger voters for all of these organizations.

Apart from the direct impetus of BCRA and the activities of other new 527 organizations, America Votes also grew out of dissatisfaction with the level of coordination among issue groups in 2000 and 2002. In particular, it drew its inspiration from surveys of union members in battleground states or districts in the 2000 and 2002 elections (Richards 2004). Participants in these surveys saved and dated political mail they received and noted television advertisements, phone calls, and direct contacts. These surveys demonstrated the problems involved in a lack of coordination between groups—many groups that shared a political agenda sent their mailings or ran advertisements at the same time, thus preventing each group's message from being received clearly. In other cases, some groups used political approaches that had been rejected after focus group testing by like-minded groups. By sharing information about these matters, the participating groups hoped to improve each other's messages, ensure that groups were clear about the timing of each other's efforts, and compare notes on what approaches or strategies worked best.

Uncertainty. Finally, one aspect of BCRA that influenced many smaller advocacy groups was uncertainty—uncertainty about what was and was not permissible under the new law and uncertainty about how much of the law would stand after *McConnell v. FEC.* Many groups supported BCRA without fully understanding the chain of events it might initiate. The 2003 and 2004 Take Back America conferences (gatherings of liberal groups sponsored by the umbrella organization Campaign for America's Future) included several workshops devoted to what nonprofit organizations and PACs would need to do to comply with BCRA. According to attorney Holly Schadler (2003), who led these workshops, the ongoing litigation over BCRA and the complexity of the law had stalled the efforts of many smaller groups and had caused many groups without large budgets to divert so much money into merely understanding the law and the importance of the FEC's subsequent decisions that even their least controversial advocacy efforts would be hampered. Newer citizen groups, including offshoots of Dean's primary campaign organization, faced daunting start-up costs as they worked to comprehend what they could and could not do.

Uncertainty about how much of the law would stand was reflected primarily in donor reluctance. While the new liberal 527 groups were in the process of being formed, many political directors expressed uncertainty about whether BCRA would influence donations to the groups—whether they would raise more money from donors who otherwise would have given to the parties, or whether this money would be directed toward other groups. There is no way to know how well group fund-raising would have gone had ACT and MoveOn.org not emerged, but the increased emphasis on grassroots activity can be seen as a logical response to established groups' failure to bring in donations of the type that fueled electioneering advertisements in 2000.

MoveOn.org

The most conspicuous new group in table 5.4 is MoveOn.org. MoveOn was often discussed in the media along with the new 527 organizations, but it was not quite a "new" 527, since it had been formed in 1998. But it also does not fit the profile of most of the ongoing advocacy groups since its reason for being is not advocacy related to a signature issue niche. When it was formed in 1998 by two Silicon Valley entrepreneurs, MoveOn.org's signature issue was its opposition to the impeachment of President Clinton and its desire for Congress to "move on" to more important political issues. Following the president's impeachment, the group then started a PAC and began bundling contributions aimed at supporting challengers to the Republican impeachment managers. By 2000, MoveOn had developed into a bottom-up organization championing a variety of progressive causes, but it continued to emphasize bundling. According to one estimate, it raised an estimated $1.85 million for Democratic candidates from forty-three thousand donors (Harris and Pressman 2000). According to the group's estimates, it raised $2.3 million, with an average donation of $35, and in 2002 it raised $4.1 million for candidates (Boyd 2003). In 2002 and 2004, MoveOn retained its emphasis on raising money in smaller donations but diversified its activities. According to the group's Wes Boyd, the group's 527 organization, the MoveOn Voter Fund, continued to raise an average of only $60 per donor, excluding large contributions from George Soros and Peter Lewis (Carney 2004). As table 5.4 shows, in 2004 MoveOn had become the second-largest advertiser on the left. Like the Dean campaign, MoveOn sought to use its advertisements not only to influence voters but also to raise money to run more advertisements (Boyd 2003). Also like the Dean campaign, MoveOn funded and publicized these ads through participatory events for members. The group held numerous meet-ups during the 2004 primaries, conducted an online primary, and held a contest for the best anti-Bush advertisement.

If one looks simply at membership, MoveOn has become one of the largest pro-Democratic groups; even before the 2004 campaign began, the group reported that it had 2.4 million members (Janofsky and Lee 2003). This membership was essentially a mailing list, however. During the 2004 election cycle, MoveOn had seven employees, only one of whom was in

Washington, D.C. The group was active in several of the pro-Democratic coalitions and sought volunteers for canvassing by ACT and America Votes (Blades 2004). Yet MoveOn was primarily distinguished from other groups by its emphasis on its function—use of the Internet to communicate with members and raise money—rather than on a single issue area. While some 527 groups may have been responses to BCRA, MoveOn clearly was not, even though its emphasis on function resembles that of some of the Democratic 527s. In 2004, MoveOn was uniquely positioned to take advantage of BCRA, of the new mobilization possibilities provided by the Internet, and of the polarized political climate.

Conservative Advocacy Groups

The National Rifle Association. The NRA resembles many liberal advocacy groups in that it has engaged in substantial issue advocacy in the past and in that its issue priority leads it to be relatively but not exclusively partisan. Unlike many other advocacy groups, however, the NRA was a major soft money donor, giving $1.5 million to the Republican Party in 2000. According to many accounts, the NRA went deeply into debt to spend an estimated $20 million in combined PAC contributions, soft money contributions, television advertising, and other activities related to the 2000 election (Miller and Miller 2000). By 2003, the NRA was also carrying an estimated $100 million in debt as a consequence of legal fees in gun manufacturer liability suits (Strom 2003). As a consequence, the NRA spent far less in 2002 and 2004 but nevertheless remained a major force. The NRA's PAC receipts declined from a high of $17 million in 2000 to between $10 million and $12 million in 2002, 2004, and 2006. The NRA clearly has the ability to engage in substantial electioneering through its PAC, but the group reoriented much of its advocacy work toward member communications, direct mail, and other forms of advocacy. In many states, this change resulted not from electioneering restrictions but from a desire to target its audience. In Pennsylvania, for example, advertising in the major media markets, where many viewers would likely be hostile to the NRA, would be far less effective than narrowly targeted appeals in rural areas.

Following the passage of BCRA, the NRA took two steps to push the limits of the law. First, it argued unsuccessfully that it should be exempted from the electioneering restrictions on the grounds that it could segregate corporate and labor funds from individual contributions. Second, the NRA purchased a satellite radio station, enabling it to qualify as a media organization and present programming during the election season (Dao

2004). The NRA, then, remained quite active following BCRA but notably shifted its activities. It is unclear, however, whether this shift resulted from changing resources or changing political priorities or from new legal restrictions, and many of the group's activities in response to BCRA were clearly rooted in a desire to challenge the law rather than to reorganize political activity to comply with the law.

The Club for Growth. Although the Club for Growth (now the Citizens Club for Growth) also argued vigorously against BCRA, the group's executive director, David Keating, made a compelling case that the Club's PAC was helped in some ways by the legislation. As the preeminent bundling organization on the right, the Club's PAC capitalized on increased candidate contribution limits to increase the size of its bundled candidate contributions. The Club's PAC has traditionally selected a small number of House and Senate candidates who espouse economically conservative views and has done advocacy work out of its PAC and its 527 for these candidates. The Club for Growth was a 527 organization prior to BCRA, but it and its PAC grew following passage of the law, spending approximately two million dollars from its PAC, largely in independent expenditures, and twelve million dollars from the 527. Because the group has targeted so few races, and because it often becomes involved in primary elections, it has had the ability to almost singlehandedly bring about the victory of its preferred candidates, in some cases even when running against candidates supported by the NRCC or the DCCC. The Club, unlike many other groups, increased its clout following BCRA and engaged in substantial electioneering work out of its PAC. However, the FEC fined the Club for some of its activities between 2000 and 2004, and in 2006 a new Club for Growth was formed as a 501(c)(4) organization.

Other Conservative Groups. The dominant social conservative groups of the 1990s—the Christian Coalition, National Right to Life, and various coalitions of evangelicals—had become less influential as campaign contributors and in terms of issue advocacy by the time of the 2000 election. BCRA thus had less obvious effects on them than on other groups, in some cases (e.g., the Christian Coalition) because the group's financial resources had declined, and in other cases because the groups had traditionally engaged in grassroots work that fell outside BCRA's scope. Several new organizations—PACs, (c)(4) organizations, and 527s—were formed in the 2004 elections. Prominent new organizations included the Campaign for Working Families, a PAC created by social conservative activist

Gary Bauer, and Let Freedom Ring, a (c)(4) organization supported by the John Templeton Foundation. Some 527 organizations were also created to work to advance state-level constitutional amendments against gay marriage. Most of the 527 groups on the right worked toward immediate political goals and lacked the broad focus or intent to remain in business of many left-leaning groups.

Summary

As was the case for other group types, BCRA pushed many advocacy groups in a direction they might well have gone even without changes in the law. BCRA reduced television advertising by some groups, increased the importance of raising and spending hard money, and increased coordination among groups. BCRA's increase in contribution limits aided some groups, although overall it worked to privilege individual donors at the expense of groups. Yet to the extent that these phenomena occurred, they cannot necessarily be considered solely responses to legal changes. Political events, such as the fervid anti-Bush sentiment among liberals during the latter half of Bush's first term, also may explain increased coordination between groups. Changes in the television market and in the level of television advertising in the 2000 and 2002 elections may explain much of the shift away from television advertising. And changes in the prominence of many groups' signature issues may also explain the reluctance to rely on issue advertisements and the desire to link issues and efforts to a broader grassroots effort.

Group Adaptations in the 2006 and 2008 Elections

By 2006, many of the political conditions that had brought about the outpouring of group activity in 2004 had changed dramatically, and with these changes, advocacy groups, business groups, and labor unions found that they again needed to reconsider their strategies. The shift in the political climate, which eventually brought about Democratic majorities in the House and the Senate, requires little elaboration here, but two less obvious changes also affected groups' priorities. All of the Democratic Party campaign committees increased their fund-raising substantially in 2006, to the point that the DSCC had a forty-million-dollar advantage over its Republican counterpart, and the DCCC went from being outspent about two to one in 2004 to spending approximately 77 percent of what the

NRCC spent. The party committees' increased ability to support their candidates meant that interest groups were less important in the 2006 campaigns than had previously been the case (Franz 2008b) and that parties regained the upper hand in supporting competitive congressional candidates (Corrado 2006a).[8] Second, in 2005 the Federal Election Commission levied substantial fines on several of the highest-spending 527 groups of 2004 (Phillips 2006). In 2006, 527 activity was largely confined to smaller groups that sought to influence individual elections rather than to shape the overall political climate (Boatright 2007; Magleby and Patterson 2008, 42). The absence of a presidential race may have made such groups as America Coming Together less consequential even without FEC intervention, but whatever the reason, the bulk of 527 spending came from organizations directly tied to ongoing groups.

Many changes in group behavior in 2006, then, are more easily linked to changes in the political environment than to any ongoing response to BCRA. The AFL-CIO provided an estimated $40 million in support to Democratic candidates (Vandehei 2006). The shift in the Democrats' fortunes gave labor less reason to consider supporting sympathetic Republicans. And despite forecasts to the contrary, the split between the AFL-CIO and the Change to Win coalition may have led to more labor spending on the 2006 election than would otherwise have been the case (Magleby and Patterson 2008, 53; Roof 2008).[9] Also sensing a shift toward the Democrats, business groups responded by increasing their support for centrist Democratic candidates (Magleby and Patterson 2008, 43). Among advocacy groups, despite the demise of America Coming Together, evidence indicated that groups were continuing to work in concert. America Votes spent $14.4 million on the year's congressional races; Democracy Alliance, a new "cooperative" of liberal donors led by George Soros and others, directed an estimated $50 million toward various think tanks and advocacy groups (Vandehei and Cillizza 2006); and Catalist, a for-profit firm founded by Harold Ickes, provided voter information of the sort gathered by ACT to a variety of liberal groups (Ambinder 2006). All of these activities suggest that groups did not necessarily turn their backs on their 2004 strategies, but they approached the 2006 elections in a slightly less coordinated manner and with goals that are not easily traced back to BCRA.

The Supreme Court's *FEC v. Wisconsin Right to Life* decision, handed down in June 2007, loosened BCRA's restrictions on electioneering advertisements by groups that accept corporate funds. The Court did not strike down BCRA's relevant provisions but held that it restricted groups' right to encourage the public to lobby legislators on issues. Many commentators predicted that the decision would bring about a new onslaught of issue ads in the 2008 election (Carney 2007; Vogel 2007). This decision and the Court's June 2008 ruling in *Davis v. FEC*, which struck down BCRA's "millionaire's amendment," signified to many observers that the Court was open to reviewing many aspects of the current campaign finance regime, as indeed it did after the election.

In 2008, groups remained subordinate players to the parties and the candidates, in part because of BCRA's expansion of hard money limits (by 2008, the inflation-adjusted cap on individual contributions to candidates was $2,300). But it had also become apparent that Internet fund-raising would allow parties and candidates to raise money far more efficiently than they had in the past. At the presidential level, groups were less consequential on the Democratic side in large part because of Barack Obama's unprecedented fund-raising. The Obama campaign and the Republican National Committee absorbed much of the money that would otherwise have gone to outside groups. As of the end of 2007, 527 groups were raising money at a faster pace than they had in 2003 (Campaign Finance Institute 2008), but no constellation of groups appeared that resembled the groups of 2004. Much of the Democratic mobilization work occurred within the Obama campaign, and despite a smattering of attack ads on Obama that appeared in early September, no single group emerged to focus Republican efforts.[10]

Other groups continued the patterns they had established during the previous decade. After organized labor had coalesced behind Obama, unions poured an unprecedented amount of money into the 2008 campaign, with almost all of this money going toward voter contact and mobilization efforts. The AFL-CIO spent an estimated $200 million on the election, and in a reflection of the Obama campaign's effort to expand the playing field, it identified twenty-four states for contact (Wayne 2008). The SEIU and other Change to Win groups also spent more than $100 million on mobilization. Estimates of total union spending reached as high as $450 million (Greenhouse 2008). Union efforts were particularly important in Ohio and Pennsylvania, where some analysts worried that race might be an issue for union members. The International Brotherhood of Electrical Workers and the United Mine Workers countered these fears by sending out DVDs to members reassuring them of Obama's commitment to labor issues (Zenilman and Smith 2008). Although some unions invested in television advertising for competitive Senate races—for example, both the SEIU and the NEA spent heavily on television ads for the New Hampshire Senate race—most union money was spent on mobilization. The fact that Working America had grown to 2.5 million members (making it larger than any union but the NEA) meant that the AFL-CIO could now reach far more members than in 2000 or 2004 and could more easily find campaign workers outside of unions (Moberg 2008).

The major resource-sharing vehicles developed in previous elections, America Votes and Catalist, continued their 2006 roles. America Votes reported being active in fourteen states, and under the leadership of former DCCC chair Martin Frost, it ensured that group efforts complemented each other (Kosterlitz 2008). Likewise, Catalist, which had been used by groups in individual races in 2006, was used by liberal groups to target undecided voters in the presidential race and in Senate races. Catalist's activities are not necessarily as visible as those of groups or candidates, but candidate and group disclosure forms indicate that Catalist can serve as an informal means of coordination between candidates and groups, which can purchase data or mailing lists from the firm, giving all participants access to the same information (see Mosk and Kane 2008).

Although some advocacy groups clearly spent enough to have an impact—MoveOn.org, for example, spent more than thirty-five million dollars on the election—the fact that Obama's spending so far exceeded group spending meant that many of the groups that received the most attention were noticed not because of the extent of their activity but because their actions fit in with news media priorities. For example, Defenders of Wildlife was among the first environmental groups to criticize Republican vice presidential nominee Sarah Palin, developing a television advertisement condemning wolf hunting practices in Alaska. Defenders of Wildlife was not necessarily the most active environmental group in the election, but it developed a strategy for making itself heard above the fray of candidate and party advertisements.

Business groups responded to changing Democratic fortunes in 2006 and 2008 in two different ways. The Chamber of Commerce spent little on the 2008 presidential race, but it spent an estimated thirty-five million dollars on 2008 Senate races, seeking to prevent the Democrats from reaching sixty seats in the Senate (Mullins and Davis 2008). While the Chamber had supported some Democrats in 2006, two years later it supported only one Democrat, Louisiana incumbent Mary Landrieu. The Chamber's effort was far smaller than that of labor, and approximately one-third of the Chamber's spending went into television advertising. BI-PAC, which has sought to lead more by example than through financial clout, endorsed only one Democratic Senate candidate (open-seat candidate Mark Warner in Virginia) but supported six Democratic House candidates. BIPAC issued a series of press releases cautioning member companies that Democrats would increase their margins in the House and Senate in 2008 and urging members to seek out pro-business Democrats. BIPAC's press releases in both years touted the Prosperity Project as a means of facilitating employee communication with legislators, devoting less attention to electoral outcomes. BIPAC, then, sought to advocate for its method without overtly tying itself to Republican victories.

Following the 2008 election, several business coalitions shifted their attention to working against the health care and climate change legislation promoted by the Obama administration. A new group, 60 Plus, with similar form and funding to United Seniors and CBM, aired advertisements in the districts of wavering Democratic House and Senate members while the health care bill was being debated (Pershing 2009), and the Chamber of Commerce announced plans to run advertisements criticizing Democrats for their stances on emissions caps (Broder 2009). Because these advertising campaigns took place well before the 2010 election, they were completely legal under existing law; for that matter, ads run closer to the 2010 election would also be legal following the *Citizens United* decision.

The 2006 and 2008 elections show a consolidation of the group strategies pioneered in 2002 and 2004, but the distance of these elections from the passage of reform legislation makes it difficult to identify effects of reform for groups. The increased hard money limits clearly had a powerful effect on candidate fund-raising, as did the abandonment of the public financing system by many of the 2008 presidential candidates. The partisan balance, whether measured in terms of fund-raising or electoral success, shifted so abruptly between 2004 and 2008 that any changes in group behavior were submerged by the shift in party and candidate activities. Yet many of the strategies pioneered by groups in the years immediately before and after BCRA—among them labor's renewed emphasis on mobilization, MoveOn.org's development of online fund-raising and activism, and BIPAC's effort to use the Internet for mobilization purposes—were echoed by the parties and by candidates in 2006 and 2008.

6 | The Canadian Response

Many scholars have noted that the major periods of campaign finance reform in Canada and the United States have coincided. Yet the rationales for reform have differed substantially in the two countries. The Canadian reforms of the early 2000s had their roots in the Lortie Commission's (1991) recommendations, but the path from recommendation to implementation was not nearly as tortuous as that followed by the McCain-Feingold legislation, and curbing the role of interest groups was not as central to the reformers' goals in Canada as in the United States. The passage of the Canada Elections Act Amendments of 2003, the most comprehensive of the package of the Canadian reforms, appears to have been an attempt to mitigate the effects of scandal, in this case the Gomery Commission report on the funneling of advertising money by the Liberal Party to sympathetic firms in Quebec. BCRA, too, represented a response to scandal, but whereas the Bush administration accepted BCRA reluctantly, with little fanfare, the Chrétien government actively discussed the CEA amendments as a panacea for the "democratic deficit," the disconnect between citizens and government.

Whatever the impulses behind the two nations' campaign finance laws, Canadian campaign finance problems evidently had not reached the scale of American problems, in large part simply because the sums of money spent in American elections in the 2000s dwarf the sums spent in Canadian elections.[1] Canada's reforms curb the role of groups but appear designed to ward off the specter of American-style elections, even though the financing of Canadian elections had not come to resemble that of American elections. When one adds to the mix a party system that was very much in flux as of 2003, with the splintering of the Progressive Conservative Party in the early 1990s and the as-yet-incomplete reunification of the Conservatives under Stephen Harper, it seems unlikely that Canadian parties or groups could have adequately thought through the consequences or ways around reform legislation to the same extent as American parties and groups.

Canada has experienced three elections since the passage of the CEA amendments. Canadian groups' political activities, traditionally harder to observe than American groups' activities, have shifted somewhat, but, as in the American case, it is difficult to isolate the reasons for these changes. Canadian groups have also made some changes that parallel those in American groups' activities; while no Canadian groups directly claimed to have adopted American groups' strategies, the coincidence of shifts in election-related behavior, particularly among business groups and labor unions, indicates that some sharing of information probably occurred. For the most part, however, Canadian groups appear to have made small changes in their activities; as with American groups, many of these changes might have occurred absent the passage of reform legislation.

In this chapter I draw on interviews with several of the most politically active Canadian groups to draw comparisons with American groups' adaptations. The comparison is instructive insofar as it shows the effects of differences in political institutions and political culture on groups' responses to reform. Beyond this comparison, however, Canadian groups' adaptations show how little room exists for group influence in a strong party system and, at least according to many of these groups, the consequences for issue-oriented politics and activism when groups are sidelined.

Organized Labor

Organized labor in Canada, as in the United States, initially appeared to be the group that had the most to lose from party finance reform. Labor unions are much more likely to "push" money into the political system than are business groups or advocacy organizations, and labor clearly has the money and the incentive to engage in third-party advertising as well. In addition, organized labor is the only group that has an ongoing formal connection with one political party, the NDP. Most labor unions, however, did not object to the 2003 CEA amendments, in fact arguing that the law should in some regards be stricter. In testimony before Parliament, the CLC's Hassan Yussuff (2003) noted that restrictions on contributions would level the playing field between business and labor. Yussuff argued that the one-thousand-dollar limit would make bookkeeping difficult and that an outright ban might be better; in labor's case, unions would have to keep careful track of contributions by their locals. And just as business groups argued that branches of businesses should count as separate entities with regard to the contribution limit, Yussuff argued that union locals should be counted as separate entities. Yussuff further argued that the limit on individual contributions should be lowered and that although the CLC supported public funding for parties, the threshold for parties to qualify for funding should be lower.[2] The CLC's director of political action, Daniel Mallett, noted that Yussuff and the CLC were briefed by Liberal cabinet minister Don Boudria before the CEA amendments were introduced, enabling labor to make changes in anticipation of the bill's passage.

Just as campaign finance reform in the United States likely pushed the AFL-CIO in a direction it had already been headed, so reform in Canada reinforced the CLC's increasing emphasis on member communication. Unions in both countries have not always been successful in persuading their members to vote for union-endorsed parties or candidates (see, e.g., Archer and Whitehorn 1997, 260–62). The CLC sought an advisory ruling shortly after the 2003 CEA amendments were passed to ensure that member communications were not counted as contributions or independent expenditures; the court ruled that such communications are protected, even if they are partisan (Jansen and Young 2009). This meant that the CLC's Labour Issues campaign, in which the union polled members on issues of concern and then used these issues to frame internal communications and radio advertisements, was all the more important. Labor therefore poured most of its efforts and the money it otherwise would have given to the NDP into what it calls the Better Choice campaign, which grew out of dissatisfaction on the part of union leaders in Saskatchewan and Ontario who believed that in instances where the NDP has governed, it has not always been responsive to labor issues. At the provincial level, the CLC distributed summaries of the parties' positions on issues, encouraging members to "vote their interest." The CLC made this approach an integral part of its national campaign in 2004, focusing its efforts on competitive ridings—primarily those where the NDP had a chance of victory and with sufficient labor density. The CLC also has undertaken extensive radio advertising in the weeks immediately preceding the issue of the writ of election; Mallett estimates that the CLC spent four hundred thousand dollars on radio advertising in 2004. The limits on advertising after a writ has been issued make it impossible to advertise at all in urban areas, but the CLC has done targeted radio advertising in a few rural areas.

Finally, many CLC unions have run member lists against party lists to gather more information on members' voting tendencies, using this information for face-to-face contacts.

While labor maintains a close relationship with the NDP, the Better Choice campaign's focus on engaging in political action all of the time, not just during elections, leaves open the possibility of dialogue with the other parties. Absent the financial ties with the NDP, other parties may also see labor as a constituency to be courted, particularly in Ontario, which features high union density but much poorer NDP performance than the prairie provinces. The Better Choice program has also focused more on municipal politics and on recruiting and training promising candidates; this approach also leaves open the possibility that labor can influence issues without solely being a client of the NDP.

This strategy closely resembles the AFL-CIO's strategy, but Mallett emphasizes that the CLC had been developing the Better Choice campaign since the early 1990s and that it was not a consequence of the AFL-CIO's efforts. Although the CLC president always attends the AFL-CIO's annual meeting, most of the direct contact between CLC unions and AFL-CIO unions happens at the local level, often on border-related issues, on issues related to a common employer, or on other issues of shared concern. Some CLC unions continue to belong to internationals headquartered in the United States, but during the 1980s and 1990s, many Canadian unions—most prominently the Canadian Auto Workers (CAW)—disaffiliated from the internationals. The CLC's political strategy differs from the AFL-CIO's strategy in several important respects. First, the CLC has made less of an effort to improve voter turnout. Union members are slightly more likely to vote than nonmembers, but Mallett attributes this phenomenon not to mobilization but simply to the fact that union members tend to have other characteristics that make them likely to vote. Second, the CLC has made fewer efforts than have American unions to do advocacy work among nonmembers, largely because union density is much higher in Canada than in the United States. (As of 2006, union density was 30.8 percent in Canada and 12.5 percent in the United States).[3] And third, again because of greater union density, Canadian unions have been less concerned with declining membership or with tying political activity to organizing.[4]

The CEA amendments effectively severed financial ties between labor and the NDP, although the NDP continues to accord labor unions a prominent role in the party leadership.[5] Since the party's formation in the 1960s, tension has existed between union and nonunion NDP members and between unions and NDP leaders over strategy (Smith 2005, 69; Tanguay 2002). Following the 1988 election, many union leaders expressed their unhappiness that NDP leader Ed Broadbent did not make the FTA the focus of the NDP's campaign, even though the NDP claimed that its polls showed that an appeal based on other issues would be more effective (Archer and Whitehorn 1997, 47; Fraser 1989, 450; Whitehorn 1992, 228). Similarly, some in the CLC noted that under current leader Jack Layton, the NDP did better in 2006, when it ran on issues that the CLC was also promoting in its Labour Issues campaign, than in 2004, when it ran on different issues. Tensions between some labor unions and the NDP have much to do both with the different incentives of groups and parties and with contributors' expectations of the parties. The CLC tended to be a major contributor to the NDP (giving $684,000 in 2000, the last election year before the CEA amendments), but the majority of NDP funding has come from individual unions. According to Mallett, one of the reasons for the Better Choice campaign is that many of the fastest-growing or fastest-changing unions are those that have not been major NDP contributors. The CLC has done extensive analysis of Canadian census data, which show that the non-NDP unions are also more representative of younger Canadians in terms of gender, ethnic background, and so forth. Demographics, in other words, will continue to advantage unions that have never had strong ties with the NDP. The NDP, as the lone party that underperformed, relative to its finances, in the elections preceding the CEA amendments, will be hurt by the structure of the new public funding provisions, but the CLC appears to have adjusted its strategy to account for this development.

Some of the unions that belong to the CLC had somewhat more ambivalent responses to the Better Choice campaign, not so much because they disagree with its intent but because they are more entwined in the NDP or because they maintain their own mobilization programs. Both Sue Milling of the United Steelworkers and Bob Linton of the United Food and Commercial Workers noted that the greater emphasis on mobilization has generally been beneficial to their unions but emphasized that the limitations imposed by the new CEA primarily affect transfers of goods, money, and services, not general campaign information and strategy. The Steelworkers run a Steelworkers Vote campaign that identifies people within the union to prepare for NDP campaigns; these people are then trained for political work, encouraged to join the NDP, and released from their jobs and paid by the party. As in the U.S. model, the Steelworkers have stressed the importance of maintaining contact with members between elections—for example, by jointly publishing a regular newsletter with the NDP discussing NDP priorities. Likewise, the United Food and Commercial Workers (UFCW) has emphasized in its training the need to begin conversations with nonpartisan or nonpolitical issues before moving to issues germane to federal politics. Steelworkers Vote differs from Better Choice in that it explicitly advocates voting for the NDP. According to Milling, the nonpartisan nature of the Better Choice campaign is in part a consequence of disagreements among the CLC unions. In her view, expressly telling workers whom their best choice is may make sense in a two-party, polarized system, but in a multiparty system, workers may be confused about whether the "better choice" really is the NDP, particularly in ridings where the NDP is not competitive and voting strategically may appear attractive. Milling disputes the notion that strategic voting can make sense in the long run. Like Better Choice, Steelworkers Vote is not designed with direct consideration for reaching out to nonunion members, but Milling contends that to the extent that the program provides political training to members and encourages them to identify politically first and foremost with the goals of the union and the NDP, they may well use their training to reach out to nonmembers.

The USW's and UFCW's responses to the CEA amendments are in part a consequence of the fact that union leaders often maintain official positions within the NDP. Both the Steelworkers and the Canadian Union of Professional Employees have representatives on the NDP executive board. Union representation at NDP conventions is determined by the number of union members who are also NDP members; prior to the enactment of the CEA amendments, unions could affiliate with the NDP and have all of their members counted toward their NDP membership totals. Now, unions (not the NDP) must determine how many of their members are NDP members. While this change may result in an imprecise accounting of representation, it encourages unions to find out more about the political leanings of their members and to encourage members to join the party. Such knowledge can help unions in building NDP riding associations and can aid unions in coordinating campaigns with other unions. For example, unions can work together to release members to work for the party, to identify issues of specific concern to locals, and to give feedback to NDP candidates and leaders about which issues might best be discussed in particular ridings. The CEA amendments were written with the acknowledgment of existing arrangements between unions and the NDP, so the effects have again been felt primarily in terms of the resources transferred from unions to the national NDP.

One consequence of the new restrictions that may not have been obvious when the law was passed has been the law's push of the NDP toward nationalization. While some analysts (Stewart 2005) have argued that the CEA amendments may fracture the political Left, leaving the Green Party and the NDP to fight over left-leaning voters much as the Reform Party and the Progressive Conservatives split the conservative vote in the early 1990s, union leaders have noted that the public funding provisions of the CEA amendments increase the value of NDP votes in ridings where the party has historically not been competitive. Because public funds are awarded based on vote share rather than seat share, unions can tell members that a vote for the NDP even where it is unlikely to win a riding can help the party financially. Both the USW and the UFCW dismissed the notion that members might be encouraged to vote strategically—to vote for "anyone but Harper" at the federal level, just as Ontario unions sought to encourage strategic voting to oppose Ontario premier Mike Harris's re-election in 1999—because they felt that the Liberal Party would not reliably look after union interests if it succeeded in these elections. One long-term effect of encouraging NDP votes across the board may be to make the party competitive in more ridings. A thornier problem, however, is the relationship between national unions and the Bloc Québécois. Prior to the 1997 by-elections, the NDP had not been particularly successful in fielding candidates in Quebec, yet the BQ and the Parti Québécois have generally supported labor issues, and Quebec labor laws compare favorably to those of other provinces.[6] As a result, the USW and the UFCW have acknowledged Quebec's "distinct culture" and have not pushed for NDP votes there. Even national unions that might encourage strategic voting have acknowledged the need to treat Quebec differently; the existence of the BQ makes strategic voting more complicated than in other provinces. Both unions noted that there may be a need to reevaluate the NDP's role in Quebec now that even fielding unsuccessful candidates there will have financial consequences for the NDP.

The CAW is perhaps the most visible of the unions that have moved away from the NDP in recent elections. CAW president Buzz Hargrove made several public appearances with Paul Martin in the 2006 election and was subsequently kicked out of the NDP, taking the CAW with him. USW president Ken Neumann (2006) criticized Hargrove's move, arguing that "in the long term, endorsing the Liberals, even if only in a 'strategic' way, will lead Canada down the road to a two-party system like in the United States, where labor's interests are always shortchanged by the Democratic Party and ignored by the Republicans." Neumann goes on to note that individual CAW locals have remained loyal to the NDP (a claim disputed by CAW leaders). The concept of strategic voting, then, remains very much a sore point for NDP supporters. In response, the CAW has sought to demonstrate that the program works and that it will advance the Left's interests. In 2006, for example, the CAW posted on its Web site a lengthy PowerPoint display of the results of a Decima poll on the CAW effort in Ontario.

According to the CAW, however, the basic premise of its strategic voting push was not an endorsement of the Liberals but an acknowledgment that in ridings where the NDP cannot win, the Liberals may be the second-best choice. Hargrove (2005) claimed that he was "somewhat puzzled as to why" his contention that a minority Liberal government with a substantial NDP contingent would be the best possible outcome of an election was problematic for other unions. Hargrove contended that while he endorsed electing a Liberal minority government, this endorsement was not the same as an endorsement of the Liberal Party. Furthermore, he contended that he was merely giving voice to a sentiment shared by many on the left, including some NDP leaders. The public funding provisions may make support for the NDP in hopeless ridings more important to the party, but such support will not necessarily benefit individual unions. CAW economist Jim Stanford argues that the strategic voting pitch in 2006 was a natural outgrowth of the CAW's Ontario campaigns and had nothing to do with the CEA amendments. Likewise, the third-party spending restrictions ensure that the CAW cannot advertise to the extent it did in 1988, but Stanford contends that the CAW had been moving more toward issue-based communication with members, particularly outside of election periods, long before the restrictions were put in place.

In terms of its mobilization efforts, organized labor has thus adapted to reform in much the same way as its American counterparts but does not appear to have done so as a response to American efforts. The most obvious institutional difference—labor's ties to a party that has never governed at the national level—has had far less of an effect in bringing about differences in American and Canadian group strategies than one might expect if one were to look at internal union strategy. The major differences in Canadian and American adaptations derive from labor's different histories in the two countries and differences in union density. Despite the fact that Canadian labor may be disadvantaged by its ties to a minor party, there is less desperation to the CLC's member mobilization efforts largely because labor in Canada has faced neither as sharp a decline in membership as have U.S. unions (although union density did decline during the

1980s and 1990s) nor the degree of antilabor sentiment that has flourished among American conservatives. According to some analyses (see Yates 2008), concern within the labor movement about decline and the need to organize has dissipated in the past decade. The Steelworkers' Milling notes that after "an initial panic" about what the CEA amendments might do to unions, they have begun to settle into their new arrangements. The NDP faces some difficult logistical questions in reorganizing its conventions and its finances, but much of the dissension between Canadian unions may well be linked more to personalities and to the economic challenges faced by individual unions than to changes in the law. The current turmoil among Canadian unions about NDP support bears some resemblance to the shake-up undergone by the AFL-CIO following the 2004 U.S. election. In both cases, restrictions on unions' political activities may play a role in these conflicts, but participants have been quick to argue that these disputes predate campaign finance reform and likely would have been aired anyway.

Business Groups

The major Canadian peak business associations supported or were at least indifferent to the general thrust of the 2003 CEA amendments. Most groups took no official position on the bill. The Canadian Federation of Independent Businesses (CFIB) publicized survey results showing that a majority of members supported restricting contributions and increasing the tax credit. In testimony before Parliament, David Stewart-Patterson (2003) of the Canadian Council of Chief Executives (CCCE) reported that two-thirds of the group's members supported expanding the tax credit and imposing a "reasonable cap" on corporate or individual contributions, but Stewart-Patterson expressed some concern that the one-thousand-dollar-limit was too low for national corporations. A thousand-dollar cap might be sensible for a group active in only one riding, but for a national company, the limit worked out to only three dollars per riding. Stewart-Patterson wondered whether this amount would make even token contact with legislators—for example, purchasing a cup of coffee—illegal. The CCCE's survey of its members defined a "reasonable cap" as being between one thousand dollars and ten thousand dollars. Stewart-Patterson argued that making branches of companies separate entities for the purposes of the law would solve the problem. Echoing other groups, he argued that corporations did not expect access in return for contributions and that many

CCCE members recognized that public disclosure laws effectively prevented any sort of quid pro quo, but he worried that the public perceived that contributions bought favors or access. In his testimony, Stewart-Patterson deflected questions about whether an outright ban might be better than a small limit, while other group leaders argued that banning contributions solved many of the problems that a low limit and the attendant possibility of accidentally exceeding it might create.

Similarly, few groups objected to the limits on third-party spending. Although several groups had spent substantial amounts during the 1988 campaign, few business groups spent money on advertisements in subsequent elections, and business groups did not foresee another election in which they would want to air advertisements. Stewart-Patterson noted that many business leaders might object to the third-party spending restrictions on free speech grounds but did not anticipate any policy consequences as a result of the ban.

However, business groups objected to several other provisions in the CEA amendments and the Accountability Act. The CFIB survey results showed substantial opposition to the public funding provisions; the CCCE also opposed these provisions. The Chamber of Commerce objected to the Accountability Act's disclosure provisions for lobbying, and Canadian Manufacturers and Exporters (CME) objected to the measure's restrictions on lobbying by former government officials.

Business groups' political activities changed slightly following the passage of the various reform laws, but it is hard to pinpoint the legislation's effect on group activity. Since before the passage of the CEA amendments, the CFIB has pursued a somewhat restrained version of American groups' Web-based voter information campaigns. The CFIB Web site includes a Legislative Action page that provides summaries of party platforms, party leaders' responses to questions posed by the CFIB, and voter registration information. The CFIB does not use this information in even a casual attempt to steer voters toward any party, and it does not track usage of this information by member companies. This approach is very much in keeping with the CFIB's historical mission to measure and publicize members' views; the CFIB has sought to create a niche for itself through frequent surveys of members on issues of concern. The group often compares members' views to those of the general public, and while these views reflect the fact that the group's 105,000 members are businesspeople, their views frequently do not differ dramatically from those of the country as a whole. The CFIB, as is the case for many other business groups, is relatively indifferent between the business policies of the two major parties.

Likewise, the Canadian Chamber of Commerce has sought to present party platforms to members and has occasionally rated the parties on business issues but limits the use of this information to press releases. The Chamber has not pursued the aggressive mobilization strategy of its American counterpart. Neither the Chamber nor the CFIB is formally connected to the U.S. Chamber or the NFIB, and while both groups reported being vaguely aware of American groups' mobilization strategies, neither reported discussing these strategies with American groups. The Chamber has a slightly more fractious history in regard to political activity than does the CFIB; during the 1960s, the Chamber launched Operation Freedom, an aggressively political free trade effort, but backed off in response to members' objections (Engelman and Schwartz 1975, 149). During the 1990s, some local and provincial Chambers (most notably the Alberta Chamber) objected to third-party advertising restrictions, but the national Chamber took no position on the matter.

The CCCE, historically the most politically active of the major business groups, has differed from the CFIB and the Chamber in that it has not felt a need to educate its members on party policy in any sort of systematic way. CCCE vice president Ross Laver attributes this approach to the CCCE's membership, which comprises the CEOs of approximately 150 of the largest Canadian corporations. The CCCE thus does not need to recruit or retain members as larger groups do and can thus pick and choose its issues rather than responding to party platforms. The CCCE has a greater ability to introduce issues and seek to persuade government (or the public) to act on them. Some observers have argued that during the 1980s, the CCCE, then called the Business Council on National Issues, was the major group responsible for encouraging the parties to work on what became the FTA (Salutin 1989, 10). Laver points out that the CCCE has always taken a strictly nonpartisan stance. As a consequence, the group has worked independently of election politics to frame issues and develop consensus positions among CCCE members; recent examples include policy on climate change and energy issues. This focus also ensures that informal contacts between politicians and the CCCE and its president, Tom d'Aquino, are common but not consequential for election politics.

Perhaps one of the CCCE's most notable recent political activities was its letter to Prime Minister Paul Martin calling for substantial changes in the organization of Parliament (Canadian Council of Chief Executives 2004). Specifically, the CCCE has recommended strengthening parliamentary committees by having them consider legislation earlier in its drafting and solicit greater input from opposition parties; increasing parliamentary scrutiny of government appointments; and making free votes more common. One consequence of such changes, as the CCCE has admitted, would be to make politics both more open and more fractious. In terms of elections or of lobbying, this change would make individual members, including backbenchers, more consequential and would increase the number of access points for groups. It is easy to see such policies creating a more American-type system, where individual races for Congress are important for groups. According to Laver, however, the CCCE is motivated not by its own gain in lobbying but by the goal of increasing the government's perceived legitimacy. Parties and party members would be compelled to be more responsive to groups and to the public, and the creation of policy would be more democratic. Laver notes that the combination of contribution limits, lobbying restrictions, and the third-party advertising restrictions effectively circumscribes corporations' ability to direct money toward elections. In this sense, parliamentary reforms of the sort advocated in the CCCE letter could not result in increased electioneering.

Some business group leaders noted that the party financing reforms not only were enacted without intent to influence business but were very much in keeping with the parties' lack of interest in letting groups help to formulate policies. Jeff Brownlee, vice president for communications of CME, notes that most businesses are not engaged in politics in large part because they feel that parties formulate business policies and only then consult with businesses, either in a pro forma fashion or to encourage the groups to support the policies that have already been selected. For a group such as CME, with a base than includes many troubled or rapidly changing manufacturing businesses in Ontario, the crucial problem is branding of the industry—what Brownlee calls "PR and GR" (public relations and grassroots). CME's political efforts can influence elections but tend to go on independently of them. CME's strategies involve encouraging members to discuss the group with MPs and to frame the way in which manufacturing and the organization are perceived. Brownlee contends that the restrictions on corporate contributions have removed even the casual contact with party leaders that went into attending fund-raisers, so that businesses have needed to increase their lobbying simply to remain visible to lawmakers.

All of these responses show the limits of comparing businesses' political strategies in the United States and Canada but also provide several reasons why such comparisons are important. The most notable differences in business groups' responses to reform are rooted in the nature of Cana-

dian institutions; business groups see interest groups' traditional consul-
tative role with Parliament as an invitation to become involved in politics
only when asked (see, e.g., Young and Everitt 2004, 100, 151). Party discipline and parties' brokerage role also ensure that corporate groups have
little at stake in either national-level or riding-level elections.[7] Although
the groups with which I spoke did not mention being shaken down for
money by the parties in the same manner as some American soft money
donors, none of my interviewees expressed any regret at having contributions prohibited; at most, many regarded contributions as a sort of civic
function. They could therefore learn little from American groups because
of the institutional constraints on Canadian business groups.

All of the political directors with whom I spoke mentioned one unique
historical factor. Groups are guaranteed somewhat more access in a minority government, and all three elections since the passage of the CEA
amendments have produced minority governments. Minority governments strengthen parties' interest in using groups to build coalitions and
increase groups' ability to lobby multiple parties. Groups traditionally
have had little reason to have any contact with opposition parties, but in a
minority government, matters are different. In addition, the somewhat
greater number of private members' bills and free votes under minority
governments increases groups' incentive to have contact with individual
MPs. The CCCE's Laver expressed his group's view that minority governments have historically been unstable and susceptible to demands from
minority parties, but for groups concerned with more immediate issues,
minority governments create a greater opportunity that can translate into
electoral support or at least goodwill.

Advocacy Groups

The lack of consistent differences between Canada's major parties and the
co-optation of interest group demands by the parties has limited the scope
of advocacy group activities in Canada. While groups have, at times, been
closely allied with a party, Canada lacks the enduring clusters of advocacy
groups characteristic of the American system,[8] and many group movements have been ephemeral. For example, much of the literature on interest groups of the 1980s focuses on the National Action Committee, a
group that still exists but has nowhere near the visibility that it once pos-
sessed; other studies highlight the advertising efforts of the National Citizens Coalition, but even before the advertising ban, the Coalition did not

consistently run advertisements in every election year. And because of the lack of consistent contributions or electioneering efforts by Canadian groups, it is difficult to compile a list of the most prominent or politically powerful groups; such a list would change over the course of election cycles much more thoroughly than would a list of such American groups. The groups discussed here, then, cannot be said to be representative of advocacy group strategies to the same extent as Canadian business and labor groups. Nonetheless, I highlight groups with distinct ideological profiles: groups of the political Left (the Sierra Club and the merged Animal Alliance/Environment Voters group) and Right and, within the groups that might be associated with the Right, a group with socially conservative views (the Campaign Life Coalition) and two with more libertarian or economically conservative views (the Canadian Taxpayers Federation [CTF] and the National Citizens Coalition).

Some advocacy groups have previously engaged in third-party advertising and are thus subject to the advertising limitations, but none were major donors to the parties. Group attitudes toward the CEA amendments, the original CEA advertising restrictions, and the Accountability Act are thus more a consequence of groups' ideological or philosophical stances than of self-interest. The Sierra Club, for example, adopted the same stance as its U.S. counterpart, noting its approval for contribution limits on the grounds that limits would restrict business groups' ability to influence policy. In contrast, the CTF stated its opposition to public funding and advertising restrictions while contending that tax credits should be extended to any contribution to a group or charity. Groups were affected only on the margins; some groups reported seeking advisory opinions on the legality of some traditional practices, ensuring that travel to promote issues, for example, did not violate the third-party spending restrictions. The groups most vehemently opposed to the new party finance laws were not necessarily the largest groups; rather, these groups not only saw their activities restricted but also objected to the new rules not so much out of self-interest as out of philosophical opposition to restricting the speech of nonparty groups. These groups had less interest in lobbying and more interest in the electoral process itself.

Several more established groups included lobbying as a major component of their activities. The Sierra Club of Canada, formed in 1963, is an offshoot of the American Sierra Club. The Sierra Club of Canada established a national office in 1989 and was incorporated independently of the U.S. Sierra Club in 1992. It continues to engage in issue-specific collaborations with American chapters, primarily on border issues, but has no other official ties with the U.S. club. The Sierra Club's election-related activities primarily comprise of distributing and evaluating questionnaires to party leaders, although the group at times rates individual candidates according to their track records on the environment. Though not the largest environmental group in Canada, the Sierra Club has a reputation that ensures that it can generate substantial earned media. The Sierra Club has never engaged in third-party advertising. The major development for the Sierra Club since the passage of the CEA amendments has been the formation of the Green Party, whose current leader is the club's former executive director and whose former executive director, Jean Langlois, is now the campaigns director for the Sierra Club. According to Langlois, such close connections mean that the Green Party can expect to attract Sierra Club members, but the Sierra Club must be careful to maintain the perception that it is independent. According to some scholars (Stewart 2005), the Green Party has grown dramatically in large part because the public funding provisions of the CEA amendments encourage nascent parties to run candidates in as many ridings as possible. The Greens' 2004 showing (4.3 percent of the vote) likely drew votes away from the NDP; as a consequence, says Langlois, the NDP has sought to strengthen its environmental platform: In 2006, the Sierra Club rated the NDP platform higher than that of any other party.

The Campaign Life Coalition,[9] Canada's largest antiabortion group, has focused its political activities largely on distributing voter guides describing candidates' positions on abortion, gay marriage, and other family-related issues. The group's primary spokesperson, Jim Hughes, runs the group's headquarters in Toronto, but the Coalition also maintains a federal office in Ottawa. Despite a general lack of support from the major parties for restricting abortion and despite the fact that abortion is a less divisive issue in Canada than in the United States, the Campaign Life Coalition has been one of the most politically active Canadian advocacy groups. The group's voter guides do not officially endorse candidates but present a very clear picture of the Coalition's preferred candidates. According to the group's federal director, Aidan Reid, the group selects approximately thirty ridings each year in which to mobilize volunteers based on the differences between the candidates and the viability of the riding's antiabortion candidate. Reid admitted that the mobilization efforts are neither costly nor necessarily of great influence but argued that the group could swing several hundred votes in a close election. Although the effectiveness of the Campaign Life Coalition's targeting has been studied in the past (Tanguay and Kay 1991), according to Reid, the scale of the efforts and the fact that they rely primarily on volunteer labor have rendered them too small to be covered by the third-party restrictions. While the voter guides resemble those used by American groups such as the Christian Coalition, collaboration with such groups has been largely informal; Reid noted that he had attended the socially conservative Morton Blackwell Leadership Institute in Virginia, that he and other group members had some contact with antiabortion groups in Michigan, and that Hughes has long-standing ties with Gary Bauer, Ralph Reed, and other prominent American activists.

Perhaps because of the paucity of abortion-related votes at the federal level and the fact that both major parties have argued that votes on abortion should be free votes, the Campaign Life Coalition has taken great pains to encourage its members to vote for the candidate, not the party. The group's 2006 ratings of the party leaders noted, "It doesn't make any sense for pro-life voters to oppose a candidate who defends the sanctity of human life simply because of party affiliation."[10] While Reid believes that most Coalition members today are likely to vote for the Conservative Party, the Coalition has previously supported many Liberal candidates, especially members of the Liberals for Life faction (see Young 2000, 18), and the group's strongest support has traditionally come from Ontario, where the Liberals have dominated. The group has also sought to encourage members to become involved in nomination campaigns; most notably, the Coalition aggressively supported Stockwell Day's bid to lead the Canadian Alliance Party (Flanagan 2007, 59). Some Coalition members have been involved in the creation of minor parties, such as the Family Coalition Party and the Christian Heritage Party. Some other groups with which the Coalition works, such as REAL Women and the Canada Family Action Coalition, have been associated with the Reform and Alliance Parties. The Coalition views minor parties as a useful alternative only when neither of the major parties will address abortion issues, and it has not done any mobilization work that would benefit these parties.

By some measures, the CTF is now one of the two or three best-financed advocacy groups in Canada, with an annual budget approaching four million dollars. The CTF began in Saskatchewan in 1990, merged with a similar group in Alberta soon after that, and subsequently established offices in other provinces and an alliance with the Quebec Taxpayers' League. This federated structure ensures that many of the group's efforts are not focused on the national level or on national elections; indeed, the group's Ottawa office was established only in 1997. The CTF, although philosophically opposed to many of the components of the party finance reforms, does not engage in activities that would be affected by them; the group relies primarily on earned media, using its reputation to generate press coverage. Former CTF federal director John Williamson contends that the CTF has drawn on the expertise of several conservative and libertarian think tanks, including the Fraser Institute and the C. D. Howe Institute, but that it is more focused on activism during the election cycle than are other groups or think tanks.

CTF leaders have been part of American antitax activist Grover Norquist's weekly gatherings in Washington and are friendly with American groups such as the National Taxpayers Union and Americans for Tax Reform. The CTF shares these groups' interest in reducing the size of government as well as their reticence about becoming too involved in election politics; in fact, the CTF, like several other Canadian groups discussed here, has sought through its rhetoric and organization to emphasize its independence from the parties. Several Reform or Conservative Party members have been active in the CTF; Conservative MP Jason Kenney was formerly the Alberta CTF director, and Williamson was the press secretary for Stephen Harper in 2001 before becoming the CTF's Ontario director and in 2004 its federal director. In September 2009, Williamson was appointed Harper's director of communications. CTF board members are prohibited from being members of any party, and Williamson emphasized that the CTF has criticized Conservative governments in Alberta and at the national level just as much as it has criticized NDP provincial governments and Liberal provincial and national governments.

Each of these groups has an interest in elections, but that interest is not necessarily a primary goal. In contrast, the National Citizens Coalition, which may have played a role in inspiring the third-party advertising restrictions, has always had electoral change as one of its major goals. Since its formation in 1975, the NCC has aired political advertisements concerning several major causes, including immigration reform, energy policy, health care, and taxes, but it has also regularly made arguments about the electoral process, including arguments against campaign spending limits and in favor of Senate reform. It is difficult to argue that the new funding rules in the CEA amendments and the CEA's advertising restrictions harm the NCC financially or in terms of its visibility; the group has reacted much as has the CTF, increasing its use of its Web site and its efforts to garner media attention through group-sponsored tours. NCC CEO Peter Coleman argues that the contribution restrictions in the CEA amendments increase the group's revenues in that citizens may seek out groups to which to donate after reaching the limit for party contributions.

Since the 1980s, however, the NCC's best publicized activity has been its candidate-specific advertising; while many groups ran advertisements in 1988 discussing the FTA, the NCC ran ads that explicitly encouraged voters to vote against the NDP and Ed Broadbent. Similarly, in 1993, the NCC spent an estimated fifty thousand dollars on ads targeting Progressive Conservative incumbents in Alberta, including sitting prime minister Kim Campbell (Jeffrey 1999, 410). There is little evidence that these advertisements were particularly effective; Coleman contends that the ads probably did not sway a large number of votes but nevertheless forced candidates to discuss the group's issues and the media to cover these issues. The NCC has challenged the government's efforts to restrict third-party spending since 1984, culminating in the group's suit against the government in *Harper v. Canada (Attorney General)* (so named because Stephen Harper led the NCC at the time). Although the legal challenges failed, the group's efforts have clearly raised the visibility of the NCC and of the issue of third-party spending. It is no surprise, then, that now that the Supreme Court has settled the issue, the NCC's response to the third-party spending restrictions has included a concerted effort to call attention to the law's limits. This effort has included exploring the possibility of Internet advertising, pursuing the idea of advertising immediately before a writ is issued (which, Coleman notes, will be easier if fixed election dates are established), and supporting the defendant in the *R. v. Bryan* case concerning early disclosure of election results. Coleman contends that the NCC was deliberately less active in 2006 not so much because of changes in the law but because of Harper's former leadership of the group and the NCC's decision to avoid making itself a campaign issue.

The NCC had one other group as intervenor in the *Harper* case, a small Toronto-based environmental group, Environment Voters.[11] The NCC has frequently referred to Environment Voters, noting that opposition to third-party spending restrictions is not a matter of self-interest or of advancing its general fiscal conservative ideology but of preserving the right of citizen groups to influence what the parties discuss in elections. Environment Voters, which merged with the animal rights group Animal Alliance in 1999, has spent far less than the NCC in elections—it has never spent more than twenty thousand dollars on an election—but has also sought to directly connect its issues to politicians. Following the *Figueroa* decision and Parliament's subsequent legislation allowing any party that runs at least one candidate to provide tax credits to members, the group realized that if it reconstituted itself as a political party it could spend money to discuss issues in a manner that nonparty groups could not. In 2006, the Animal Alliance–Environment Voters Party (AA-EVP) ran one candidate, group leader Liz White, and to the extent that White campaigned, she discussed other candidates for whom people should vote.[12] The AA-EVP, with a budget of only about three hundred thousand dollars, is likely not large enough to play the spoiler or to win any seats on its own; White argues that the group does not even have an interest in winning a token number of seats. By registering as a party, however, the group qualifies for a small amount of free air time, can spend money discussing issues such as the Canadian seal hunt that politicians may not address, and the new party's donors can receive tax credits. Moreover, White notes, there are no restrictions on belonging to multiple parties (so AA-EVP members may remain members of the NDP or other parties) and no requirement that candidates must spend all of their money in their own riding, so an AA-EVP candidate might be able to spend money in other media markets.

White vehemently denies that the AA-EVP is exploiting a loophole in the law; she argues that while the group opposes third-party spending limits as undemocratic, it is merely taking the law as it is and using it to pursue a longer-term strategy, and she expects other organizations to follow suit. Establishing itself as a party has no obvious downside for a group the size of the AA-EVP; White reports that the group has seen little change in politicians' receptivity to its lobbying efforts, and although individual members now are limited in what they can contribute to the group, White noted that the group had few donors who gave more than the new eleven-hundred-dollar limit.

These groups' varied reactions show that institutional factors in Canada have precluded the type of electioneering that characterizes American advocacy groups' strategies during elections; some groups have used these strategies but have not done so frequently enough or spent enough money to claim success. Canadian political culture and geography also play a role in these groups' strategies. The Campaign Life Coalition and the CTF, for example, have origins in provincial politics and may be stronger at that level than at the national level. While advocacy groups in any nation may find more success pursuing their issues at the local or regional levels, the federated structure of Canadian politics, the differences in political culture across regions, and the lack of receptivity on the part of the federal government to some of these groups' issues may persuade them to focus less on federal elections and more on generating attention for their issues. Each of these groups spoke of its reputation and its effect on gaining media attention; whatever the cause of these groups' restrained approach to advertising and electioneering, the media can serve as a far more effective vehicle for publicizing issues and encouraging parties to pick up on the groups' issues. In instances where advocacy groups advertise, the advertising buys are often small enough to be geared more toward attracting media attention than toward influencing voters.

Just as business groups and labor unions spoke of the consequences of minority governments for their policy issues, so advocacy groups addressed changes in how their issues were received in a minority Parliament. In particular, the Campaign Life Coalition, with its "the candidate, not the party" approach, benefits the most from any relaxation in party discipline or in control over which issues are addressed. And while these groups expressed frustration with the major parties' discipline and agenda control, the organizations' relationships with minor parties are more ambiguous. Each of these groups has some connection with minor parties, although in the case of the CTF and the NCC, the relationship was with a minor party that eventually supplanted the old PC Party. In some cases, the line between groups and parties is somewhat blurry. As the AA-EVP example shows, party formation is a far more attractive option in Canada than in the United States because of the tax benefits that come with forming a party. In the cases of established groups that seek to influence the major parties through lobbying, such as the Sierra Club and the Campaign Life Coalition, the formation of minor parties that address those groups' issues poses a far more direct threat to the election prospects of Liberal, Conservative, or NDP candidates than would any sort of group effort. Yet all of these groups except for the AA-EVP stressed the importance of maintaining distance from minor parties; to the extent that the groups value their reputations as sources of attention from both the media and the major parties, the organizations cannot afford to be seen as captive to a party that has no chance of winning elections. The AA-EVP, which explicitly encourages voters to choose someone else, is an exception that proves the rule.

Canadians on the American and Canadian Responses

Little in the rhetoric of Canadian politicians suggests that group influence was as much of a consideration in the passage of the Canadian party finance reforms as it was in the American reforms. It seems appropriate, then, that few of the groups with whom I spoke felt that the CEA amendments had a major effect on them. Advocacy groups were scarcely affected, and some advocacy group leaders who were not well versed in the American campaign finance reform story expressed some puzzlement at this research project. Canadian business groups, like their American counterparts, were not wholly opposed to reform, although it clearly had some effect on them. And Canadian labor unions were the major groups affected by the legislation, but they nonetheless voiced some support for reform. It may well be that the CLC would have preferred to continue to support the NDP, but insofar as the CLC had little lobbying influence in determining the scope of the legislation, it adopted a fairly constructive attitude.

Table 6.1 presents a comparison of Canadian and American groups' responses to reform. As the table shows, the response to reform has been far more muted in Canada than in the United States. Canadian corporations and unions have largely eschewed grassroots work, while American peak business associations and labor unions have been far more aggressive in mobilizing their members. Direct financial support for parties and candidates in both countries has largely disappeared; this change has met little resistance from business but generated some regret from labor. Unions'

TABLE 6.1. The Responses of American and Canadian Groups Compared

Group Type	Prereform Activities, United States	Postreform Activities, United States	Prereform Activities, Canada	Postreform Activities, Canada
Corporate	PAC contributions, grassroots work	Little increase in PAC contributions. Increased grassroots work.	Contributions to parties; very limited grassroots work	Contributions removed from system. No change in grassroots work.
Labor	Grassroots work, PAC contributions, soft money contributions, TV and radio advertising	Increased member mobilization, some early advertising. Contributions to 527 organizations.	Grassroots work, contributions to parties (NDP), some radio advertising	Increased grassroots work; some early radio advertising. Disputes over relationship with NDP.
Advocacy	TV and radio advertising, endorsements, some grassroots work	Increased grassroots work; some early advertising. Development of multigroup coalitions and more complex organizations.	Most did little advertising or grassroots work around elections.	Little increase in grassroots work or coalitional work. Slight increase in efforts to use the media to advocate for electoral goals.

attempts to push money into the system have resulted in increased grass-roots work in both nations, although in both, the emphasis on mobilization may well have preceded reform. Advocacy groups' responses have varied: American groups have sought to overcome their small memberships by pooling resources and engaging in coalition work, while Canadian groups, traditionally less likely to develop cross-issue coalitions, have mostly retreated even further from the political arena. Exceptions exist in the Canadian case, but the groups that have sought to push the limits of the law or to develop partylike structures are less consequential than the major American groups.

According to my interviewees, the variation in responses can largely be explained by two factors. First, Americans have historically been more receptive to interest groups than have Canadians, as the institutional status of groups in the United States testifies. The existence of PACs, the constitutional protections for group speech, the lack of party discipline, and the corresponding candidate-centered nature of campaigns and campaign finance in the United States have given groups far more of an incentive to take an interest in elections. Canadians, as Jeffrey Simpson (2002, 181) notes, have seen groups as competitors with rather than allies of the parties, and Canadians have generally seen parties rather than groups as the appropriate vehicles for and brokers of competing interests. Second, the American two-party system, the ideological gap between the parties, and the fevered competition for control of Congress and the presidency in the 1990s and 2000s forced American groups to take sides and led politicians to encourage groups to do so. The existence of competitive minor parties, the lack of ideological differentiation between the Liberals and Conservatives, and the radical changes within what is today the Conservative Party have correspondingly discouraged Canadian groups from sorting themselves according to electoral preferences. As Simpson (2002, 182) argues, Canadian groups can be seen as an alternative to electoral politics, while American groups are virtually synonymous with electoral politics.

Canadians have been suspicious of regionally defined groups, but few of the interest groups discussed in this chapter derive their identities from regional causes. The organizations that do so have tended to constitute themselves as parties, not as interest groups, or have tended to steer clear of national politics. Organized labor, for example, may be stronger in some areas of the countries than in others, but the CLC has taken pains not to become associated with one particular region. The Canadian federal system is constituted to allow substantial regional autonomy, and groups have at times responded by pursuing their goals at the provincial level. The primary source of regional dissension, the difference between Quebec and anglophone Canada, has few repercussions for the national campaign finance system or for group activities at the national level (see Boatright 2011).

While most differences can be explained by institutions or the historical development of groups, one notable difference in responses may be rooted in political culture. In the United States, groups were well aware of the gray areas in the law before it passed, and some groups sought to exploit these areas even while knowing that their actions could subsequently be declared illegal. Several Canadian group leaders offered assurances that some loopholes must exist and that someone, someday, would exploit them; a few offered their opinions on what these loopholes might be. But no groups claimed actively to seek loopholes, and there was no consensus on how groups might continue to support the parties or engage in electioneering. This state of affairs speaks to one major difference between the two countries in political culture or in the political events surrounding the enactment of reform. Canadian interest groups have only sporadically been involved in Canadian elections, and many groups insist that they change nothing in their strategies after a writ has been issued. And while the development of the Reform Party into today's Conservative Party constituted a relatively dramatic event in Canadian politics, potentially ending the unbalanced party system of the 1990s and creating what may be an enduring set of minority governments, the 2004, 2006, and 2008 elections were nowhere near as polarizing as the same years' elections in the United States. The stakes may have been higher in the United States in 2004, leading groups to do all that they could to influence the outcome regardless of new legal restrictions. Such an argument would be somewhat subjective, however, in the sense that American elections are almost always more polarizing than Canadian elections. Group alignments with the parties are far stronger in the United States than in Canada, and there are no obvious instances of presidential elections in the past three decades where groups largely sat on the sidelines.

In sum, according to my Canadian respondents, party finance reform in Canada had consequences for what groups *can* do, while reform in the United States has had consequences for what groups *actually* do. The effects of BCRA remain a subject of discussion in the United States; many Republican politicians and activists remain deeply unhappy with the law, and efforts to overturn the law, especially through the courts, continue. Some Canadian groups worked to have third-party advertising restrictions declared unconstitutional, and many groups have voiced dissatisfaction with the public funding provisions of the CEA amendments. Most notably, in November 2008, the Harper government proposed removing public funding for parties as a cost-cutting move, a proposal that was quickly withdrawn after the threat by the Liberals, NDP, and BQ to seek to form a coalition government (see Curry 2008; Russell and Sossin 2009). This incident seems a sign more of the Conservative Party's dissatisfaction with public financing than of a broader dissatisfaction on the part of organized interests or the public. Most of the groups with which I spoke professed to have accepted the current campaign finance regime and to have moved on. Some of the dire consequences these groups had predicted did not occur, and no organized effort appears to exist outside of Parliament to overturn the reforms, in part or in full.

Beyond the U.S.-Canada Comparison

Many intriguing themes in the responses of Canadian groups are of note beyond the U.S. comparison. In many regards, as I was frequently reminded by the group leaders I interviewed, Canadian interest groups may well be more typical of interest groups generally than are American groups. That is, more countries have groups that resemble Canadian interest groups than have groups that are like American groups.

In the United States, the term *interest groups* encompasses organizations with a variety of different tax statuses. Canada has no functional equivalent to political action committees; the majority of large Canadian groups have a tax-exempt, charitable status and cannot engage directly in politics. If a group wishes to be overtly political, it can become a political party. In the United States, however, even groups that are officially nonpartisan become, by virtue of the two-party system, associated by the public and by politicians with one party or the other. The lack of differentiation between the major parties ensures that groups can become critics of governmental policy without being seen as partisans, although even groups that scrupulously avoid election-related activities can find their ideas taken up by opposition parties and can find themselves cast by those parties as foes of the governing party (see Boatright 2009).

The Canadian party system remains highly fragmented; there are few ridings in which more than two parties are competitive, and the competitiveness of the parties varies substantially across the country. The unification of the political Right by the Conservative Party has reduced this variation somewhat, but those who criticize one party in a national forum cannot necessarily predict which party will benefit from their criticisms. In the case of organized labor in particular, the parties that benefit from a group's activity may differ across provinces.

The opposition between parties and groups in Canada is thus much more fundamental than simply a case of policy differences. If each party saw some groups as allies and others as critics, an argument by politicians that groups are too powerful might be construed to mean that some groups—those that disagreed with a particular party—wield too much clout. But to the extent that Canadian parties have at times co-opted groups' positions, and to the extent that many scholars have claimed that Canadian groups provide an alternative to electoral politics, the functions of Canadian parties and groups seem to be in conflict.

It is possible, of course, to overstate this opposition. The argument by organizations such as the NCC that groups have too much power surely contains the argument that that particular organization is not a "group"— that it is a collection of citizens and that other organizations are the "groups" being criticized. In this argument, a group is an organization that speaks for citizens who are defined by a trait, not a set of ideas. It is hard to know whether the Trudeau government foresaw this sort of backlash when it instituted federal funding for groups, but even so, it might not have rethought the program. Empowering groups that speak for Canadians in a manner that is not geographic, that admits a multiplicity of identities beyond the French/English division, certainly had its political uses, but it seems unlikely that any government would have encouraged federally funded groups to play a substantive role in policy-making.

Have the Canadian reforms gone too far in silencing groups? For an American observer, hearing the comments of Canadian groups such as Environment Voters, there is always the possibility of "going native," of being drawn into an ideological debate that differs fundamentally from those taking place among American groups. Nevertheless, it is striking that the Canadian reforms dramatically circumscribe group contributions and advocacy without substantially improving the transparency of the political process. The restrictions on contributions and third-party speech and the public funding now provided for candidates ensure that voters can learn little about a candidate or party by looking at that candidate's supporters. A crucial heuristic step is thus lost. This situation may force voters to pay attention to what the parties are saying and to their platforms without worrying about their base of support, but it is difficult to argue that the limits on groups bring politicians closer to the voters. This topic is one of several normative issues in the U.S.-Canada comparison that will be examined in this book's closing chapters.

7 | Lessons

Some Canadian group leaders noted that they had learned from observing their American counterparts. As an Americanist, I do not second-guess the lessons drawn by Canadians about the relevance of U.S. politics to them. What, however, can Americans, notoriously inattentive to the politics of our northern neighbor, learn from this comparison? In this chapter, I summarize what can be learned from the case studies here with reference to the three levels of analysis presented earlier in this book—differences in group strategy across time periods, across group types, and across nations. These levels of analysis may be presented in several different ways to draw out the most important information. In the previous two chapters, I argued that a coherent story line charted U.S. and Canadian groups' responses to their nations' reform laws. That is, I prioritized the first type of comparison, comparisons across time within each system. Here, I organize concluding remarks on the effects of reform around group types—the second level of the comparison—to place similar groups operating in the United States and Canada side by side. This approach makes the effect of political institutions—the third level—more obvious and shows campaign finance reform's limitations in modifying group behavior in each country.

Group Characteristics and Reform

Organized Labor

Labor unions differ from the other group types discussed here in that they have different criteria for membership, different goals, and different ways of making decisions. They also differ from other organizations because in both nations, the majority of labor unions share a common governing body—the AFL-CIO in the United States and the CLC in Canada. These federations are relatively weak. Given the AFL-CIO's and CLC's inability to bring about changes within their member unions and the two unions' similar internal conflicts over organizing and political strategy, however, it can be difficult to speak of one labor strategy in each country. Some American unions perceived the AFL-CIO as not aggressive enough in responding to political developments or to labor's declining density within the population, while other unions saw the AFL-CIO as reacting in an overly partisan manner. Conflict within the CLC over support for the NDP has provided evidence of similar divisions.

Membership. The primary strength of labor unions in both countries is their ability to mobilize their members. Because AFL-CIO member unions have been privy to briefings from the AFL-CIO's political department, most have worked with the AFL-CIO on canvassing operations or have implemented similar programs. The basic simplicity of the mobilization model and message that AFL-CIO leaders have communicated to unions and to other sympathetic groups makes its core message easy for any union to latch onto. Unions differ in their ability to mobilize their members effectively—some unions are too small for a mobilization program to be particularly useful, while others lack staff resources to generate much effect. Large unions such as the SEIU can set up evaluation programs that parallel those of the AFL-CIO—testing a particular message, training volunteers, and so on. For unions such as the National Postal Mail Handlers Union or the National Air Traffic Controllers Association, this process entails merely having political directors make a pitch to members at union meetings, by mail, or even by telephone. Unions' direct contact operations clearly resonate among many members, corresponding to their idealized notion of what unions used to provide to their members. As such, most unions can support this activity.

In the Canadian case, mobilization is a similarly easy issue, although it intersects with party politics. American unions have little variation in the message they give to workers about which party to support, while Canadian union messages do vary. This difference is a function not only of the fact that the NDP is competitive in some areas of the country but not others but also of the fact that unions have had difficulty coordinating their messages—some have encouraged strategic voting, while others have not. Strategic voting is a more difficult issue around which to mobilize voters, and unions have reached little consensus about what to do in areas where the NDP is not competitive.

Financial Resources. Resource differences among unions largely correspond to union size, albeit with some exceptions—in the American case, white-collar unions have tended to raise more PAC money, controlling for size, than have blue-collar unions, simply because members have more money and may also be more politicized. The abolition of soft money contributions has given large unions more of an opportunity to target independent spending. Large unions with distinct geographic bases, such as the United Auto Workers, have also pursued different programs or supplemented AFL-CIO efforts. Smaller unions or those with little ability to gain new members have tended to prioritize PAC contributions over independent expenditures, and unions without distinct geographic bases but substantial resources (such as AFSCME or the SEIU) have emphasized independent expenditures in competitive races with less regard for geography.

Resource differences are less easily mapped onto political activity in Canada, in part because Canada has no equivalent to PACs, in part because of party discipline, and in part because the parties' regional fragmentation has influenced groups' political calculations. Prior to the passage of the CEA amendments, Canadian unions' major spending decisions concerned giving to the NDP and mobilization. Financial support for the NDP was largely a routinized matter—with fewer spending choices, contributions to the NDP were clearly dictated by group size, but the targeting of any other type of spending was and remains more a matter or provincial politics and the nature of provincial elections than of federal elections.

Union Goals and Partisanship. Although some American unions are more supportive of the Democratic Party than others, few went so far as to support President George W. Bush or to support more than a small number of Republican candidates. Despite Bush's attempts to court Douglas McCarron of the Carpenters' Union and James Hoffa Jr. of the Teamsters, neither union reciprocated with an endorsement in either 2000 or 2004. According to several political directors, under John Sweeney, the AFL-CIO has also taken strides to ensure that unions work cooperatively on issues—that unions that lack an immediate stake in another union's major issues will nonetheless support that union. This approach has ensured that while unions have had different policy concerns, they have been relatively united in their partisan preferences. And the centralizing of political activity within the AFL-CIO has ensured that unions are more aware of other unions' actions and can work in a more coordinated way than was previously the case. Access-seeking unions, such as the various postal workers unions, have tended to limit their support of Republicans to making PAC contributions.

The existence of the NDP has clearly separated policy goals from partisanship for Canadian unions; as Yates (2008) recounts, organized labor has at times lobbied the Liberal Party in regard to policy issues, but labor has never tied its campaign activities to particular policy objectives to the same extent as American unions.

Technological Context and Communications.   Labor unions have mobilized members in political campaigns, but because unions are not strictly political or ideological entities, as is the case with advocacy groups, they have not consistently moved beyond face-to-face communication to speak to members or sympathetic nonmembers. The Web pages of all unions discuss political issues, but they are not the sites' major focus. And despite the growing use of e-mail to contact members, unions have not used such communications to encourage political activities to the same degree as have other groups. The major technological development that has aided unions, however, is the creation of lists of members with information gathered from personal contacts about political views and concerns. Because of the size of union membership—and, in particular, the size of union membership in heavily unionized areas—gathering data on members has been vital to unions and has been a more effective tool for unions than for smaller or more issue-driven groups. While the coincidence of Internet-based campaigning and campaign finance restrictions has meant that other types of groups moved toward online organizing, union communication has remained more of an in-person activity.

Leadership and Organization.   Finally, somewhat intangible differences among unions have affected how they approach politics. In the United States, the Painters Union and the Teamsters have cultivated a particular image that is reinforced by having a large number of activists who are visible at campaign events. This strategy is partially group self-image, but it is likely also a function of group leadership. Some unions have enthusiastically supported the AFL-CIO's mobilization program, while others have not. Some unions have dramatically increased the percentage of their budget devoted to organizing, while others have not. In many cases, this decision is a function of group leadership. According to many analysts, Andrew Stern's decision to take the SEIU out of the AFL-CIO, for example, was as much a matter of Stern's personal views as of any sort of enduring divisions within the AFL-CIO. It appears that Sweeney's successor,

Richard Trumka, may work toward a rapprochement with Stern and the other union leaders who have left the AFL-CIO, again bringing personality into play. Many accounts of Canadian union strategy boil down to matters of personality—most obviously, Buzz Hargrove's support for Paul Martin and the Canadian Auto Workers' departure from the CLC.

Union Characteristics and Reform. Given the intensity of American unions' opposition to BCRA, what is ultimately surprising about union activities after 2002 is how much unions' changes reflected the calls of Sweeney and other AFL-CIO leaders during the 1990s. In other words, the union effort in 2004 and beyond seems more like a natural outgrowth of unions' evaluations of their 2000 and 2002 campaign efforts than a sudden shift to comply with the new law. Between 2000 and 2004, labor unions gradually reduced their television advertising and sought to focus more on member mobilization. And recognizing that member mobilization had perhaps reached the limits of its effectiveness, they sought to use their program to mobilize nonunion voters. BCRA certainly reduced the AFL-CIO's ability to communicate with the general public and to support the Democratic Party, but organized labor's direction was remarkably consistent with the agenda Sweeney and others within the AFL-CIO had advocated well before BCRA's passage.

Canadian unions were initially less hostile to reform, so it is perhaps less of a surprise that they continued to develop their mobilization strategy. Canadian unions have tended to use the NDP as their vehicle to communicate with the public, and although they could no longer provide financial support for the party, the replacement of their funds with public money, coupled with the fact that in-kind contributions to the parties were not affected by the new law, meant that Canadian unions, too, could focus more on member communication. Still unknown, however, is whether the severing of financial ties between unions and the NDP will enable the party more aggressively to court nonunion voters.

Business Groups

Because of the number of business groups, it is difficult to make a general statement about how these groups changed; many did not change at all over these election cycles. In the United States, however, a substantial number of business groups altered their activities, and the fact that these changes were coordinated by the larger peak associations ensured that business groups, like unions, sought to do a better job than had the parties at targeting their resources. Unlike unions, however, business groups do not necessarily have individual members to mobilize, although they sought to expand their communication with employees. During the 2004 and 2006 elections, most of these groups' targeted political spending and communication were partisan in nature, although groups' spending and communication in 2008 revolved more around issues such as the Employee Free Choice Act and economic stimulus policies.

Resources.   Differences in the size of the business or business association are an obvious source of differences in contributions in the two countries, but in the United States, these differences diminished for two reasons. First, more and more business PACs took advantage of PAC development training provided by peak associations. Second, with the shift toward voter mobilization, the size of a business's PAC is now less important than is the business's ability to communicate effectively with its employees. Resources, then, are less important than business leaders' skills in getting their employees to vote and to become politically active. In prereform Canada, the legality of corporate contributions to the parties meant that Canadian businesses needed to invest less energy in raising political money than did their American counterparts, and the prohibitions on business spending following reform mean that businesses now cannot make contributions. This change advantages peak associations such as the Canadian Council of Chief Executives, which can expect to command some free media should they wish to speak about political issues.

Goals.   The conventional American distinction between groups seeking access to lawmakers and groups seeking to influence elections, which closely tracks the differences in business group partisanship, has become a major source of differences in group strategies. Many corporate PACs still primarily seek access, a situation that has prompted some reluctance to communicate aggressively with employees, while trade associations and peak groups, which are more concerned with election results, have worked to mobilize in support of candidates. This distinction was apparent in the list of groups supporting President Bush, but it has also been evident in the list of the groups most enthusiastic about encouraging employee communication. And for those access-seeking groups that still seek to affect elections, peak associations or front groups such as Citizens for Better Medicare, United Seniors, and Americans for Job Security have become a prominent venue for combining the two goals, allowing groups that want to be perceived by their members and by lawmakers as access-seeking organizations to allocate a larger share of their resources to electioneering. Canadian peak associations can play a similar role, but the lack of major differences between Liberals and Conservatives has produced a system in which all business groups can concentrate on access.

Evaluation and Learning.   The American business groups that have gone beyond simply making PAC contributions to more aggressive campaign tactics have used many tools to measure the effects of their political activities. For peak associations and trade groups, evaluation has taken the form of member surveys, independently commissioned studies of the effects of independent expenditure campaigns on voters, and analyses of contribution or voting records. For corporate PACs during the time period considered here, evaluation was generally conducted by the larger peak associations or trade groups to which they belonged. I do not contend that all groups care only about effectiveness; the Associated Builders and Contractors, for example, places partisan goals above some considerations of effectiveness. Conversely, less ideological trade associations such as the Realtors may limit their evaluation of political efforts to a relatively small number of the races in which they are involved on the grounds that securing access to whatever candidate is successful is more important than influencing election results.

Because Canadian business groups have never made political expenditures in amounts designed to influence elections—corporate contributions to the parties have been framed by the parties as a civic responsibility and explicitly decoupled from policy—they have not been encouraged to make cost/benefit calculations about their political spending. Although Canadian groups have also developed Internet-based evaluations of the party platforms, they have shown little interest in measuring the effectiveness of these tools.

Business Group Characteristics and Reform.   Business spending has been substantially affected by reform in both countries. There are numerous other outlets for the money that had previously been earmarked for the parties—in the United States, some of the decrease in party donations has been offset by the growth of business PACs, the larger amounts of hard money used for independent expenditures, the growing contributions to leadership PACs, and the record-high spending on the party conventions. But a sizable percentage of business money has simply left the system in both nations. While businesses have had the option of redirecting that money toward internal communications, anecdotal reports suggest that not all of this money has gone in this direction, and such is the case for two reasons. First, internal communications are generally far less costly than the former soft money donations (in the American case) or direct contributions (in the Canadian case), so businesses likely feel that they can adequately communicate with their employees without exhausting that money. Second, much of this money was pulled by the parties—it was a fee that businesses were willing to pay to gain access to lawmakers, but few companies were enthusiastic about making these contributions. Even well before the implementation of BCRA, many U.S. companies had grown reluctant to give soft money; in the Canadian case, businesses had likewise supported a limit on corporate contributions. It should not be surprising, then, that these companies directed this money toward non-political purposes.

Many business groups in both countries voiced displeasure with the electioneering restrictions, but they appear to have had little effect on business groups. The American groups that previously had advertised extensively ran advertisements through their PACs, but the most striking feature of the 2000, 2002, and 2004 election cycles is the degree to which even before BCRA's passage, the business community had already begun to explore mobilization work and to reduce its dependence on television and radio advertising. In the wake of the *Citizens United* decision, peak groups such as the Chamber of Commerce will certainly spend more on direct advocacy and issue advocacy. The *Citizens United* decision, however, was handed down on January 21, 2010, when peak business groups were especially eager to become more politically aggressive as a consequence of their increased frustration with the Obama administration, a decline in the president's favorability ratings, and the surprising Republican victory in the Massachusetts special election to replace Senator Edward Kennedy. Business associations, in other words, would have had a more pressing reason to direct money into politics in 2008 and 2010, regardless of the status of campaign finance law, than they did in the elections surrounding BCRA.

In both countries, peak business leaders noted their fear that issue speech would likewise be restricted, a concern that is no longer relevant in the United States. Canadian groups have not worried about this issue in recent elections because the parties have not cast these votes as referenda on contentious economic issues.[1] In both countries, business groups are free to address issues outside of the election cycle, as Canadian groups have done with border and federal budget issues and U.S. groups did in 2009 as Congress addressed the Obama administration's environmental and health policy goals.

Advocacy Groups

General statements about advocacy groups are difficult to make in part because their success depends more on the popularity of their primary issues of concern than on their membership or resources. Advocacy groups also tend to do well financially when they face legitimate threats. Many organizations have prospered under administrations that were hostile to their interests—in the United States, liberal groups gained members during the Reagan administration by vilifying the president and members of his staff and cabinet, conservative groups did the same under Bill Clinton, and many liberal groups drew attention to their issues through attacks on John Ashcroft or on President George W. Bush and Vice President Richard Cheney's connections to various oil interests. Canadian groups on the left have sought to vilify Stephen Harper, but Canadian politics lacks the sort of villains present in the United States, and group efforts can be difficult to separate from party politics when attacks on individual politicians are made.

Likewise, some group issues may be pushed into or out of the spotlight regardless of groups' efforts. In the United States, the heightened national focus on terrorism, national security, and the war in Iraq temporarily made it more difficult for many advocacy organizations to draw attention to their issues in 2002, but within two years, these organizations returned some attention to their issues. In Canadian politics, the lack of clear partisan differences on many major issues, coupled with parties' ability to ignore potentially divisive issues, is even more consequential for groups—if the parties do not pay attention, groups may make issue-based appeals to the public and seek to raise the profile of their issues, but their issues still may not matter in elections. Minor Canadian parties have been more effective in injecting issues into campaigns than have groups.

The variation among advocacy groups notwithstanding, several important group variables must be considered when comparing American and Canadian advocacy groups.

Membership and Resources. Many larger American advocacy organizations saw their resources decline somewhat from 2000 to 2002, and although group spending increased in 2004, many organizations failed to reach their 2000 spending levels. This decline was somewhat offset by the spending of 527 organizations, but several groups that engaged in major advertising buys in 2000 would have been unable to duplicate these efforts even had they wanted to. The other major group resource relevant to political activity, the size of a group's membership, also dictated political strategy. Groups consciously sought to build their membership over this time, perhaps more than is usually the case, and to mobilize their members. Advocacy groups do not have large enough concentrations of members in particular states or congressional districts to make a difference, but they must do less to mobilize their members than other groups might—those who join advocacy groups can already be expected to share the organization's political objectives. Scholars have conducted little analysis of systemic changes in Canadian advocacy group membership or resources over this period, but the involvement of groups in electoral politics has been episodic enough that it seems unlikely that changes in campaign finance law or in the political context had a major effect on group membership or resources.

Goals. Apart from election-related goals, however, many advocacy groups become involved in campaigns to establish themselves, place their issues on the political agenda, or reshape their public images. Organizations that feel their issues are not receiving sufficient attention tend to advertise well before elections begin or to engage in activity designed to garner media coverage. The restrictions on Canadian advocacy spending also make this option attractive—groups may advertise in part to gain media coverage, which they can then use to bolster their images.

Partisanship. Although most of the more prominent American advocacy groups share an overriding partisan leaning, all are officially nonpartisan. However, most of these groups tend to support moderates of the opposing party. In a handful of conspicuous cases, these organizations backed Republican incumbents who were no more supportive of the groups' issues than were Democrats as a consequence of a proincumbent policy and a desire to maintain a foothold in the Republican Party. This approach has little bearing on the presidential race or on the margins of control on Congress, but it is an appealing way to prevent a group from being completely shut out of the deliberations of either of the major parties. Canadian groups have traditionally been less partisan, so they tend not to be forced to make such decisions. In some instances, groups have deliberately made this choice, while in other cases, parties have specifically sought to avoid associating themselves too closely with groups (Farney 2009). The downside of keeping some distance from the parties, however, is that groups can be perceived as being hostile toward the governing party—as one interviewee told me, any critical assessment of government policy can lead to accusations that the group is partisan (see also Boatright 2009).

Evaluation and Learning.   Resources and the nature of the activities in question affect advocacy groups' ability to evaluate the success of past activities. Perhaps the most important change in American advocacy group behavior was the increased coordination between liberal groups beginning in 2004, which ensured that groups could benefit from each other's evaluations and minimized differences in groups' individual abilities. Groups that spend heavily on television often can test their advertisements on focus groups, compare their advertising buys with tracking polls, and survey voters regarding the ads. Groups that conduct registration or mobilization drives can measure their strategies' effectiveness after the election, although they do not always do so in a rigorous manner. Most of the group innovations discussed here have been a consequence of learning from other groups. As a result of the increased coordination and sharing of information among groups in 2004, many groups focused on the same races and similarly adjusted their strategies based on groups' evaluation of the strategies of organizations such as the AFL-CIO, the NAACP-National Voter Fund, and even conservative organizations.

These types of networks are driven either by shared interests or by partisanship. In the American case, these two factors tend to reinforce each other. In the Canadian case, the lack of group partisanship makes forming such networks problematic unless it occurs under the auspices of the government. Environmental groups, for example, can learn from other environmental groups but have more difficulty learning from other types of groups. These groups may have less of a need for information about election strategy, but the absence of such networks means that groups may be slower to innovate or that sharing of political information across issue areas takes place within the parties.

Advocacy Group Characteristics and Reform.   The fragmentation of advocacy groups in both countries ensures that adaptations to reform will certainly be slower than for labor or business. Few American advocacy organizations were directly affected by the soft money prohibition, and no Canadian groups were directly affected by the restrictions on contributions to the parties. Electioneering restrictions, however, had different consequences in the two countries. With the exception of America Votes, few U.S. advocacy groups were among the initial founders of or contributors to the new 527 organizations, but the existence of these organizations restricted what many advocacy groups could do. Groups could worry less about large-scale mobilization efforts because other groups would undertake these efforts and less about electioneering restrictions because other groups would engage in electioneering on behalf of their preferred presidential candidates.

As is the case for other group types, changes in campaign finance law pushed American advocacy groups in a direction they were likely to have gone even without reform—that is, their shared characteristics mattered more than did differences between the groups. In the American case, many of these organizations had expressed a need to increase their grassroots organizing capabilities. Many groups on the left had realized for several election cycles that they lacked the networks or shared resources that groups, politicians, and think tanks on the right have developed over the past three decades, and the campaign finance laws offered an avenue that enabled organizations on the left to increase their coordination. And many groups had explored bundling for several election cycles; the increased hard money limits gave groups an even greater incentive to do so. Many organizations realized that legal developments might ultimately work to their disadvantage—that regardless of their strengths, the decline in the Democratic Party's ability to raise and spend soft money could have the long-term effect of harming their preferred candidates. The increased emphasis on grassroots mobilization may have worked to the disadvantage of groups with smaller memberships. Finally, these groups' strategies were both less flexible and less measurable.

In the Canadian case, the greater fragmentation among advocacy groups and the fact that advocacy groups were less affected by reform decreased the need for the development of networks or for changes in strategy. Groups' options are clearly more limited, however, and some organizations, including the Animal Alliance–Environment Voters Party, have worried that the lack of ability to raise issues is a serious democratic concern, even for groups that did not engage in advocacy on a scale large enough that reform mattered. Despite the fact that Canadian groups have focused less on turning back the clock or on undoing the reform legislation than have Americans, the normative issues raised about group speech are at least as compelling as those raised by American groups, in part because they seem less derived from self-interest.[2]

For each of these group types, the Canadian response bore some resemblance to the American response—labor adopted a mobilization strategy, albeit with somewhat less urgency; business groups withdrew somewhat more of their money from the political system; and advocacy groups also turned somewhat further away from campaign activity (although they were never as active). These changes are in keeping with the institutional incentives provided to groups by the different systems and with some of the differences between the two pieces of reform legislation.

Institutional Characteristics and Reform

The third level of this comparison is of the variables of importance in looking at the relationship between political institutions and interest groups. This comparison offers several useful lessons for interest group scholars that can be applied in comparing behavior in other nations or in assessing the potential effects of institutional changes within each country.

Institutional Structure as an Independent Variable

Several basic features of American and Canadian political institutions have produced different responses to campaign finance reform. The parliamentary structure of the Canadian system discourages groups from becoming involved in elections. Even if Canadian groups care which party governs, electoral activity is highly unlikely to be particularly influential. Groups have responded by seeking to avoid alienating either of the major parties, thereby maintaining some influence in any government. Labor unions are the exception to this rule, but organized labor's history of support for a party that does not have the strength to govern at the federal level ensures that any claims to influence are complicated; labor can have some influence if the NDP holds the balance of power in a minority government, but such an argument cannot easily be translated into messages to the electorate, as the conflict between the Canadian Auto Workers and NDP unions shows. American groups, conversely, can influence particular policies by working for or against particular legislators, and their influence has something to do with the size of the majority party, even if they are unlikely to influence who governs.

Another institutional difference, the frequency of elections, also influences group activity. American groups can plan their election strategies over a two- or four-year period and can steadily implement a plan for communicating with voters, an approach that is not available to Canadian groups. This difference has implications for how groups raise money, allocate resources, identify issues on which to focus, and develop coalitions.

Campaign finance reform in the two countries thus had different implications for different groups. American groups could grasp the general contours of the 2004 election soon after the passage of BCRA and could test responses to and gray areas in the law well before they needed to begin electoral activities. Canada, however, had two elections in relatively quick succession, a phenomenon that surely influenced groups' fund-raising efforts and strategic calculations in a much different way. The governing party's ability to call an election at any time can undercut opposition party strategies as well as any coordinated group strategy. Groups' fund-raising, contribution, and issue advocacy strategies depend on defined timetable. Absent this timetable, Canadian groups were much more quiescent about reform than were American groups, leading to responses that were similar in direction but less dramatic.

Party System Differences as an Independent Variable

Similarly, groups' alliances with the parties can determine how groups allocate resources. The American two-party system encourages groups to ally with the parties, while the Canadian brokerage system discourages such alliances. The Canadian exceptions—the relationships between labor and the NDP and between some conservative groups and the nascent Reform Party—again prove this rule. Groups can ally with minor parties, but doing so can impede any sort of lobbying activity. Most established Canadian advocacy groups tend to avoid such alliances, while less powerful, less institutionalized groups may take this approach.

In the United States, campaign finance reform has been a relatively partisan issue from the early days of the McCain-Feingold reform proposals. Much of the debate regarding this reform as well as other reforms has centered on which party would gain and which party would lose and on which party constituencies would gain or lose. The less partisan a group, the more likely it would stay on the sidelines, as was the case for business groups. Canadian reforms, too, had winners and losers among the parties, but the legislation, and particularly its public financing component, was crafted to reinforce the status quo in party strength in at least the short term. The severing of ties between parties and groups in the United States, as exemplified by the soft money ban, the privileging of individual donations over PAC donations, and the limits on electioneering, did not necessarily make groups less partisan and may have strengthened ties among groups with shared partisan leanings. In the Canadian case, groups clearly sought to avoid partisanship to a greater degree than in the United States.

At least in the short run, BCRA encouraged the formation of 527 groups, organizations that have tended to be strongly partisan and to pursue party goals within a particular niche (e.g. to focus on voter contact or advertising) or in a particular geographic area (Boatright 2007). Very few independent 527 groups persisted across all of the first three post-BCRA election cycles. Such groups, then, can be said to be ephemeral in nature, an argument that has been made about Canadian interest groups as well. A crucial difference, however, is that the formation of ephemeral 527 groups has largely resulted from a weakening of the parties, while the ephemerality of Canadian groups has been a consequence of party strength. To put matters in other terms, American party activists have at times created short-lived groups to pursue goals that the parties lack the legal ability or the resources to pursue; in the Canadian case, while the parties have at times encouraged group formation, they have not seen groups as a means of pursuing electoral goals.

Federalism as an Independent Variable

The variation in provincial campaign finance laws is much more consequential than are any differences among the American states. These differences reinforce or are reinforced by the geographic pockets of group strength and the greater autonomy of provincial governments. While many American groups have definable bases of strength, BCRA did little to push groups into state politics and away from federal politics. U.S. federal politics is simply too important for groups to ignore, regardless of whether they can achieve some of their objectives at the state level. Because the Canadian provinces tend to have greater power in regard to environmental laws, labor laws, health care, and some aspects of social policy, the limitations imposed by the CEA amendments encouraged some groups to refocus their efforts on provincial politics. Organized labor, in particular, had already been heavily engaged in provincial elections; the CEA amendments may well have pushed labor further in this direction. Differences in provincial laws regarding union affiliation with the NDP or any party, for example, influenced union efforts in several provinces. Moreover, several Canadian provinces prohibited group contributions to the parties prior to passage of the federal law, so some groups already had experience with restrictions similar to those imposed by the 2003 CEA amendments.

Courts as an Independent Variable

American political scientists have explored the difference in legal regimes between the United States and Canada, with many commentators noting the U.S. Supreme Court's more elastic definition of speech in elections. In both countries, courts have struck down various pieces of reform, and they have enabled interest groups to engage in actions that Parliament or Congress would prefer to prohibit. The Canadian Parliament has, however, simply been more persistent than the U.S. Congress in pursuing its goals despite court opposition, and Parliament has succeeded in limiting interest group advocacy where the U.S. Congress has not.

All of these institutional features are relatively immutable. Few serious discussions of changing them have taken place in the United States, and although such discussions have occurred in Canada (during the nation's constitutional debates, in proposals regarding the status of the Canadian Senate, in the proposals of the Reform Party, and in Ontario's referendum on proportional representation), any such changes face significant obstacles. Smaller variations also exist, however—the large gap between Canada's disciplined party system and the less disciplined American system, for example, allows room for some variation. The level of party discipline in the United States has varied over the past few decades, even though the nature of American elections ensures that the parties cannot enforce slavish obedience to the party line. Courts' interpretations of constitutional law likewise shift over time, the terms under which governments can be dissolved and elections called in Canada have changed somewhat, and the degree of autonomy granted to states and provinces is not completely constant. In some ways, the stark oppositions established here serve as guideposts in looking at how interest group behavior may be influenced by smaller variations.

Similarities in the Reform Packages . . . to a Point

Finally, I return briefly to the first level of this comparison, the measurement of changes in the interest group systems of these countries across time. Throughout much of this book, I have treated the American and Canadian laws as roughly equivalent, but in regard to each of the group types, the public financing component and the tax credit component of the Canadian legislation provide an extra wrinkle to group strategies. In addition, the Canadian legislation is more comprehensive in the sense that it bans group contributions entirely and prohibits issue advocacy much more thoroughly than did BCRA (even before the *Citizens United* decision). The more comprehensive Canadian legislation shows the potential effects of some proposals circulated in the United States. In regard to the public financing component, the Canadian experience has shown that, on the negative side, parties have much more freedom to ignore groups than was previously the case. On the positive side, the nationalization of party strategies, as in the cases of the NDP and the Green Party, can push parties to pay attention to geographic demands that might otherwise be ignored. And the fact that the tax credit applies to parties, not groups, has made party formation more attractive. In some cases, including organized labor, groups can encourage members to support parties. In general, Canadian campaign finance laws already privilege parties over groups. No serious discussion of changing the status of PACs has taken place in the United States, but the Canadian system shows that where groups have no legal status in campaigns, they cannot establish themselves as an enduring presence.

The tighter regulations present in the Canadian law, however, have shut off one of the hydraulic valves present in American politics. Some Canadian business groups noted that corporations cannot redirect the money they had contributed into any sort of alternate political vehicle; nothing like 527 groups can exist in Canada. A group such as the NCC, which has previously received some support from corporations or corporate leaders, may still be able to argue that those who gave large sums of money to the parties can turn to ideological groups, but absent the ability to engage in issue advocacy, such groups can do less with donations than American 527 groups did in 2004. Loopholes may still exist in the Canadian system, but Canadian groups have far less of an incentive to find them than do American groups.

These two components of Canadian campaign finance law also do not quite match existing public financing programs or tax credit programs in the American states. Although six American states provide tax credits for political contributions, in all cases, these tax credits are far more modest than the Canadian tax credit (Boatright and Malbin 2005; Rosenberg 2002). These programs cannot be said to work to the disadvantage of groups; although only one program (the Oregon tax credit) provides tax credits for contributions to PACs, the amounts in question for all the U.S. state tax credits, generally of fifty dollars or less, tend to be small enough that the goal is clearly to encourage small contributions, not to privilege particular recipients of money. In contrast, many group leaders perceived the Canadian tax credit as privileging parties over groups. The American states that have public financing tend to reward candidates, not parties. The American systems, limited as they are, may reduce the role of groups in campaigns but do not influence the group/party relationship, particularly insofar as groups can still engage in substantially more issue advocacy work in the states than is the case in Canada.

The public funding component of the Canadian legislation, however, has had a substantial impact on what parties need from interest groups. Parties do not need to encourage interest groups to divert their contributions into other types of election-related work and have the means to dominate the agenda during elections without relying on interest groups as proxies, as American parties may have. This state of affairs is somewhat in keeping with the conflict many Canadian observers have posited between parties and interest groups—Canadian parties do not need interest groups, while American groups do. In this regard, American groups are somewhat unusual among Western nations because of their role in providing financial support for parties and candidates.

Again, Campaign Finance Reform as a Natural Experiment

This chapter shows that although the effects of reform cannot be precisely measured in either the United States or Canada, the fact that the two nations undertook similar changes at similar times provides a rare opportunity to look at, on the one hand, the role that group characteristics play in determining campaign strategy and, on the other, the role that institutions play in providing incentives to different types of groups. The two reform packages are not identical but are similar enough that one can hold the broad features of the legal changes constant to focus on groups and institutions. And the differences in the two laws provide an instructive example in their own right of the ways in which different components of substantially similar laws can have major consequences.

Campaign finance reform has provided a mixture of foreseeable and unforeseeable consequences for group activities. The broad contours of groups' immediate postreform adaptations, such as the rise of 527 groups in the United States in 2004, likely were foreseeable. And the increase in Internet fund-raising by American candidates, groups, and parties likely was not completely surprising, but the magnitude of the increase and the resilience of the Democratic Party clearly were unexpected. It is unclear how the increasing use of the Internet for fund-raising and for advertising will mesh with the Supreme Court's removal of the limits on corporate spending in elections. In the Canadian case, the consolidation and political success of the Conservative Party can now be tied in part to its superior fund-raising base and network of supportive groups, but it is not clear that the Liberal Party could have anticipated this development in the early 2000s.

Changes in the fortunes of political players may be among the goals of reform efforts but do not provide sufficient explanation for the development of reform proposals. All of the major movements to change American and Canadian campaigns have originated in a normative critique of the role of money in elections. The normative story of the past decade of campaign financing in the United States and Canada is complicated, but the final chapter of this book evaluates how closely postreform interest group behavior has accorded with reformers' goals.

8 | Reform Goals and Values

It would be natural for anyone evaluating the effects of campaign finance reform on interest groups to choose sides among the groups—to breathe a sigh of relief that the groups one likes have remained effective despite limitations on their activities, or to note with frustration that groups one dislikes continue to play a role in campaigns. It is far more difficult to stand outside the fray and to draw normative conclusions about the role of groups in general. This phenomenon is natural—as we have seen throughout this book, politicians and citizens tend to believe that "special interests" corrupt the political process, while other groups ("not-so-special" interests, perhaps) merely serve as a vehicles for concerned citizens who wish to play a role in politics. Because groups bring such different types of resources and concerns to their political activities, governments cannot help but choose sides as well; any change in campaign finance practices will confer advantages on some group types while disadvantaging others. Even reforms that limit the activities of all groups are hardly neutral; as the Canadian example has shown, reducing the role of organized interests can strengthen the role of political parties, and given that parties may well have their own issue preferences, distinct from those of nonparty groups, it is still hard not to view such reforms without seeing them through the lens of one's partisan or ideological preferences.

How, then, can the merits of the American and Canadian reform laws be weighed? Is it troubling or reassuring that so many of these groups adapted relatively easily to the new laws? Many of these adaptations were apparent, or at least should have been apparent, to the authors of the two nations' reform proposals. These authors' intentions may not coincided precisely with the values espoused by reform advocates, but these advocates did use a common language. What values should we use in looking at reform, and how can we separate them from lawmakers' partisan calculations?

For many types of legislation, an easy way to avoid messy discussions of values is simply to measure public support for legislative changes, to assume that laws that find support in public opinion data are "good" laws. In the case of campaign finance laws, however, doing so is not possible. Opponents of reform have argued that public support for reform is shallow and uninformed; supporters of reform have responded that while the public may care more about more substantive issues, the fact that substantial majorities in both countries have supported these reforms remains important. Both sides are undoubtedly correct. The democratic deficit literature summarized in the introduction, however, shows that the public's desire for changes in campaign financing is unlikely to be sated—disaffection with government responsiveness may be manifested in calls for change, but campaign finance reform is unlikely to be a powerful enough tool to stem public dissatisfaction. As Ikstens et al. (2002) have noted, reforms, even when relatively successful, can make the situation worse. The public may observe instances of corruption, which may still occur in even the most transparent, egalitarian system, and conclude that little has been accomplished. In other words, it is natural to conclude not that individual politicians are corrupt but that the system itself is corrupt.

The values inherent in any debate over campaign finance laws, then, must embody more than simple references to public support. This is not to say, however, that distinctions cannot be made among different types of laws, that those who research campaign finance cannot draw normative conclusions about changes in campaign financing practices. In the comparison between the United States and Canada, the broad trends in public sentiment toward money in politics and toward the role of groups in political campaigns are relatively similar, but the basic values espoused by reformers differ slightly. Lisa Young (2004) frames Canadian campaign finance reform in light of four different goals: accountability of politicians, transparency of the political system, integrity of both the system and its participants, and equity among participants. American analysts of reform have adopted slightly different criteria. Critics and proponents alike have emphasized the goal of limiting corruption (arguably similar to Young's "integrity" criterion) but have also stressed the opportunity for and quality of political expression. John Samples (2006) has argued that reformers have always sought to improve discourse, although he believes that few reform proposals meet this goal; Diana Dwyre and Victoria Farrar-Myers (2000) also argue that improving discourse is a major goal of reform, although they take a more positive attitude toward BCRA and other reforms' ability to meet this goal.[1] Michael Malbin (2008) argues that any post-BCRA reforms should seek to increase participation, competition, and engagement in campaigns—that is, citizens should be provided with greater opportunities to become involved and interested in campaigns. To the extent that group involvement can further these goals, it should be welcomed, and to the extent that groups impede citizens' ability to play a constructive role in campaigns, their activities should be regulated.

Of these arguments, Malbin's most directly takes on the democratic deficit argument. For Malbin, as for many American scholars, the relevant opposition is between groups and citizens. American reform proposals have generally weighed the merits of privileging or discouraging individuals' rights to support candidates against groups' rights to communicate about politics and to influence discourse among candidates. Americans have traditionally been less enthusiastic about viewing groups and parties as competitors, while Canadians have often framed campaign finance regulation in this light. Arguments about strengthening or weakening parties have been made in regard to BCRA but have rarely contended that strengthening parties necessarily implies a diminution of groups' opportunities for campaign involvement. The argument in favor of retaining soft money, for example, has been that it strengthened parties' ability to influence congressional elections at the same time that it strengthened groups' ability to shape party activities.

Most democratic theorists would agree that a reform that gives groups and parties added incentives to communicate directly with voters is beneficial to democracy. American theorists have long preferred parties over interest groups on the grounds that parties can be a unifying force while groups can often fragment the electorate. Yet many students of interest groups have argued that this preference is misguided (see Baumgartner and Leech 1998, 40–46). It is hard to argue, given today's American politics of red and blue states, gerrymandered congressional districts, and excessively partisan congressional policy-making, that parties currently serve as a unifying force.[2] The major Canadian parties have seen part of their mission as providing this sort of national unity, and although most students of Canadian politics have contended that the fragmented nature of the Canadian party system has made this process difficult for the past twenty years, they have generally argued that the next stable party system in Canada will only take root when one or more parties can accomplish this goal.

These distinctions make sense in light of the different natures of the American and Canadian political systems. In both countries, unfettered group communication serves as an alternate channel for defining the issues around which the election can revolve. In the 1988 Canadian election, for example, groups defined the election as being about free trade, no matter how much parties might have wished to avoid this frame. In the 2008 U.S. election, spending by labor unions and business clearly was linked to organized labor's push for passage of the Employee Free Choice Act, although many group advertisements on both sides did not make this motivation explicit.[3] If we imagine an absence of group spending, however, the results are different. In the Canadian case, the danger is that the parties will define elections in a narrow, issueless way—they will simply avoid taking positions on topics of importance to groups, although the presence of the NDP ensures that labor will retain a party vehicle. In the American case, an absence of group spending can lead to a cacophony of candidate appeals—an election that involves a great number of issues, often parochial in nature, but does not necessarily have the sort of nationalization that groups can provide. It is a choice between too few issues, in the Canadian context, and too many issues in the American context.

If we consider the values inherent in reform debates, then, we have two sets of values—those we should use to judge reform legislation or proposals, and those we should use to evaluate the role of groups within the political system.

Reform Values

A striking paradigm shift occurred in the United States in the years between the passage of BCRA and the Supreme Court's *Citizens United* decision. Americans have traditionally been skeptical of the equation between money and speech, but the unrestricted spending in the 2008 presidential election elicited few claims that the election was being "bought" or that fund-raising raised the specter of corruption. Although the core components of BCRA may not have had a direct relationship to the increase in candidate spending apart from the increase in individual contribution limits, the removal of soft money and the decline of 527 spending as a subject of media inquiry meant that the 2008 election put at least a temporary halt to many reform plans. Both major-party presidential nominees made the subject of lobbying an issue in the campaign but did so in such a way that lobbyists were criticized not necessarily for their financial clout but for their involvement in policy-making. It would be tempting to say that the moment for reform had passed—that although even before the *Citizens United* decision many reform advocates thought further changes were needed, no unified campaign finance reform movement would have arisen in the decade to come. The expansion of corporate and group speech ushered in by *Citizens United* has resulted in some talk about working to find constitutional means of reining in groups yet again, but such changes would at best merely reinstate the imperfect campaign finance regime as it stood before the decision.

It would be a mistake, however, to argue that just because some reformers' concerns have receded from public view, the United States and Canada took steps over the past decade toward normatively better campaign finance systems. Campaign finance laws are not necessarily *about* the values reformers have posited—these laws have something to do with these values, but the goals of candidates, parties, and groups intersect in such a way that any change in campaign finance law cannot go very far in changing our normative assessment of what takes place during elections. These values are connected, but they vary in the degree to which they are related to politicians' actions, as an examination of these values and the effects on them of changes in campaign finance law shows.

Transparency, Corruption, and the Appearance of Corruption

Transparency and corruption are in many ways the same issue. If the public observes a relationship between large campaign contributions and policy-making, the incentive for politicians or parties to accept suspect contributions is reduced. Neither BCRA nor the Canadian reforms sought directly to address issues of transparency, but the abolition of unrestricted campaign contributions ensures that in a system where contributions are a matter of public record, no line can be drawn between contributions and politicians' actions. The reforms in both the United States and Canada have led to a more transparent system in many regards and have limited the appearance of corruption—which many observers perceive as just as important as limiting corruption itself. Neither country had produced compelling arguments that contributions from individuals or groups lead to corruption on a large scale, but because the public often makes this link, the removal of suspect categories of fund-raising may increase citizens' confidence in the system.[4] Canada has traditionally had as transparent a financing system as does the United States, but it has not yet seen a large-scale mobilization of small donors to match that of American parties and candidates. The institution of public financing may have removed the need for parties to undertake such efforts, but the absence of such a movement may also be a consequence of a lack of galvanizing personalities and issues.

The avenues for unrestricted spending that remained in the American system before *Citizens United* are among the least transparent areas of spending—expenditures, for example, by 501(c) 4, 5, and 6 organizations—but are also sufficiently removed from politicians' campaigns that they do not necessarily corrupt. Much of the spending by the Chamber of Commerce and the AFL-CIO during the 2008 election was directed toward congressional campaigns, and it was clearly driven by these groups' concerns about the Employee Free Choice Act. On the one hand, these expenditures were not scrutinized very extensively by a public concerned with the presidential election and the issues at stake there. Not until several months after the election were relatively precise spending totals for these groups made available, and it is still unclear exactly where this money was spent or what it was spent on (see Campaign Finance Institute 2009). This issue, however, is hardly a matter of corruption, in that neither side would deem a successful candidate who took a position for or against the issue to be corrupt. The donors receive no immediate benefits that can be tied to their contributions, in the manner that some analysts feared individual soft money donors to the parties might have during the 1990s. Removing the link between candidates and high-spending groups, then, removed smaller issues from the agenda and ensured that the issues brought up are those whose benefits are dispersed, not concentrated.

Some observers have contended that *Citizens United* will reintroduce the possibility of such quid pro quo arrangements (see, e.g., Hasen 2010; Teachout 2010), but the sums involved in a strong electioneering campaign ensure that only a small number of groups (such as the Chamber of Commerce) could engage in such practices, and such groups are, by their nature, representative of a broad coalition of businesses and interests. Some allegations of quid pro quo will likely arise, particularly in races where local issues are dominant, but many businesses had expressed a distaste for having their money pulled into the system before BCRA and may not be willing to engage in such activities.[5] This distaste, in fact, raises the possibility that while corporations will have a new avenue for independent spending, the decision will not necessarily "open the floodgates for corporate cash," as Vogel (2010) puts it. Despite harsh criticism from reformers in the week following the decision, some campaign operatives expressed skepticism that *Citizens United* would have much of an immediate effect for precisely this reason (Cummings 2010; Ben Smith 2010).

Similarly, there are few reasons to suspect that the Canadian campaign finance system facilitates corruption, although this problem was less severe before the reforms. The imposition of spending restrictions in leadership campaigns (as part of the Accountability Act) has closed off one loophole, and the cases where corruption has been alleged in Canadian politics were areas where corrupt behavior was not necessarily related to campaign finance laws.

Mobilization and Engagement

A common theme for all types of interest groups discussed in this book has been the turn toward voter mobilization. This trend could well have occurred without the passage of reform laws, but BCRA and the CEA amendments clearly encouraged group mobilization. Group mobilization allows groups greater control over their message than do contributions and is generally more effective than persuasion, the major goal of electioneering advertisements. As some media accounts have noted (see Coyne 2010), the political consulting industry has little understanding about how well electioneering ads work, while mobilization can yield measurable consequences.

Mobilization may be seen as a value in its own right insofar as greater citizen participation in elections is generally held to be good for society. Yet the turn toward mobilization has not come without costs. The increase in voter turnout in the American elections of 2004 and 2008 reversed a decline several decades in the making. Yet mobilization is also both a cause and a consequence of the polarization of the American electorate; thus, Canada's less polarized political climate meant that voters did not turn out in greater numbers in the past three Canadian elections than had been the case in earlier elections.[6] Prohibitions on large contributions also have fostered greater citizen engagement efforts by the parties and by groups. The increase in small donations in both countries has been in part a consequence of parties' scramble to raise money in small amounts. In the United States, the *Citizens United* decision does little to alter this trend; BCRA's soft money restrictions remain in place, and even if candidates or parties benefit from group advocacy, they are unlikely to turn their backs on successful get-out-the-vote or small donor programs.

Mobilization efforts can be viewed through two lenses. On the one hand, face-to-face communications are generally held to be part of a "nicer" version of democracy insofar as the most effective face-to-face fund-raising and turnout efforts have depended on citizens, who are in some sense "like" the targets of mobilization. Fellow union members or employees or, for advocacy groups, activists who share social traits with those whom they seek to engage have greater credibility than someone unknown to the voter. A turn toward mobilization thus can strengthen social ties, but mobilization and the accompanying microtargeting mean that citizens lose any sort of shared information source or ability to use the political information they have gathered in conversation with those who do not already share their views. Second, mobilization efforts, especially face-to-face fund-raising efforts, have been analogized to wagering at a horse race. Voters who have made a small commitment to a particular candidate—making a small contribution, signing a petition, taking some small step to voice support, or simply stating their intention to vote—may make increased effort in the campaign because they feel they now have a stake in it.

Viewed through both of these lenses, any reform that increases citizen engagement is beneficial. Again, it is not clear that campaign finance reform on its own had a substantial effect on parties' or candidates' propensity to work to engage citizens, and different groups have different abilities with regard to this sort of activity. Mobilization may, then, be felt unequally among citizens. It is one thing to claim that mobilization of the public is good; it is another to argue that mobilization of, for example, union members, is beneficial for those who are not sympathetic to unions' political goals. The importance of the source of mobilization efforts is also up for debate. In the United States, both parties and groups have an incentive to mobilize voters; in Canada, organized labor has more of an incentive to engage in mobilization, but the parties and other types of groups have either been unaffected or have seen their incentive to mobilize decreased.

Competition and Campaign Discourse

In the United States, few saw BCRA as a measure designed to increase competition in elections. Little evidence indicates that it has influenced competition at the presidential level, in large part because the ongoing breakdown of the presidential public financing system has overshadowed any of the legislation's potential effects. At the congressional level, many observers argued that both of BCRA's major provisions would reduce competition—the removal of soft money and the increased restrictions on electioneering would ensure that candidate fund-raising became more important than ever before, and incumbents would have an easier time raising money than would challengers (Campbell 2003). The 2006 and 2008 elections do not necessarily support this claim; in many of the most competitive congressional races, party campaign committees made up for candidate fund-raising differences, and interest group spending in several races remained a major equalizing factor. Because Canadian elections have historically been more about the parties and less about the candidates or about group goals, restrictions on group activities have likewise had little effect on competition. In both cases, however, shifting the funding sources has implications for discourse. That is, it is unlikely that lopsided elections will feature issue-related discourse among the candidates or will educate the voters. Competitive elections may feature more discourse, but here the issue of the quality of discourse becomes a factor. Even if candidates are forced to talk about an issue or voters are forced to think about it, this does not mean that it is an issue that *should* be an important factor in the election.

The predictions about BCRA's effects on competition and discourse pose a dilemma. On the one hand, an election where the lion's share of spending is done by the candidates may result in an advantage for the incumbents and may result in diminished discourse on issues. On the other hand, party electioneering in 2006 and 2008 suggests that the party campaign committees are more likely to air attack ads and less likely to discuss issues than are candidates. Parties can be a nationalizing force and can present a set of overarching issues, but there is little reason to suspect that they will do so, with or without soft money or electioneering help.

Canada also provides little evidence that restrictions on party spending have any consequences for discourse. The country's political system offers no real alternative to party spending since candidates tend not to engage in their own electioneering, but the record of party electioneering there certainly does not suggest that any of the alterations in funding sources for the major parties have consequences for discourse. The public funding criteria in Canada, however, raise the possibility that third parties with evenly distributed but shallow public support—such as the Green Party—may achieve greater visibility in future elections and that parties with regional support, such as the NDP, may find it advantageous to take some steps to present issue-based appeals in regions where they cannot necessarily expect to win seats. In this second tier of competition—competition for funds and for (losing) votes, not for seats—competition and discourse may coincide.

In both nations, however, the most persuasive claims about the consequences of reform for discourse have been made by groups, not parties. The comments of issue-based groups such as Canada's NCC and Animal Alliance–Environment Voters Party suggest that groups see themselves as injecting issues into campaigns. Steve Rosenthal of the AFL-CIO has made similar claims about electioneering in the United States; he notes that groups can most effectively raise issues while campaigns are being waged. If this is the case, both reforms limit discourse. However, the American restrictions (as they stood before the *Wisconsin Right to Life* decision) explicitly limited electioneering only where candidates' names are mentioned, potentially resulting merely in coded messages about the candidates, as was the case in the 2006 SEIU advertisements proclaiming "time for a change." The restrictions may also result in more purely issue-oriented advertising during elections, as exemplified by the health-care-related advertisements run by the Divided We Fail coalition, which included the AARP, the Business Roundtable, the SEIU, and the NFIB. These advertisements ran during the summer of 2008, discussing issues and noting the unusual coalition behind the ads, but did not single out candidates. More advertisements of this nature may well be positive development, but they also comprised a small percentage of the postreform ads, may well have been unique to the circumstances of the 2008 election, and would also have been permissible before BCRA, let alone before *Citizens United.*

In addition, any claims regarding the relationship between money and discourse face the difficult question of how to identify relevant and legitimate issues and legitimate (or discourse-enhancing) ways of framing them.[7] The 2004 Swift Boat Veterans for Truth ads concerned issues, albeit issues that were inseparable from one of the candidates, as did 527 advertisements in 2008 concerning the Reverend Jeremiah Wright, Bill Ayers, or other unpopular figures connected with Barack Obama. Drawing the line between legitimate and illegitimate issues is difficult, and the Divided We Fail ads can be seen as the product of a particularly deep-pocketed set of organizations. Groups that have fewer resources but want to promote their issues may grab the most attention only when their advertisements make strong claims about candidates, as was the case with Defenders of Wildlife's highly publicized attack ads on Sarah Palin in 2008. The quality of discourse ultimately may well have far more to do with the candidates and the nature of the election than with changes in electioneering regulations.

It is easy, then, to connect the American and Canadian reforms to the values discussed within the two nations' campaign finance reform movements, but it is hard to draw strong conclusions in part because so many of these values are affected by so many factors other than the campaign finance system. Limiting the potential for corruption or fixing documented abuses are in themselves legitimate goals for any set of reform proposals, but such fixes are unlikely to influence public sentiment about elections. BCRA and the Canadian reforms are the most sweeping changes to the two nations' campaign finance laws in the past three decades, and their passage may have exhausted reformers in both nations. Such a state of affairs would be especially unfortunate for American reform advocates, who could point to few obvious results directly attributable to BCRA even before the Supreme Court began to chip away at the law.[8] Any American reforms that would go beyond limiting the damage of the *Citizens United* decision—for example, pressuring the television networks to provide free airtime for candidates, adjusting the public financing system for presidential candidates, or changing tax laws governing political contributions— may be worthy goals, but they are modest in scope.

The Value of Organized Interests

The lack of strong effects of reform laws on campaigns or public sentiment certainly would come as no surprise to those who have documented the growth of the democratic deficit in Western countries. The Dalton (2004) and Nevitte (1996, 2002) arguments contend that disenchantment with the role of money and organized interests in politics has much to do with trends in citizens' political awareness and engagement and little to do with discrete events. Any introductory political science course in the United States will likely document the long history of politicians' criticism of organized interests and lobbyists. Such attacks have at times been warranted but have remained popular even when they are not. Many—perhaps most—students of electoral politics may be pluralists at heart, but most citizens are not. A defense of the role of interest groups in election politics may fall largely on deaf ears, then, but such a defense may nevertheless be necessary. Many of the most cogent defenses of interest groups' election activities have come from controversial groups such as the National Rifle Association or the Swift Boat Veterans for Truth. Interest groups remain unpopular in both U.S. and Canadian politics in part because these groups have few advocates who will command a receptive audience: it is difficult to imagine, for example, an American presidential candidate arguing that most lobbyists are simply advancing their clients' interests.

The resilience of American and Canadian interest groups may thus be a strength instead of a weakness of the two nations' reforms. The reforms may be evaluated on the more limited terrain of transparency and corruption rather than on whether they have produced wholesale changes in interest groups' influence. To the extent that interests have been silenced, particularly in the Canadian case, this development is a weakness of the reform laws. The claims about the beneficial nature of interest groups help to put campaign finance reform as it pertains to groups in proper perspective.

Groups as Information Providers

Perhaps the most common means of framing the argument that groups are a benign or even beneficial part of the political process is to argue that they provide information to politicians. This way of framing group activity is most common in literature on lobbying, but it can apply to campaigns as well. In an environment where groups have an unfettered ability to discuss issues, several informational consequences may result. Groups can introduce issues that the public genuinely ought to think about. Groups can make issue appeals that, if successful, can alert politicians to concerns they should address or, more cynically, to tactics to be used in discussing issues. To perform this function, groups must be somewhat autonomous. If interest groups seek to push money into the political process, whether through contributions to candidates or through advocacy, then the issue motivation is clear, while pulled money is somewhat more suspect as a correlate of speech. In other words, to adjust the *Buckley* paradigm, group money can be but is not always speech.

In this regard, both provisions of BCRA may have enhanced groups' capacity to provide information, although the results have been mixed in practice. In terms of electioneering, an appealing issue message does not need to be connected to candidates to provide information, although connecting a message to politicians is no doubt more effective in influencing vote choice. The soft money provisions clearly reduced the amount of pulled money in the system and freed some groups who were reluctant givers to redirect their money into advocacy. The types of communications advantaged by BCRA's electioneering provisions, however—face-to-face contact and Internet appeals—may be effective in influencing voters but are more mixed in their consequences for information provision. Such communications can provide more detailed information for recipients but are less observable by politicians, and to the extent that they have been targeted at voters already sympathetic to the group's objectives, they have mobilized rather than educated voters. The advantage that BCRA provides to targeted communications will likely endure following the *Cit-*

izens United decision—as is the case for the parties, groups are unlikely to abandon a strategy that has worked over the past few years just because they have new means (or rather, a restoration of an old means) of communicating with voters.

The Canadian reform laws limit the role not only of pulled money but also of pushed money. But Canadian groups have rarely seen their educative function as tied to electoral campaigns. Canadian politics has provided enough teachable moments to groups outside of the electoral process—the Quebec secession votes, the Charlottetown and Meech Lake Accords, and the prorogation crisis, to name a few—that groups have tended to see their role in providing information as something that can be undertaken with little attention to politicians' issue stances. The Canadian reforms may well limit groups' ability to influence elections, but groups there have pursued this avenue to a lesser extent than have American groups, so the groups most opposed to these reforms (and most involved in elections) have been more peripheral political actors than established groups. Many American group communications are and have been sham issue appeals. The Canadian reforms prevent such appeals, which may irk politicians but have rarely had consequences in Canadian politics. These appeals called attention to groups more than they influenced elections. The Canadian contribution restrictions and public funding provisions reduce groups' power both to have their money pulled into the political system and to push money into the system, but the Canadian system never featured as much pushed money as the American system.

In regard to the informational content of group advocacy and contributions, then, the American reforms (and, more importantly, since the electioneering restrictions are no longer in place, groups' adaptations to those reforms) have shown the potential to be beneficial, although they have not clearly been so in practice. The Canadian reforms have the potential to be harmful, although, again, they have not clearly been so in practice.

The Party/Group Conflict

The Canadian literature is far more likely than the American literature to allege a conflict between interest groups and political parties. Canadians have engaged in little overt discussion about strengthening political parties or penalizing groups, in part perhaps because few observers thought that Canadian parties need to be strengthened. The American reforms featured much discussion of whether parties would be weakened (by prohibiting soft money contributions, which had been a major source of party support) or strengthened (by forcing parties to improve their hard money fund-raising and thus their appeals to voters for financial support). Groups and parties have differing incentives. Parties seek to win elections and use issues as a means to do so, while groups seek to provide benefits to members. These benefits may penalize nonmembers or may spill over and advantage the public.

In both nations, most interest groups seek to provide material benefits to members. Groups that have tended to be involved in the activities regulated by BCRA, however, are not typical of the universe of groups; the dominant soft money donors were corporations or labor unions, providers of material benefits. The dominant electioneering groups have had a greater tendency to include advocacy groups, which provide purposive benefits to members. Analysts did not regard soft money as an effective tool for many larger groups, although some individual donors who sought narrowly targeted benefits saw the ability to make large donations as advancing their interests. BCRA's soft money provisions took aim at the appearance of corruption and so sought to limit the ability to trade contributions for material benefits. The Canadian restrictions on corporate contributions have had similar aims.

In both countries, the trade-off is not completely clear. American parties have been strengthened by their newfound effort to raise money in smaller amounts, and the dramatic increase in party committee spending in the past two elections shows that parties are more consequential in terms of electioneering than was previously the case. It is not clear that this development is solely a consequence of BCRA—the Democratic Party's fund-raising success may result in part from its renewed emphasis on raising hard money but likely has more to do with the changing American political environment. The Canadian reforms have instituted a stable public funding source for parties, thus removing the need to raise money. This change may strengthen parties, but I am skeptical of this idea. Canada already provided favorable tax treatment for small donors to the parties, and absent the need to be in frequent contact with voters to raise money, parties may lose their capacity to mobilize voters or address their concerns. At the same time, however, Canadian groups have clearly ceded ground to the parties in the ability to affect elections.

Both nations' reforms, then, illustrate the limits of the notion of conflict between parties and groups. To the extent that American party committees have improved their ability to raise money and mobilize voters, they have done so by adopting tactics used by groups. The fund-raising practices of Democratic candidates and the Democratic Party committees, for example, share much with Internet-based groups such as MoveOn.org. The American parties start from a weaker position than Canadian parties, and they start from unequal footing—the Democratic Party has traditionally been more intertwined with advocacy groups of all sorts and with labor unions than has the Republican Party. The difference between 2004 and 2008 is instructive, however; interest groups sought to fulfill some of the basic party functions in 2004, but the Democratic Party and the Obama campaign reasserted control over these activities in 2008. The Canadian group most connected with organized interests has always been the NDP, which is clearly in the process of adjusting to the changes in its relationship with organized labor. Canadian parties may have greater ability to frame elections but may have gained this strength at the risk of alienating voters and weakening party ties to the electorate. Canadian parties were already the winners in the party-group conflict, at least as far as elections are concerned, and it is not apparent that further weakening groups or strengthening parties is in the parties' long-term interests.

In defense of the Canadian party system, however, that country's parties may provide more of a unifying force than do their American counterparts. Were outside groups to play a greater role in Canadian elections, many observers fear that the issues to which they gave voice would be destabilizing, regional grievances. American politicians, including both Obama and Bush, have recently given some voice to urging the country to move beyond partisanship. The need to do so and politicians' and party leaders' ability to provide such guidance is clearly less acute in the United States than in Canada, however; in Canada, the nation's future may well be at stake. The differences between the means by which politicians have sought this sort of unification are also glaring. In Canada, the fragmentation of the third party system has meant that calls for national unity have generated a perception that parties are avoiding talking about difficult issues. In the United States, the success of a movement-based presidential campaign may have generated more excitement for moving beyond partisan conflict but may also have generated unrealistic voter expectations that will result in bitter disappointment and a sharpening of partisan conflict in the long run.

Group Support as a Heuristic for the Public

Finally, groups can provide the public with a convenient shorthand for evaluating parties and candidates. An endorsement from a prominent advocacy group may convey little in the way of substantive information to voters, but it is arguably almost as important as a candidate's party label as a simple shortcut for voters and is less pernicious than heuristics such as race or gender. This sort of heuristic has little to do with contributions except in that a list of a candidate's contributors may send a signal about that candidate's policy views. Such a heuristic certainly has little to do with the permissible size of contributions; it has something to do with electioneering insofar as a substantial advertising budget informs voters of a candidate's group support, but endorsements can certainly matter without electioneering.

Groups in both nations have issued endorsements or de facto endorsements; American groups have tended to make direct endorsements, while many Canadian groups provide voters with report cards on or ratings of parties or candidates. Such communications matter only in a context where meaningful distinctions exist between parties or candidates and where groups have a recognizable, durable brand. In the less disciplined American system, many groups have argued that an endorsement of a candidate running as the nominee of a party they tend to oppose—a Democrat endorsed by the NRA or a Republican endorsed by the Sierra Club or the Human Rights Campaign—is more influential than an endorsement of the nominee of a party they tend to support. The greater discipline and the lower degree of polarization in the Canadian system has made endorsements both more fluid (for example, Sierra Club Canada has at times made favorable statements about all of the major parties) and less valuable. A candidate endorsement, as Aidan Reid of the Campaign Life Coalition has noted, has negligible value because the system encourages voters to think first about parties, not candidates.

In both nations, group endorsements are a relatively unobjectionable form of activity, but to the extent that they involve contributions and electioneering, a need exists to discern when groups have an acceptable means to communicate their preferences. Allowing groups to use hard money to air electioneering advertisements may be an acceptable compromise for the American system insofar as a group's ability to speak correlates somewhat with its base of support, as the Supreme Court reasoned in *Austin v. Michigan Chamber of Commerce* and *FEC v. Massachusetts Citizens for Life*. This view played a prominent role in Justice John Paul Stevens's dissent in the *Citizens United* case. Advertising by 527 groups may be particularly objectionable in this regard, because they may be supported only by a small number of wealthy donors, and the endorsement of a 527 is also of questionable heuristic value insofar as these organizations are not durable and often are largely unknown to the public.[9] The lack of an equivalent means for Canadian groups to engage in such speech may be harmful, but again, the Canadian system limits the effectiveness of this tool. Canadian groups generally have been less durable than the prominent American advocacy groups, but some of the larger Canadian organizations (particularly organized labor) have sufficient durability that their support for a party may have some heuristic value.

Despite antigroup rhetoric in both nations, groups unquestionably should play a role in the political process. The American and Canadian reforms changed groups' options, but changes in political context may well have overshadowed groups' adaptations. In regard to each of the three group functions noted here—providing information, providing a counterweight to the parties, and providing a heuristic to voters—neither American groups nor the public interest has been demonstrably harmed. But this result is hardly a ringing endorsement for BCRA (as it stood before *Citizens United*) in that the rapid shift in American politics complicates the argument that the law has been (or was) beneficial except perhaps in limiting the appearance of corruption (a worthy goal but likely not the most important value to extract from this comparison). In one of the three functions, information provision, the potential exists for Canadian groups and the Canadian public interest to be harmed. In regard to the other two, it is more difficult to draw firm conclusions.

Conclusions

The comparisons in this chapter point back to the basic problem established in the introduction—the American experience has provided instructive lessons to Canadians on what might take place in their political system, but warding off these effects when they are unlikely can be harmful and unnecessary. Canadians might simply learn not to take American elections as indicators of a likely Canadian future. For Americans as well, this comparison may inspire some caution. Some of the areas in which Canada has gone in the direction liberal reformers might prefer—providing tax credits for small donors, limiting candidate and party spending, and dramatically reducing contribution limits—may provide a model or at least a wish list for future American reforms. If the Federal Election Campaign Act served as a model for the EEA and for Canadian reformers in the 1970s, it is hard to argue that it was not a good exemplar. Similarly, some aspects of the EEA may serve as a starting point for American reforms. The 2003 Canada Elections Act Amendments and the other related recent reforms serve an important function in Canadian politics, and, again, some aspects of these laws are well founded. The major components of these laws, however, are not exportable to the American case. The consequences of public funding and heightened restrictions on groups, while understandable in the Canadian context, should cause skepticism of similar programs in the United States.

This book shows that differences between countries' institutions can influence group responses to laws that on their face seem similar. In addition, the volume demonstrates that at least in the case of the United States and Canada, comparing political cultures that are similar enough to have generated similar legal approaches can show the effects of small differences within the laws. To the extent that institutional differences matter, they indicate that the basic contours of group responses to campaign finance reform were similar but that groups will be far more aggressive in their adaptations in a system with weaker parties and regular elections. To the extent that differences in the two countries' approaches to reform matter, they indicate that some of the fears of campaign finance reform opponents in the United States have some merit; the Canadian system, with less of an emphasis on the *Buckley* paradigm of equating contributions with speech, has produced laws that effectively increase the privilege of parties over groups, perhaps to the detriment of public engagement and the discussion of issues.

In closing, it is tempting to argue for a middle ground between the two sets of reforms—to develop a means of allowing group speech on campaign issues that educates voters and opens up the discourse of the campaign but to do so without enabling big-spending groups to hijack campaigns through their contributions or their independent advocacy. Were there a means of using campaign finance law to influence not merely the quantity of group speech but its quality, such a means might be a suitable middle ground. Arguments can be made about modifications to both nations' laws that can take this goal as an end. I am skeptical, however, that this approach provides much of a starting point for a future campaign finance agenda for two reasons. First, this book and the campaign finance literature more generally provide little evidence that partisan goals can be removed from legislative debates about campaign finance. Second, neither country's reforms really fit either the interest groups' and politicians' most problematic activities or voters' major concerns. Group activities were influenced by reform, but these reforms took place within a much less malleable institutional context. To the extent that groups wield power, they do so because of the institutional rules within which they operate. The reforms described here provide a means of thinking about American and Canadian institutions but do little to change the major features of these institutions. This book ultimately testifies to the resilience of interest groups and the limitations of campaign finance reform. Those who advocate limiting the role of money in politics can read this conclusion as pessimistic (campaign finance reform will not have substantial effects) or, following the *Citizens United* decision, as optimistic (striking down limitations on spending will not radically change the campaign finance landscape). This book may also be seen as an invitation for reformers to think big—to start to talk about changing national institutions, to challenge claims that the "big" institutional features of our political system are really impervious to change.

Appendix: A Primer on Brokerage Parties

Throughout this book, I refer to Canadian "brokerage" politics. As one reviewer of the original manuscript has pointed out, this is a "peculiarly Canadian concept."[1] This appendix provides some context for readers unfamiliar with the idea. The basic notion is that the two governing Canadian parties throughout the twentieth century saw it as their mission to "broker" divisions between anglophone and francophone Canada, to serve as vehicles of national unity. This focus has, according to some observers, led to a substantial amount of policy convergence between the parties and a pragmatic focus on placing national unity above ideological goals.

The brokerage system, then, has two components. First, the Liberal Party and the Progressive Conservative Party, while nominally representing the Left and the Right in the manner of the Democratic and Republican Parties in the United States, have not been as easily characterized as left and right parties as have the American parties. And second, the parties have not been as ideologically consistent as have American parties and have had an easier time reversing policy positions. Although comparativists often contend that American parties tend to converge far more than left and right parties in other systems, my characterization of the Canadian parties throughout this book assumes an even smaller degree of consistency or distinctness than American parties have historically shown.

This distinction will likely puzzle American readers. Americans tend to assume that "responsible" parties display a remarkable degree of unity while presenting voters with clear ideological choices. Canadian parties clearly are responsible in the first sense, in that party-line voting is the norm, but they clearly are not responsible in the second.

I allude throughout chapter 1 to Canadian party responsibility in the first sense. The parties do at times allow "free votes," where members are permitted to vote against the party leadership, but most major legislation is considered akin to a confidence vote, and party discipline prevails. In regard to the second sense, however, I consider here some of the arguments documenting the lack of difference between the parties.

Several articles have documented the degree to which Canadian voters fail to see consistent, meaningful differences between the parties. Blais et al. (2002) assess differences between supporters of the five (at the time) Canadian political parties regarding government policy toward businesses, unions, social programs, and several other issue areas that are harder to place on a left-right continuum. They conclude that a left-right ordering of the parties exists and that the Liberals tend to be slightly to the right of the Conservatives. The differences, however, are very slight—to the point that "on most issues, there is hardly any difference between Liberal and Conservative voters" (193). A similar group of authors (Gidengil et al. 2006) has argued that despite the lack of ideological differentiation, voters form enduring attachments to the parties. As Clarke, Kornberg, and Scotto (2009, 71) note, voters identify with the parties but do not necessarily do so on the basis of ideology or enduring issue cleavages. Far fewer Canadians than Americans can place themselves or the parties on a left-right ideological scale, and for those who do, no correlation exists between citizens' ideological stances and their party preference.[2]

If party members do not display different ideological views, however, it does not necessarily follow that the parties are not radically different in what they do in office. Precise comparisons (of the nature of Blais et al. 2002) are more difficult when measuring parties' policy stances; the fact that one party may vote as a bloc against the policy of its opponent does not necessarily indicate ideological disagreement if that party does not adopt a different course of action when in office. That is, making meaningful distinctions between the parties based on their platforms requires comparing the activities of the parties across time, and doing so is complicated because the precise nature of the issues being debated may change. Several works have made general claims about a lack of difference in Canadian party platforms or government actions. Brodie and Jenson (1989, 33) present this aspect of the brokerage argument concisely, arguing that events of the 1970s and 1980s indicate that

> the party system is one in which the Liberal, Progressive Conservative, and, to a lesser extent, the New Democratic parties do have similar platforms which change from election to election. The Liberals and Tories have often abandoned their promises once the exi-

gencies of office demand something else, and they do not emphasize ideological differences because they appeal to many, often the
same, interests—whether they be linguistic, regional, or economic—in their perennial struggle to construct a winning coalition. Party platforms vary over time, following politicians' perceptions of what will work at any particular moment. Therefore,
although parties may sometimes develop quite coherent and even
principled positions, these constructions are fragile and easily reversed when conditions change.

To support this claim, the authors cite several policy reversals by the Liberals and Progressive Conservatives during the 1970s; later work by the
same authors (Brodie and Jenson 1990) has referenced the Liberal Party's
opposition to the FTA while in opposition in 1988 and support for the
agreement while in office during the 1990s. Other works of the 1990s, such
as Johnston et al. (1992, 96–110) have noted that the parties can be placed
in different positions in a multidimensional issue framework but that
these differences are not necessarily related to differences in other elections. And Clarke et al. (1996) offer an argument about an "absent mandate" in Canadian elections that mixes the two types of claims—if voters
do not choose parties based on ideological differences or explicit ideological appeals, the parties have no mandate to adhere to consistent ideological positions in making policy.

Finally, many of these arguments (with the exception of Gidengil et al.
2006) were made with reference to the Liberal Party and the Progressive
Conservative Party, not necessarily the Conservative Party of the 2000s. As
many authors have noted (see Blais et al. 2002), the Canadian media have
characterized the Conservative Party as a party of the Right, perhaps more
than the Progressive Conservatives. While the major Canadian parties
may not consistently stand for anything, minor parties, such as the NDP
and the Reform Party, generally have made strong ideological critiques of
the major parties from the left (in the case of the NDP) or the right (in the
case of Reform). A stronger case might exist for the argument that the
Conservative Party, as a product of the "uniting of the right" between Reform and the Progressive Conservatives, has a consistent ideological identity. Be this as it may, however (and few academic studies back up this
claim), any such arguments capture only current differences between the
major parties, not long-term consistency.

Again, any claims to consistency or differentiation are by their nature relative—the differences between American parties might be seen as small relative to those of many other nations, and U.S. parties may in fact show a tendency to reverse positions over time—but the Canadian literature indicates that differences between the major Canadian parties have historically been smaller and that the Canadian parties' ability to make sudden reversals is greater than that of American parties.

Notes

INTRODUCTION

1. See the Gomery Commission Report summary, at http://epe.lac-bac.gc.ca/ 100/206/301/pco-bcp/commissions/sponsorship-ef/06-02-10/www.gomery.ca/en/ phase1report/summary/default.htm.

2. Although Grabb and Curtis argue that there are four distinct cultures, these cultures are converging or at least moving in parallel directions on most of the political trust and political efficacy indices—see Grabb, Andersen, Hwang, and Milligan 2009.

3. These are the author's calculations from the ANES cumulative file; time series trends for some of these variables can also be found on the ANES website (www.elec tionstudies.org). See Sapiro, Rosenstone, and the American National Election Studies 2005.

4. That is, the candidate with the most votes wins an election, even if that candidate has not won a majority of the votes, as can be the case in an election with more than two candidates.

5. There are two related types of studies of procedural change that are worth noting here. First, Franklin (2004) and Wattenberg (2001) have used changes in the minimum voting age in Europe and the United States to study declining voter turnout. These studies are most similar to this one in their ability to use a common change in political rules to compare different nations. Second, there is a substantial comparative politics literature on European Union membership—but here we have an identical international agreement being ratified by different countries, as opposed to, in this case, a comparison of two nations' laws aimed solely at regulating domestic politics.

6. And the Canadian provinces as well, as in the case of Cross (2004) and Hamm and Hebda (2006).

CHAPTER 1

1. Note that the data in table 1.2 are from different years; the financial data are from 2008 while the *Fortune* Magazine ratings are from 2001—*Fortune* commissioned the survey for these rankings for several years but ceased doing so after 2001. Because I seek to show variations in group resource types in this table, rather than to show the strength of particular groups, the difference in time here does not seem to me to be a problem.

The *Fortune* ratings remain a common citation for those seeking to discuss group strength even ten years after their last publication.

2. The categories shown in tables 1.2 and 1.3 are not, however, particularly transferable to other contexts. Although Canada has no equivalent to PACs, it is possible to acquire data on the largest corporate or labor contributors to the parties prior to 2004 (see, e.g, Cross 2004, 149), but these data merely reveal that corporations have supported the Liberal and Progressive Conservative Parties while unions have supported the NDP. Independent expenditure data are also available, but, as shown by Eagles (2004), such expenditures tend to be so small that they are not particularly indicative of the sponsoring groups' size or goals.

3. Throughout this book, American campaign finance data are drawn from the Center for Responsive Politics (www.opensecrets.org) unless otherwise noted.

4. The K Street Project was an effort by the Republican congressional leadership in the 1990s to pressure lobbying firms to hire more Republican lobbyists and to direct a larger share of their campaign contributions to Republican candidates; see Hacker and Pierson 2005, 142.

5. Canada has not had formal coalition governments as several other parliamentary democracies have, and as a consequence minority governments have been short lived. The past three minority governments (one led by the Liberals and two by the Conservatives) have relied upon minor parties who were unwilling to bring down the government (although, as discussed later in the book, the three out-of-power parties threatened to do so, or to form a coalition government, in late 2008).

6. This is not to say that Canadian elections are entirely without issues, only to argue that few have been dominated by one overriding issue or that Canadian parties have the option of scheduling elections so as to downplay the effect of issues on which they have taken unpopular stands; see Clarke, Jensen, LeDuc, and Pammett 1996.

7. For a discussion of the party brokerage concept, see the appendix.

8. See Rozell, Wilcox, and Madland 2006, 115, for discussion of the Christian Coalition and the NAACP, two groups that were investigated by the Internal Revenue Service and the Justice Department for their political activity.

9. For American readers unfamiliar with the term, *prorogation* is the suspension of parliament. In this case, Prime Minister Harper requested that the Canadian governor general suspend parliament in December 2008 after the three opposition parties stated their intention to bring down Harper's government and form a coalition government just weeks after the October 2008 election. The immediate impetus for this threat was the Conservative Party's budget, which contained no stimulus funding to confront the recent market crash but which included several small spending cuts, including a provision removing public funding for the parties. The governor general agreed to Harper's request, suspending parliament until January 26, 2009. At that time, the Conservatives introduced a new budget that restored party public funds, and the Liberal Party withdrew its threat to bring down the government. The Russell and Sossin (2009) book includes, among other things, a summary of events, an explanation of the connection between the prorogation crisis and the Conservatives' adoption of fixed election dates, and an explanation of constitutional issues involved in the prorogation.

10. The primary case of this is the National Rifle Association's campaign against Al Gore in 2000—see Patterson and Singer 2007, 56.

11. These categories overlap closely with those provided by Gagnon and Tanguay (1989) in their discussion of minor or protest parties.

CHAPTER 2

1. Union density for 2008 is 12.4 percent.

2. These figures are the author's calculations from the American National Election Studies cumulative file (Sapiro, Rosenstone, and the National Election Studies 2005); they are for union members, not union households.

3. These are Center for Responsive Politics numbers; see also Masters and Delaney 2005.

4. Casey is referring to the fact that members of the United Auto Workers were given a paid holiday on Election Day and to estimates that 42 percent of votes in this race were cast by union members.

5. The only organization that could be termed a "liberal advocacy group" among the *McConnell* plaintiffs was the American Civil Liberties Union.

6. To provide a sense of scale here, consider that eleven corporations (and seven labor unions) gave over $1.5 million to the American political parties in 2000.

CHAPTER 3

1. For discussion, see Manfredi and Rush 2008; also see the Elections Canada summary, at http://www.elections.ca/content.asp?section=loi&document=ec90512&dir=ref&lang=e&textonly=false.

2. In the United States, the Revenue Act of 1971 did establish a small tax credit ($12.50, indexed to inflation) for political contributions; this tax credit was repealed in 1986 (see Boatright and Malbin 2005 for discussion).

3. Expense limits are set according to the number of registered voters (or "electors") in each riding, with some adjustment for geographic size. There is no equal population requirement for ridings in Canadian law as there is for congressional districts in the United States, and so ridings can vary somewhat in size; see Cross 2004, 155, for details.

CHAPTER 4

1. I exclude primary candidates in order to show the funding for comparable numbers of candidates across time. This excludes a substantial amount of fund-raising, but it also ensures that idiosyncratic variations across years do not complicate the time series here. This is a particular concern for the 2008 election, discussed later, in which the unsuccessful Democratic presidential primary candidates raised a large sum of money that would render comparisons to years where there were fewer presidential candidates such as 2000 (on the Democratic side) or 2004 (on the Republican side) misleading. Of course, some successful candidates will have had to spend money in order to win their

primaries, and that money is included here, but in my judgment this approach maximizes the ability to compare similar numbers of elections across years.

2. Section 527 groups were not required to disclose their expenditures until July 2000, and so data on spending during the entire election cycle are unavailable. The 2004 figure excludes state candidate and party expenses.

3. These tables measure the amount of money raised by the parties, regardless of when it was spent. As the parties' disclosure forms show, it is not uncommon for parties to raise more than they legally can spend during an election period (as has been the case for the Conservatives) or to take out loans in order to finance some election-related spending if they fall short of raising enough to approach the expense limit. While many Canadian election analyses focus on election spending, my concern in presenting these data is fund-raising rather than spending, hence the somewhat unorthodox presentation of the Canadian data.

4. Peak business associations, as defined by Wright (1996, 171), "typically have as members specialized groups or trade associations" and "seek to represent an entire economic sector, not simply the interests of one specialized producer." Examples in this study include the National Federation of Independent Business and the Canadian Federation of Independent Businesses, the Associated Builders and Contractors, the U.S. and Canadian Chambers of Commerce, and the Canadian Council of Chief Executives. See also Salisbury, Heinz, Laumann, and Nelson 1987.

CHAPTER 5

1. These numbers appear impressive, but as Freeman (2003) points out, union members have a variety of traits that would lead them to vote Democratic even without contact from their union. Freeman estimates that the labor "premium"—the effect of contacting union members on their propensity to vote Democratic—is about 4 percentage points.

2. As Masters and Delaney (2005) argue, however, overall PAC contributions declined during the 1990s in inflation-adjusted dollars; this may be a function of the AFL-CIO's lack of interest in PAC contributions, but it may also be due to the fact that the AFL-CIO has traditionally "maxed out" to many incumbent Democrats and the lack of inflation indexing for the maximum PAC contribution has made such contributions worth less over time.

3. See also Zullo 2004 for discussion of union contacting strategies.

4. See Panagopoulos and Francia 2008 for a discussion of these attitudes.

5. *McConnell v. FEC,* 251 F. Supp. 2d 176, 251 F. Supp. 2d 948; Monroe 2002, 65–67, 90–91.

6. Barry 2001, quoting Sierra Club political director Deanna White.

7. Malcolm (2003) claims that in 2002 a total of $25 million was raised by the group from 73,000 donors, $8 million of which was bundled for candidates. These are internal numbers; they are substantially larger than those reported to the FEC but lower than other estimates made by supporters, by the group itself, and in the media.

8. Franz and Corrado treat this as a somewhat enduring change; Parker (2008, 193) is skeptical that in the long run the parties will be able to maintain their ability to raise large sums in hard money contributions.

9. I devote little attention in this book to the causes of the departure of the Change to Win groups from the AFL-CIO; while certainly this split has had consequences for labor unions' political activities, literature on this split gives little indication that the AFL-CIO's political program was a cause of the split or that the Change to Win unions have developed a substantially different approach to voter mobilization and electioneering than the AFL-CIO has had in recent elections (see Dark 2007; Masters, Gibney, and Zagenczyk 2006).

10. Organizing for America, perhaps the best-known offshoot of the Obama campaign, is not an independent group but an arm of the Democratic National Committee.

CHAPTER 6

1. According to Griner and Zovatto's (2005, 63) estimates, a total of $4.12 billion was spent in connection with the 2004 U.S. presidential election, while $56.6 million was spent in connection with the June 2004 Canadian general election. This represents a 72 to 1 ratio. On a per capita basis, given that the United States is roughly nine times as large as Canada in population, American elections are eight times as expensive as Canadian elections. Griner and Zovatto's numbers, however, only include spending directly related to the election; the Canadian figures used here do not include party spending outside of the election period.

2. As noted in chapter 3, this threshold was subsequently lowered, following the 2003 *Figueroa v. Canada* decision, so that a registered party must run at least one candidate and otherwise comply with the terms of the law.

3. See Human Resources and Social Development Canada, http://www.hrsdc.gc.ca/en/lp/wid/union_membership.shtml, for Canadian data; Bureau of Labor Statistics, http://www.bls.gov/news.release/pdf/union2.pdf, for U.S. data.

4. According to some studies, however, there are some within the CLC who claim that this should be a greater concern; Camfield (2008) argues that this was one of the reasons for the challenge by Carol Wall to CLC president Ken Georgetti in 2005.

5. For instance, Hassan Yussuff, quoted in the text in his capacity as CLC secretary-treasurer, also serves as associate president of the NDP, and the NDP Executive Council includes representatives from the ten largest NDP member unions—see http://www.ndp.ca/federalcouncil.

6. The NDP won the Outremont (suburban Montreal) riding in a 2007 by-election and held the seat in the 2008 election.

7. I am paraphrasing my corporate interviewees here. To unpack this claim, businesses see few major distinctions between the parties in regard to their attitudes toward business—the appendix explains the general consensus in the Canadian literature regarding the lack of party differentiation. This claim also, however, presupposes that businesses will see few reasons to support one party over the other on the basis of smaller government projects or riding-level projects—to put this in an American context, businesses will not favor one party over the other on the basis of individual line items in government spending or appropriations bills. This is a more difficult claim to evaluate, but one can consider the higher level of Canadian party unity, and the corresponding lack of "pork barrel" politics on the part of individual legislators, to buttress this claim. Businesses may secure funding or government approval for particular pro-

jects, but, according to the logic here, they do not necessarily have reason to believe that this funding is contingent on which party controls government.

8. One exception to this pattern is the Canadian Environmental Network, which was formed by Environment Canada to provide a forum for environmental groups and federal bureaucrats to discuss politics (McKenzie 2008). Following the pattern noted by Pal (1993) and discussed in chapter 1, however, this organization was largely instigated by the federal government, not by the groups themselves, and McKenzie (2008) notes that many of the larger environmental groups expressed unhappiness at the democratic nature of it (i.e., being on the same footing as smaller groups) or at the potential for co-optation by the government.

9. The Campaign Life Coalition often uses the acronym "CLC," but I do not use it here in order to avoid confusion with the Canadian Labour Congress.

10. See http://www.campaignlifecoalition.com/elections/federal2006/news_items/partiesandleaders.html.

11. An intervenor is similar to an amicus in the U.S. legal system.

12. The group fielded four candidates in 2008.

CHAPTER 7

1. I am paraphrasing comments made by several of the Canadian business group leaders I interviewed; for a dissenting view on the nature of Canadian campaign issues, see Clarke, Jensen, LeDuc, and Pammett 1996, 26–49.

2. This claim does not hold, however, for political parties, as Prime Minister Harper's 2008 attempt to strip the parties of their public financing showed. While this was certainly an attempt to undo the reform legislation, it appears not to have been a proposal developed in consultation with affected groups. There was a clear self-interest component to the claim—the Conservative Party is less dependent on the public subsidy than are its opponents—but it is the self-interest, again, of a party, not a group.

CHAPTER 8

1. Court decisions striking down reform laws, have, as well, been touted as a means of improving campaign discourse; see, e.g., Bradley Smith 2010.

2. The notion that BCRA would hurt political parties was common among both reformers and political scientists. Somewhat paradoxically, similar arguments have been made regarding the *Citizens United* decision—see, e.g., Ben Smith 2010, quoting the Republican election law counsel Ben Ginsberg.

3. The Employee Free Choice Act (EFCA), or the "card check" bill, would require employers to recognize unions based on the number of employees who have signed membership cards, thereby eliminating workplace votes on whether to unionize. For many in organized labor, this represents a chance to reduce the difficulties of workplace organizing and for unions to expand their membership substantially (see Rosenberg 2009).

4. In making this claim, I do not deny the existence of corruption in the recent cases of, among others, Representatives William Jefferson, Robert Ney, and Randy "Duke"

Cunningham. I argue, instead, that these are cases where the corrupt behavior of politicians went far beyond the norm for politicians who accept legitimate political contributions. That is, these politicians were not corrupted by PAC contributions or other interest group support; they broke the law. While I do not wholeheartedly endorse the arguments of antireform authors such as Bradley Smith (2001, 52), I do second here the argument, made by Smith, that there is nothing inherently corrupting about the receipt by a politician of a contribution from a group or individual with particular goals in mind. As Smith writes, it is difficult to distinguish between "corruption" and "responsiveness" when a legislator acts in the interests of his financial supporters.

5. The possibility of quid pro quo arrangements was a major reason for BCRA's soft money prohibition, but this was not as much of a concern in regard to the electioneering restrictions. The Supreme Court's 2009 *Caperton v. A. T. Massey Coal Co.*, however, revolved around allegations that the defendant had spent approximately $3 million on advertisements attacking a state Supreme Court judge because the defendant had a case pending before the West Virginia Supreme Court and hoped to defeat that judge in an election and elect one who would, at a minimum, be aware that his election was due to the spending of Massey. Although the Supreme Court rejected the notion that electioneering can corrupt in *Citizens United,* it ruled that the *Caperton* case was a clear instance of such corruption (see Hasen 2010; and the Stevens dissent in *Citizens United,* 558 U.S. 50 [2010]).

6. According to Elections Canada data, turnout in each of the four general elections of the 2000s has been lower than in any of the elections of the 1980s or 1990s; 64.7 percent of eligible voters voted in 2006, and between 58 and 61 percent voted in each of the other three elections. Turnout during the 1990s never fell below 67 percent, and turnout in the two elections of the 1980s was over 75 percent. For a discussion of these trends, see Clarke, Kornberg, and Scotto 2009, 254–64. There are also those who have argued that Canadian politics has been sufficiently polarized that the parties have stepped up their mobilization efforts; the cause of lower turnout has not been in the mobilization work of the parties but in voter fatigue at the frequency of elections since 2004. For analysis of mobilization work by the parties, see Endersby and Galatas 2009.

7. In many such studies, the views of elected officials, consultants, journalists, and citizens diverge sharply. Partisanship and one's political incentives may cloud any effort to reach objective conclusions here. See, e.g., Bartels and Vavreck 2000; Buchanan 2004; Dulio and Nelson 2005; Maisel, West, and Clifton 2007.

8. The reader will note that later in this chapter I contend that the Democratic Party's emphasis on hard money contributions and smaller contributions may have stemmed from BCRA. One might contend that this is a result of BCRA, but we have no way of knowing that this strategy—which was also a feature of the Howard Dean and Barack Obama campaigns—would not have taken place absent reform. The ability of candidates and parties to raise small contributions via the Internet would have been present even without reform.

9. One might argue that the sort of direct advocacy permitted in the *Citizens United* decision might represent an improvement in this regard. Were businesses to advertise *as* businesses, this might be the case. Such advertising seems unlikely, however; corporate groups before BCRA tended to obscure their identities by using misleading names or joining coalitions, and there is little reason to expect that they will alter this strategy now that they have more options for electioneering. The fact that, for instance, Americans for

Job Security's Michael Dubke was among the first to announce plans to expand corporate electioneering after the *Citizens United* decision (see Cummings 2010) suggests that corporate advocacy will be dominated by "coalitions" or shell groups like AJS.

APPENDIX

1. A recent volume on the relevance of Canadian politics to the field of comparative political science also discusses the relevance of the brokerage politics paradigm to other nations; see Tanguay 2009.

2. Such survey questions in Canada are also complicated by the fact that the poles on the conventional ideology survey question—liberal and conservative—are the names of Canadian parties, thus making responses to this question of questionable value.

Interviews

AMERICAN GROUPS

AFL-CIO. Steve Rosenthal, Political Director. Washington, DC. July 25, 2002.

American Federation of Teachers. Liz Smith, Political Director. Washington, DC. May 11, 2004.

Anonymous corporate PAC directors (3). Washington, DC. Various dates, 2004.

Associated Builders and Contractors. Ned Monroe, Political Director. Arlington, VA. September 10, 2002; June 12, 2003; September 15, 2004.

Brady Campaign to Prevent Gun Violence. Alison Houle, PAC Director. Washington, DC. September 10, 2002.

Business-Industry PAC. Greg Casey, Chief Executive Officer. Washington, DC. July 10, 2002; November 12, 2003; September 22, 2004.

Campaign for America's Future. Roger Hickey, Co-Director. Washington, DC. September 19, 2002.

Citizens for Better Medicare. Nona Bear Wegner, Director. Washington, DC. September 6, 2002.

Club for Growth. David Keating, Political Director. Washington, DC. August 6, 2002; May 29, 2003.

Human Rights Campaign. Winnie Stachelberg, Political Director. Washington, DC. July 31, 2002; June 24, 2003.

International Association of Firefighters. Kevin O'Connor, Political Director. Washington, DC. April 15, 2004.

International Union of Painters and Allied Trades. Sean McGarvey, Political Director. Washington, DC. April 22, 2004.

League of Conservation Voters. Mark Longabaugh, Political Director. Washington, DC. November 24, 2003; September 17, 2004.

League of Conservation Voters. Betsy Loyless, Political Director. Washington, DC. July 9, 2002.

National Air Traffic Controllers Association. Ken Montoya, PAC Director. Washington, DC. April 23, 2004.

National Association of Letter Carriers. George Gould, Political Director. Washington, DC. June 17, 2004.

National Association of Realtors. Greg Knopp, Political Director, and Scott Reiter, PAC Director. Washington, DC. August 22, 2002; June 19, 2003; September 22, 2004.

National Council of la Raza. Clarissa Martinez de Castro, Director of Immigration and National Campaigns. Washington, DC. October 8, 2002.

National Postal Mail Handlers Union. Roger Blacklow, Political Director. Washington, DC. April 28, 2004.

National Rifle Association. Chuck Cunningham, Political Director. Washington, DC. July 17, 2002; June 23, 2003.

People for the American Way. Mary Jean Collins, Political Director. Washington, DC. September 17, 2002.

People for the American Way. Kimberly Robson, Political Director. Washington, DC. December 4, 2003.

Planned Parenthood Action Fund. David Williams, Political Director. Washington, DC. July 11, 2002; May 15, 2003; September 24, 2004.

Progressive Majority. Gloria Totten, Director. Washington, DC. October 7, 2002; July 3, 2003; October 6, 2004.

Sierra Club. Margaret Conway, Political Director. Washington, DC. August 14, 2002; June 10, 2003.

CANADIAN GROUPS

Animal Alliance-Environment Voters Party. Liz White, Leader. Toronto, ON, November 15, 2007.

Campaign Life Coalition. Aidan Reid, National Director, Public Affairs. Ottawa, ON, September 26, 2007.

Canadian Auto Workers. Jim Stanford, Economist. By telephone, November 26, 2007.

Canadian Chamber of Commerce. Shirley-Ann George, Vice President, International Affairs. By telephone, October 5, 2007.

Canadian Council of Chief Executives. Ross H. Laver, Vice President, Policy and Communications. Ottawa, ON, September 25, 2007.

Canadian Federation of Independent Businesses. Corinne Pohlmann, Vice President, National Affairs. Ottawa, ON, September 25, 2007.

Canadian Labour Congress. Daniel Mallett, National Director, Political Action and Campaigns Department. Ottawa, ON, September 26, 2007.

Canadian Manufacturers and Exporters. Jeff Brownlee, Vice President, Communications. By telephone, October 5, 2007.

Canadian Taxpayers Federation. John Williamson, Federal Director. Ottawa, ON, September 27, 2007.

National Citizens Coalition. Peter Coleman, Chairman and CEO. Toronto, ON, November 15, 2007.

Sierra Club Canada. Jean Langlois, Campaigns Director. Ottawa, ON, September 26, 2007.

United Food and Commercial Workers. Bob Linton, National Coordinator, Communications, and Andrew MacKenzie, Organizer and NDP Union Representative. Toronto, ON, November 14, 2007.

United Steelworkers. Sue Milling, Education, Equality, and Political Action Department Leader, and Lise Blanchette, Political Action Coordinator and NDP Executive Board Labour Representative. Toronto, ON, November 14, 2007.

Bibliography

Adams, Michael. 2003. *Fire and Ice: The United States, Canada, and the Myth of Converging Values.* Toronto: Penguin.

Albo, Gregory. 1990. "The New Realism and Canadian Workers." In *Canadian Politics: An Introduction to the Discipline,* ed. Alain-G. Gagnon and James P. Bickerton, 471–504. Toronto: Broadview Press.

Alden, Edward, and Neil Buckley. 2004. "Wal-Mart a Big Giver to 2004 Election." *Financial Times,* February 24.

Ambinder, Mark. 2006. "Know Thy Voter." *National Journal Hotline,* September 15.

Archer, Keith, and Alan Whitehorn. 1997. *Political Activists: The NDP in Convention.* Toronto: Oxford University Press.

Asher, Herbert B., Eric S. Heberlig, Randall B. Ripley, and Karen Snyder. 1991. *American Labor Unions in the Electoral Arena.* Lanham, MD: Rowman and Littlefield.

Associated Press. 2004. "Corporate PACs Backed Republicans 10 to 1." November 26.

Ayres, Jeffrey M. 1998. *Defying Conventional Wisdom: Political Movements and Popular Contention against North American Free Trade.* Toronto: University of Toronto Press.

Baker, Anna Nibley, and David B. Magleby. 2002. "Interest Groups in the 2000 Congressional Elections." In *The Other Campaign: Soft Money and Issue Advocacy in the 2000 Elections,* ed. David B. Magleby, 51–78. Lanham, MD: Rowman and Littlefield.

Barry, John Byrne. 2001. "Promising Steps toward Campaign Finance Reform." *The Planet: Newsletter of the Sierra Club* 10 (2). (Accessed on-line at www.sierraclub.org/planet/200103/financereform.asp.)

Bart, John, and James Meader. 2004. "The More You Spend, the Less They Listen: The South Dakota U.S. Senate Race." In *The Last Hurrah: Soft Money and Issue Advocacy in the 2002 Congressional Elections,* ed. David B. Magleby and J. Quin Monson, 159–79. Washington, DC: Brookings Institution.

Bartels, Larry M., and Lynn Vavreck, eds. 2000. *Campaign Reform: Insights and Evidence.* Ann Arbor: University of Michigan Press.

Baumgartner, Frank R., and Beth L. Leech. 1998. *Basic Interests: The Importance of Groups in Politics and in Political Science.* Princeton: Princeton University Press.

Bedlington, Anne H., and Michael J. Malbin. 2003. "The Party as Extended Network: Members Giving to Each Other and Their Parties." In *Life after Reform: When the Bipartisan Campaign Reform Act Meets Politics,* ed. Michael J. Malbin, 121–40. Lanham, MD: Rowman and Littlefield.

Berry, Jeffrey M. 1999. *The New Liberalism: The Rising Power of Citizen Groups.* Washington, DC: Brookings Institution.

Bimber, Bruce. 2003. *Information and American Democracy: Technology in the Evolution of Political Power.* New York: Cambridge University Press.

Birnbaum, Jeffrey H. 1996. "Political Money: The Rules Are Warped, Not Just Bent." *Time,* October 21.

Birnbaum, Jeffrey H., and Thomas B. Edsall. 2004. "At the End, Pro-GOP 527s Outspent Their Counterparts." *Washington Post,* November 6.

Birnbaum, Jeffrey H., and Russell Newell. 2001. "Washington's Power 25: Fat and Happy in D.C." *Fortune,* May 28.

Black, Naomi. 1992. "Ripples in the Second Wave: Comparing the Contemporary Women's Movement in Canada and the United States." In *Challenging Times: The Women's Movement in Canada and the United States,* ed. Constance Backhouse and David H. Flaherty, 94–109. Montreal: McGill-Queens University Press.

Blades, Joan. 2004. Comments at the Take Back America Conference, June 2, Washington, DC.

Blais, André, and Elisabeth Gidengil. 1991. *Making Representative Democracy Work.* Toronto: Dundurn Press.

Blais, André, Elisabeth Gidengil, Agnieszka Dobrzynska, Neil Nevitte, and Richard Nadeau. 2003. "Does the Local Candidate Matter?" *Canadian Journal of Political Science* 36 (3): 657–64.

Blais, André, Elisabeth Gidengil, Richard Nadeau, and Neil Nevitte. 2002. "Do Party Supporters Differ?" In *Citizen Politics: Research and Theory in Canadian Political Behaviour,* 184–201. Don Mills, ON: Oxford University Press.

Boatright, Robert G. 2007. "Situating the New 527 Groups in Interest Group Theory." *The Forum* 5 (2), article 5.

Boatright, Robert G. 2009. "Cross-Border Interest Group Learning in Canada and the United States." *American Review of Canadian Studies* 39 (4): 418–37.

Boatright, Robert G. 2011. "The Place of Québec in Canadian Interest Groups' Election Campaign Strategies." *American Review of Canadian Studies* (forthcoming).

Boatright, Robert G., and Michael J. Malbin. 2005. "Political Contribution Tax Credits and Citizen Participation." *American Politics Research* 33 (6): 787–817.

Boatright, Robert G., Michael J. Malbin, Mark J. Rozell, Richard Skinner, and Clyde Wilcox. 2003. "BCRA's Impact on Interest Groups and Advocacy Organizations." In *Life after Reform: When the Bipartisan Campaign Reform Act Meets Politics,* ed. Michael J. Malbin, 43–60. Lanham, MD: Rowman and Littlefield.

Boatright, Robert G., Michael J. Malbin, Mark J. Rozell, and Clyde Wilcox. 2006. "Interest Groups and Advocacy Organizations after BCRA." In *The Election after Reform: Money, Politics, and the Bipartisan Campaign Reform Act,* ed. Michael J. Malbin, 112–40. Lanham, MD: Rowman and Littlefield.

Bosso, Christopher J., and Michael Thomas Collins. 2002. "Just Another Tool? How Environmental Groups Use the Internet." In *Interest Group Politics,* 6th ed., ed. Allen J. Cigler and Burdett A. Loomis, 95–114. Washington, DC: Congressional Quarterly Press.

Boyd, Wes. 2003. Comments at the Take Back America Conference, Washington, DC, June 4.

Brecher, Jeremy, and Tim Costello. 1999. "A New Labor Movement in the Shell of the

Old?" In *The Transformation of U. S. Unions: Voices, Visions, and Strategies from the Grassroots,* ed. Ray M. Tillman and Michael S. Cummings, 9–25. Boulder: Lynne Rienner.

Broder, John. 2009. "Storm over the Chamber." *New York Times,* November 18.

Brodie, Janine, and Jane Jenson. 1989. "Piercing the Smokescreen: Brokerage Parties and Class Politics." In *Canadian Parties in Transition: Discourse, Organization, and Representation,* ed. Alain-G. Gagnon and A. Brian Tanguay, 24–44. Scarborough, ON: Nelson Canada.

Brodie, Janine, and Jane Jenson. 1990. "The Party System." In *Canadian Politics in the 1990s,* 3d ed., ed. Michael S. Whittington and Glen Williams, 249–67. Scarborough, ON: Nelson Canada.

Buchanan, Bruce. 2004. *Presidential Campaign Quality: Incentives and Reform.* Englewood Cliffs, NJ: Prentice-Hall.

Budde, Bernadette. 1980. "Business Political Action Committees." In *Parties, Interest Groups, and Campaign Finance Laws,* ed. Michael J. Malbin, 9–25. Washington, DC: American Enterprise Institute.

Budde, Bernadette. 2004. "The Political Picture: What We Saw." *BIPAC Elections Insight* 32 (3): 3.

Bureau of Labor Statistics. 2009. "Union Members in 2008." Washington, DC: Bureau of Labor Statistics. http://www.bls.gov/news.release/pdf/union2.pdf (accessed August 15, 2009).

Camfield, David. 2008. "The Working Class Movement in Canada: An Overview." In *Group Politics and Social Movements in Canada,* ed. Miriam Smith, 61–84. Toronto: Broadview Press.

Campaign Finance Institute. 2008. "Fast Start for Soft Money Groups in 2008 Election." Washington, DC: Campaign Finance Institute, April 3.

Campaign Finance Institute. 2009. "Soft Money Political Spending by 501(c) Nonprofits Tripled in 2008 Election." Washington, DC: Campaign Finance Institute, February 25.

Campbell, James E. 2004. "The Stagnation of Congressional Elections." In *Life after Reform: When the Bipartisan Campaign Reform Act Meets Politics,* ed. Michael J. Malbin, 141–58. Lanham, MD: Rowman and Littlefield.

Canadian Council of Chief Executives. 2004. "Memorandum for Leaders of Federal Political Parties—Restoring Trust, Delivering Solutions: Making a Minority Parliament Work for Canadians." Ottawa: Canadian Council of Chief Executives, June 29.

Cantor, Joseph E. 1995. *Campaign Financing in Federal Elections: A Guide to the Law and Its Operation.* Washington, DC: Congressional Research Service.

Carney, Eliza Newlin. 2004. "Small Donors Reshape the Fund-Raising Landscape." *National Journal,* May 3.

Carney, Eliza Newlin. 2007. "High Court Reversal." *National Journal,* July 2.

Carty, R. Kenneth, William P. Cross, and Lisa Young. 2000. *Rebuilding Canadian Party Politics.* Vancouver: University of British Columbia Press.

Carty, R. Kenneth, and Munroe Eagles. 2005. *Politics Is Local: National Politics at the Grassroots.* Don Mills, ON: Oxford University Press.

Chaison, Gary N., and Joseph B. Rose. 1989. "Unions, Growth, Structure, and Internal Dynamics." In *Union-Management Relations in Canada,* 2nd ed., ed. John C. Anderson, Morley Gunderson, and Allen Ponak, 125–54. Don Mills, ON: Addison-Wesley.

Chappell, Louise A. 2002. *Gendering Government: Feminist Engagement with the State in Australia and Canada.* Vancouver: University of British Columbia Press.

Chase, Steven, Bill Curry, and Campbell Clark. 2008. "Tories Take to Airwaves; Greens Back Coalition." *Globe and Mail,* December 2.

Cigler, Alan J. 2002. "Interest Groups and Financing the 2000 Elections." In *Financing the 2000 Elections,* ed. David B. Magleby, 163–87. Washington, DC: Brookings Institution.

Cillizza, Chris. 2003. "Critics Slam 'Demzilla.'" *Roll Call,* June 5.

Clark, Joe. 2004. "What's Right and Wrong with Democracy in Canada." *Election Law Journal* 3 (3): 400–401.

Clark, Peter B., and James Q. Wilson. 1961. "Incentive System: A Theory of Organization." *Administrative Science Quarterly* 6:129–66.

Clarke, Harold D., Jane Jensen, Lawrence LeDuc, and Jon H. Pammett. 1996. *Absent Mandate: Canadian Electoral Politics in an Era of Restructuring.* 3rd ed. Toronto: Gage Publishing.

Clarke, Harold D., Allan Kornberg, and Thomas J. Scotto. 2009. *Making Political Choices: Canada and the United States.* Toronto: University of Toronto Press.

Coleman, William D., and Wyn P. Grant. 1985. "Regional Differentiation of Business Interest Associations: A Comparison of Canada and the United Kingdom." *Canadian Journal of Political Science* 18 (1): 3–29.

Coleman, William D., and Henry J. Jacek. 1983. "The Roles and Activities of Business Associations in Canada." *Canadian Journal of Political Science* 16 (2): 257–80.

Corrado, Anthony. 2005. "Money and Politics: A History of Federal Campaign Finance Law." In *The New Campaign Finance Sourcebook,* ed. Anthony Corrado, Thomas E. Mann, Daniel R. Ortiz, and Trevor Potter, 7–47. Washington, DC: Brookings Institution.

Corrado, Anthony. 2006a. "Parties Playing a Major Role in Election '06." Washington, DC: Campaign Finance Institute.

Corrado, Anthony. 2006b. "Party Finance in the Wake of BCRA: An Overview." In *The Election after Reform: Money, Politics, and the Bipartisan Campaign Reform Act,* ed. Michael J. Malbin, 19–37. Lanham, MD: Rowman and Littlefield.

Coyne, Andrew. 2010. "The Dirty Little Secret behind Attack Ads." *MacLeans,* January 25, 12.

Crete, Jean. 1991. "Television, Advertising, and Canadian Elections." In *Media and Voters in Canadian Election Campaigns,* ed. Jean Crete, 3–44. Toronto: Dundurn Press.

Cross, William P. 2004. *Political Parties: The Canadian Democratic Audit.* Vancouver: University of British Columbia Press.

Cummings, Jeanne. 2004. "Companies Pare Political Donations." *Wall Street Journal,* June 7, A3.

Cummings, Jeanne. 2010. "Day After: SCOTUS Ruling Not So Bad?" *Politico,* January 22. http://www.politico.com/news/stories/0110/31878.html.

Curry, Bill. 2008. "Coalition a Threat, PM Says." *Globe and Mail,* December 3.

Dahl, Robert A. 1961. *Who Governs?* New Haven: Yale University Press.

Dalton, Russell J. 2004. *Democratic Challenges, Democratic Choices: The Erosion of Political Support in Advanced Industrial Democracies.* New York: Oxford University Press.

Dao, James. 2004. "NRA Opens an All-out Drive for Bush and Its Views." *New York Times,* April 16.

Dark, Taylor E. 1999. *The Unions and the Democrats: An Enduring Alliance.* Ithaca: Cornell University Press.

Dark, Taylor E. 2007. "Organization Theory and Stages of Decline: The Case of the AFL-CIO, 1955–2005." *International Journal of Organization Theory and Behavior* 10 (2): 213–44.

Dawson, Helen Jones. 1975. "National Pressure Groups and the Federal Government." In *Pressure Group Behaviour in Canadian Politics,* ed. A. Paul Pross, 29–58. Toronto: McGraw-Hill Ryerson.

de Tocqueville, Alexis. 1969. *Democracy in America.* Trans. George Lawrence. New York: Harper and Row.

Dobrowolsky, Alexandra. 1998. "Of 'Special Interest': Interest, Identity, and Feminist Constitutional Activism in Canada." *Canadian Journal of Political Science* 31 (4): 707–42.

Dobrowolsky, Alexandra. 2000. *The Politics of Pragmatism: Women, Representation, and Constitutionalism in Canada.* Toronto: Oxford University Press.

Dulio, David A., and Candice J. Nelson. 2005. *Vital Signs: Perspectives on the Health of American Campaigning.* Washington, DC: Brookings Institution.

Dwyre, Diana, and Victoria Farrar-Myers. 2000. *Legislative Labyrinth.* Washington, DC: Congressional Quarterly Press.

Eagles, Munroe. 2004. "The Impact of 'Third Party' Advertising in Canada: An Exploratory Ecological Analysis of the 2000 Election." Paper presented at the Annual Meeting of the Canadian Political Science Association, Winnipeg, Manitoba.

Edsall, Thomas B., and James V. Grimaldi. 2004. "New Routes for Money to Sway Voters: 501(c) Groups Escape Disclosure Rules." *Washington Post,* September 27, A1.

Endersby, James W., and Steven E. Galatas. 2009. "Campaign Expenditures and Voter Mobilization in Canadian Elections." Paper presented at the Biennial Meeting of the Association for Canadian Studies in the United States, San Diego, CA, November 19.

Engelmann, Frederick C., and Mildred A. Schwartz. 1975. *Canadian Political Parties: Origin, Character, and Impact.* Scarborough, ON: Prentice-Hall.

Erne, Roland. 2009. *European Unions: Labor's Quest for a Transnational Democracy.* Ithaca: Cornell University Press.

Esterling, Kevin M. 2004. *The Political Economy of Expertise.* Ann Arbor: University of Michigan Press.

Farhi, Paul. 2004. "Voters Are Harder to Reach as Media Outlets Multiply." *Washington Post,* June 16.

Farney, James. 2009. "The Personal Is Not Political: The Progressive Conservative Response to Social Issues." *American Review of Canadian Studies* 39 (3): 242–52.

Ferejohn, John, and Brian Gaines. 1991. "The Personal Vote in Canada." In *Party Politics in Canada: Representation and Integration,* ed. Herman Bakvis, 275–302. Toronto: Dundurn Press.

Fisher, Justin. Forthcoming (2011). "State Funding and Political Parties: Truths, Myths and Legend." In *Election and Party Finance in Canada: Consequences for Democracy,* ed. Lisa Young and Harold Jansen. Vancouver: University of British Columbia Press.

Flanagan, Tom. 2007. *Harper's Team: Behind the Scenes in the Conservative Rise to Power.* Montreal: McGill-Queen's University Press.

Francia, Peter. 2000. "Awakening the Sleeping Giant: The Renaissance of Organized Labor in American Politics." Ph.D. diss., University of Maryland.

Francia, Peter. 2006. *The Future of Organized Labor in American Politics*. New York: Columbia University Press.

Franklin, Mark N. 2004. *Voter Turnout and the Dynamics of Electoral Competition in Established Democracies since 1945*. New York: Cambridge University Press.

Franz, Michael. 2008a. *Choices and Changes: Interest Groups in the Electoral Process*. Philadelphia: Temple University Press.

Franz, Michael. 2008b. "The Interest Group Response to Campaign Finance Reform." *The Forum* 6 (1), article 10.

Franz, Michael M., Joel Rivlin, and Kenneth Goldstein. 2006. "Much More of the Same: Television Advertising Pre- and Post-BCRA." In *The Election after Reform: Money, Politics, and the Bipartisan Campaign Reform Act*, ed. Michael J. Malbin, 141–60. Lanham, MD: Rowman and Littlefield.

Fraser, Graham. 1989. *Playing for Keeps: The Making of the Prime Minister, 1988*. Toronto: McClelland and Stewart.

Freeman, Richard. 2003. "What Do Unions Do . . . to Voting?" Working Paper 9992, National Bureau of Economic Research, Cambridge.

Gagnon, Alain-G., and A. Brian Tanguay. 1989. "Minor Parties of Protest in Canada: Origins, Impact, and Prospects." In *Canadian Parties in Transition*, ed. Alain-G. Gagnon and A. Brian Tanguay, 220–48. Scarborough, ON: Nelson Canada.

Galipeau, Claude. 1989. "Political Parties, Interest Groups, and New Social Movements: Toward New Representation?" In *Canadian Parties in Transition*, ed. Alain-G. Gagnon and A. Brian Tanguay, 404–26. Scarborough, ON: Nelson Canada.

Gerber, Robin. 1999. "Building to Win, Building to Last: AFL-CIO COPE Takes on the Republican Congress." In *After the Revolution*, ed. Robert Biersack, Paul S. Herrnson, and Clyde Wilcox, 77–93. Boston: Allyn and Bacon.

Gidengil, Elisabeth, André Blais, Joanna Everitt, Patrick Fournier, and Neil Nevitte. 2006. "Long-Term Predisposition or Short-Term Attitude? A Panel-Based Comparison of Party Identification Measures." Paper presented at the Joint Session of the European Consortium for Political Research, Nicosia, Cyprus.

Grabb, Edward, Robert Andersen, Monica Hwang, and Scott Milligan. 2009. "Confidence in Political Institutions in Canada and the United States: Assessing the Interactive Role of Region and Race." *American Review of Canadian Studies* 39 (4): 379–97.

Grabb, Edward, and James Curtis. 2005. *Regions Apart: The Four Societies of Canada and the United States*. Don Mills, ON: Oxford University Press.

Grant, J. Tobin, and Thomas J. Rudolph. 2004. *Expression vs. Equality: The Politics of Campaign Finance Reform*. Columbus: Ohio State University Press.

Green, Donald P., and Alan S. Gerber. 2004. *Get Out the Vote: How to Increase Voter Turnout*. Washington, DC: Brookings Institution.

Green, John C., and Nathan S. Bigelow. 2005. "The Christian Right Goes to Washington." In *The Interest Group Connection*, 3rd ed., ed. Paul Herrnson, Ronald G. Shaiko, and Clyde Wilcox, 189–211. Washington, DC: CQ Press.

Greenhouse, Steven. 2008. "After Push for Obama, Unions Seek New Rules." *New York Times*, November 9, A25.

Griner, Steven, and Daniel Zovatto. 2005. "The Delicate Balance between Political Equity and Freedom of Expression." In *The Delicate Balance between Political Equity and Freedom of Expression: Political Party and Campaign Financing in Canada and the*

United States, ed. Steven Griner and Daniel Zovatto, 62–69. Washington, DC: International IDEA/Organization of American States.

Gross, Donald, and Robert Goidel. 2003. *The States of Campaign Finance Reform.* Columbus: Ohio State University Press.

Hacker, Jacob S., and Paul Pierson. 2005. *Off Center: The Republican Revolution and the Erosion of American Democracy.* New Haven: Yale University Press.

Hall, Richard L., and Frank W. Wayman. 1990. "Buying Time: Moneyed Interests and the Mobilization of Bias in Congressional Committees." *American Political Science Review* 84 (3): 797–820.

Hamm, Keith E., and Kasia Hebda. 2006. "Comparative Analysis of Regulatory Regimes in the Canadian Provinces." Paper presented at the "Party and Election Finance: Consequences for Democracy" Conference, Institute for Advanced Policy Research, University of Calgary, May 25–26.

Hamm, Keith E., and Robert E. Hogan. 2004. "Legislative Lobbying: Placing Research on Legislative Lobbying in a Comparative Context." In *Research Guide to U.S. and International Interest Groups,* ed. Clive S. Thomas, 167–75. Westport, CT: Greenwood Press.

Hamm, Keith E., and Robert E. Hogan. 2008. "Campaign Finance Laws and Candidacy Decisions in State Legislative Elections." *Political Research Quarterly* 61 (3): 458–67.

Hargrove, Buzz. 2005. "Making the Most of Opportunity." *Context,* December 9.

Harrison, Trevor. 1995. *Of Passionate Intensity: Right Wing Populism and the Reform Party of Canada.* Toronto: University of Toronto Press.

Hasen, Richard L. 2010. "Money Grubbers: The Supreme Court Kills Campaign Finance Reform." *Slate,* January 21. http://www.slate.com/id/2242209/.

Heath, Joseph. 2001. *The Efficient Society: Why Canada Is as Close to Utopia as It Gets.* Toronto: Penguin.

Herrnson, Paul S. 1988. *Party Campaigning in the 1980s.* Cambridge: Harvard University Press.

Hibbing, John R., and Elizabeth Theiss-Morse. 2002. *Stealth Democracy: Americans' Beliefs about How Government Should Work.* New York: Cambridge University Press.

Hoberg, George. 1997. "Governing the Environment: Comparing Canada and the United States." In *Degrees of Freedom: Canada and the United States in a Changing World,* ed. Keith Banting, George Hoberg, and Richard Simeon, 341–88. Montreal: McGill-Queens Press.

Hofnung, Menachem. 2006. "Financing Internal Party Races in Non-Majoritarian Political Systems: Lessons from the Israeli Experience." *Election Law Journal* 5 (4): 372–83.

Ikstens, Janis, Michael Pinto-Duschinsky, Daniel Smilov, and Marcin Walecki. 2002. "Political Finance in Central Eastern Europe: An Interim Report." *Austrian Journal of Political Science (Österreichische Zeitschrift für Politikwissenschaft)* 31 (2): 21–39.

Jackson, Brooks. 1988. *Honest Graft: Big Money and the American Political Process.* New York: Knopf.

Jacobson, Gary C. 1999. "The Effect of the AFL-CIO's 'Voter Education' Campaign in the 1996 House Elections." *Journal of Politics* 61:185–94.

Jacobson, Gary C. 2009. *The Politics of Congressional Elections.* 7th ed. New York: Longman.

Jansen, Harold, and Lisa Young. 2009. "Solidarity Forever? The NDP, Organized Labour, and the Changing Face of Party Finance in Canada." *Canadian Journal of Political Science* 42 (3): 657–78.

Jeffrey, Brooke. 1993. *Strange Bedfellows, Trying Times: October 1992 and the Defeat of the Powerbrokers.* Toronto: Key Porter.

Jeffrey, Brooke. 1999. *Hard Right Turn: The New Face of Neo-Conservatism in Canada.* Toronto: HarperCollins.

Johnston, Richard, André Blais, Henry E. Brady, and Jean Crete. 1992. *Letting the People Decide: Dynamics of a Canadian Election.* Stanford: Stanford University Press.

Judis, John. 2000. "Disunion: Gore's Labor Pains." *New Republic,* August 21.

Key, V. O., Jr. 1964. *Politics, Parties, and Interest Groups.* 5th ed. New York: Crowell.

Kingdon, John. 1984. *Agendas, Alternatives, and Public Policies.* Boston: Little, Brown.

Kollman, Ken. 1997. *Outside Lobbying: Public Opinion and Interest Group Strategies.* Princeton: Princeton University Press.

Kosterlitz, Julie. 2008. "Winning the Ground Game." *National Journal,* November 8, 79.

Kotok, C. David, and Jake Thompson. 2000. "Political Ad's Donors Are Kept Secret." *Omaha World-Herald,* October 27.

Kropf, Martha, E. Terrence Jones, Matt McLaughlin, and Dale Neuman. 2004. "Battle for the Bases: The Missouri U.S. Senate Race." In *The Last Hurrah: Soft Money and Issue Advocacy in the 2002 Congressional Elections,* ed. David B. Magleby and J. Quin Monson, 137–58. Washington, DC: Brookings Institution.

Kwavnick, David. 1970. "Pressure Group Demands and the Struggle for Organizational Status: The Case of Organized Labour in Canada." *Canadian Journal of Political Science* 3 (1): 56–72.

Kwavnick, David. 1975. "Interest Group Demands and the Federal Political System: Two Canadian Case Studies." In *Pressure Group Behaviour in Canadian Politics,* ed. A. Paul Pross, 70–86. Toronto: McGraw-Hill Ryerson.

La Raja, Raymond J. 2008. *Small Change: Money, Political Parties, and Campaign Finance Reform.* Ann Arbor: University of Michigan Press.

Laxer, James. 2003. *The Border: Canada, the U. S., and Dispatches from the 49th Parallel.* Toronto: Doubleday Canada.

Laycock, David. 2002. *The New Right and Democracy in Canada.* Toronto: Oxford University Press.

Lichtenstein, Nelson. 2002. *State of the Union: A Century of American Labor.* Princeton: Princeton University Press.

Lipset, Seymour Martin. 1991. *Continental Divide: The Values and Institutions of the United States and Canada.* New York: Routledge.

Lipset, Seymour Martin, and Noah M. Meltz. 2004. *The Paradox of American Unionism: Why Americans Like Unions More than Canadians Do but Join Much Less.* Ithaca: Cornell University Press.

Lortie, Pierre. 1991. *Reforming Electoral Democracy: Final Report of the Canadian Royal Commission on Electoral Reform and Party Financing.* Ottawa: Ministry of Supply and Services Canada.

MacDonald, Ian Thomas. 2003. "NAFTA and the Emergence of Continental Labor Co-operation." *American Review of Canadian Studies* 33 (2): 173–96.

MacKenzie, Chris. 2005. *Pro-Family Politics and Fringe Parties in Canada.* Vancouver: University of British Columbia Press.

Magleby, David B. 2000. *Outside Money: Soft Money and Issue Advocacy in the 1998 Congressional Elections.* Lanham, MD: Rowman and Littlefield.

Magleby, David B., and J. Quin Monson, eds. 2004. *The Last Hurrah? Soft Money and Issue Advocacy in the 2002 Congressional Elections.* Washington, DC: Brookings Institution.

Magleby, David B., J. Quin Monson, and Kelly D. Patterson. 2005. *Dancing without Partners: How Candidates, Parties, and Interest Groups Interact in the New Campaign Finance Environment.* Provo: Center for the Study of Elections and Democracy, Brigham Young University.

Magleby, David B., and Kelly D. Patterson. 2008. "Rules of Engagement: BCRA and Unanswered Questions." In *The Battle for Congress: Iraq, Scandal, and Campaign Finance in the 2006 Elections,* ed. David B. Magleby and Kelly D. Patterson, 22–61. Boulder: Paradigm Publishers.

Magleby, David B., and Jonathan W. Tanner. 2004. "Interest Group Electioneering in the 2002 Congressional Elections." In *The Last Hurrah? Soft Money and Issue Advocacy in the 2002 Congressional Elections,* ed. David B. Magleby and J. Quin Monson, 63–89. Washington, DC: Brookings Institution.

Magnusson, Warren. 1990. "Critical Social Movements: De-centreing the State." In *Canadian Politics: An Introduction to the Discipline,* ed. Alain-G. Gagnon and James P. Bickerton, 525–37. Toronto: Broadview Press.

Mainwaring, Scott. 1988. "Political Parties and Democratization in Brazil and the Southern Cone." *Comparative Politics* 21 (1): 91–120.

Mainwaring, Scott. 1991. "Political Parties and Electoral Systems: Brazil in Comparative Perspective." *Comparative Politics* 24 (1): 21–43.

Mainwaring, Scott. 1992. "Brazilian Party Underdevelopment in Comparative Perspective." *Political Science Quarterly* 107 (4): 677–707.

Maisel, L. Sandy, Darrell M. West, and Brett M. Clifton. 2007. *Evaluating Campaign Quality: Can the Electoral Process Be Improved?* New York: Cambridge University Press.

Malbin, Michael J. 2003. "Thinking about Reform." In *Life after Reform: When the Bipartisan Campaign Reform Act Meets Politics,* ed. Michael J. Malbin, 3–20. Lanham, MD: Rowman and Littlefield.

Malbin, Michael J. 2006. "Assessing the Bipartisan Campaign Reform Act." In *The Election after Reform: Money, Politics, and the Bipartisan Campaign Reform Act,* ed. Michael J. Malbin, 1–18. Lanham, MD: Rowman and Littlefield.

Malbin, Michael J. 2008. "Rethinking the Campaign Finance Agenda." *The Forum* 6 (1), article 3.

Malbin, Michael J., and Thomas Gais. 1998. *The Day after Reform: Sobering Campaign Finance Lessons from the States.* Albany: State University of New York Press.

Malbin, Michael J., Mark J. Rozell, Richard Skinner, and Clyde Wilcox. 2002. "New Interest Group Strategies—A Preview of Post McCain-Feingold Politics?" Washington, DC: Campaign Finance Institute.

Malcolm, Ellen. 2003. "Statement by Ellen R. Malcolm on the Supreme Court Decision on Campaign Finance Reform." Washington, DC: EMILY's List. http://emilyslist.org/news/releases/ellen_court_finance_reform/ (accessed March 2, 2010).

Manfredi, Christopher, and Mark Rush. 2008. *Judging Democracy.* Toronto: Broadview Press.

Masters, Marick F., and John Delaney. 2005. "Organized Labor's Political Scorecard." *Journal of Labor Research* 26 (3): 365–92.

Masters, Marick F., Ray Gibney, and Tom Zagenczyk. 2006. "The AFL-CIO v. CTW: The Competing Visions, Strategies, and Structures." *Journal of Labor Research* 27 (4): 473–504.

Mattzie, Thomas. 2004. Remarks at the Politics Online Conference, Washington, DC, March 19.

Mazey, Sonia, and Jeremy Richardson, eds. 1993. *Lobbying in the European Community.* New York: Oxford University Press.

McKenzie, Judith I. 2008. "The Environmental Movement in Canada: Retreat or Resurgence?" In *Group Politics and Social Movements in Canada,* ed. Miriam Smith, 279–306. Toronto: Broadview Press.

Meyerson, Harold. 2000. "Rolling the Union On: John Sweeney's Union Four Years Later." *Dissent,* Winter, 47–55.

Miller, Alan C., and T. Christian Miller. 2000. "Election Was Decisive in Arena of Spending: Ever Higher Sums." *Los Angeles Times,* December 8.

Moberg, David. 2001. "This Time, Labor's Ready." *The Progressive,* February, 27–29.

Moberg, David. 2002. "Labor Plays Its Hand." *The Nation,* November 11, 14–17.

Moberg, David. 2008. "Labor's New Push." *The Nation,* August 29.

Monroe, Edward L. 2002. Deposition of Plaintiffs Associated Builders and Contractors in the U.S. District Court (District of Columbia) Three Judge Court, *McConnell et al. v. Federal Election Commission et al.,* Case 02-0582, September 12.

Morgenson, Gretchen, and Glen Justice. 2005. "Taking Care of Business, His Way: Hardball Tactics at U.S. Chamber." *New York Times,* February 20, C1.

Mosk, Matthew, and Paul Kane. 2008. "796 Insiders May Hold Democrats' Key." *Washington Post,* February 10, A1.

Mullins, Brody. 2003. "Business Changes Course: Turnout Becomes Focus." *Roll Call,* July 9.

Mullins, Brody, and Susan Davis. 2008. "Chamber of Commerce Irks Democrats with Big Push for GOP." *Wall Street Journal,* October 24.

Mullins, Brody, and Charlie Mitchell. 2001. "Saying 'No' to Soft Money." *National Journal,* March 24, 870–75.

Mundo, Phillip. 1999. "League of Conservation Voters." In *After the Revolution,* ed. Robert Biersack, Paul S. Herrnson, and Clyde Wilcox, 118–33. New York: Allyn & Bacon.

Murrilo, Maria Victoria. 2001. *Labor Unions, Partisan Coalitions, and Market Reforms in Latin America.* New York: Cambridge University Press.

Nadeau, Richard. 2002. "Satisfaction with Democracy: The Canadian Paradox." In *Value Change and Governance in Canada,* ed. Neil Nevitte, 37–70. Toronto: University of Toronto Press.

Nassmacher, Karl-Heinz. 2009. "Campaign and Party Finance in Established Democracies." *Vox Pop: Newsletter of the Political Organizations and Parties Section of the American Political Science Association* 28 (2): 5–6.

Nelson, Candice J., and Robert Biersack. 1999. "BIPAC: Working to Keep a Probusiness Congress." In *After the Revolution,* ed. Robert Biersack, Paul S. Herrnson, and Clyde Wilcox, 36–46. New York: Allyn & Bacon.

Neumann, Ken. 2006. "Why We Didn't Do What Buzz Did." *Globe and Mail,* January 31.

Nevitte, Neil. 1996. *The Decline of Deference: Canadian Value Change in Cross-National Perspective.* Peterborough, ON: Broadview Press.

Nevitte, Neil. 2002. "Introduction: Value Change and Reorientation in Citizen-State Relations." In *Value Change and Governance in Canada,* ed. Neil Nevitte, 3–36. Toronto: University of Toronto Press.

Nussbaum, Karen. 2004. Comments at the Take Back America Conference, Washington, DC, June 3.

Ornstein, Norman J., Thomas E. Mann, and Michael J. Malbin. 2002. *Vital Statistics on Congress.* Washington, DC: American Enterprise Institute.

Ost, David. 2006. *The Defeat of Solidarity: Anger and Politics in Postcommunist Europe.* Ithaca: Cornell University Press.

O'Steen, David. 2002. Deposition of Plaintiff National Right to Life, Inc., in the U.S. District Court (District of Columbia) Three Judge Court, *McConnell et al. v. Federal Election Commission et al.,* Case 02-0582, October 23.

Pal, Leslie. 1993. *Interests of State: The Politics of Language, Multiculturalism, and Feminism in Canada.* Montreal: McGill-Queen's University Press.

Paltiel, Khayyam Zev. 1989a. "Canadian Election Expense Legislation, 1963–1985: A Critical Appraisal, or Was the Effort Worth It?" In *Comparative Political Finance in the 1980s,* ed. Herbert E. Alexander, 51–75. New York: Cambridge University Press.

Paltiel, Khayyam Zev. 1989b. "Political Marketing, Party Finance, and the Decline of Canadian Parties." In *Canadian Parties in Transition,* ed. Alain-G. Gagnon and A. Brian Tanguay, 332–53. Scarborough, ON: Nelson Canada.

Panagopoulos, Costas, and Peter L. Francia. 2008. "The Polls—Trends: Labor Unions in the United States." *Public Opinion Quarterly* 72 (1): 134–59.

Parker, David C. W. 2008. *The Power of Money in Congressional Campaigns, 1880–2006.* Norman: University of Oklahoma Press.

Parker, David C. W., and John J. Coleman. 2004. "Pay to Play: Parties, Interests, and Money in Federal Elections." In *The Medium and the Message: Television Advertising and American Elections,* ed. Kenneth Goldstein and Patricia Strach, 127–54. Englewood Cliffs, NJ: Prentice-Hall.

Patterson, Kelly D., and Matthew M. Singer. 2007. "Targeting Success: The Enduring Power of the NRA." In *Interest Group Politics,* 7th ed., ed. Allan J. Cigler and Burdett A. Loomis, 37–64. Washington, DC: Congressional Quarterly Press.

Pershing, Ben. 2009. "New Campaign Targets Democrats for Health Vote." *Washington Post,* November 11.

Phillips, Kate. 2007. "Group Reaches Settlement with FEC over 2004 Campaign Advertising." *New York Times,* March 1, A16.

Phillips-Fein, Kim. 2009. *Invisible Hands: The Making of the Conservative Movement from the New Deal to Reagan.* New York: W. W. Norton.

Pierce, John C., Mary Ann E. Steger, Brent S. Steel, and Nicholas P. Lovrich. 1992. *Citizens, Political Communication, and Interest Groups: Environmental Organizations in Canada and the United States.* Westport, CT: Praeger.

Posada-Carbo, Eduardo. 2008. "Democracy, Parties, and Political Finance in Latin America." Working Paper 346, Kellogg Center, Notre Dame University.

Potter, Trevor. 1997. "Where Are We Now? The Current State of Campaign Finance Law." In *Campaign Finance Reform: A Sourcebook,* ed. Anthony Corrado, Thomas E.

Mann, Daniel R. Ortiz, Trevor Potter, and Frank J. Sorauf, 5–24. Washington, DC: Brookings Institution.

Potter, Trevor. 2005. "The Current State of Campaign Finance Law." In *The New Campaign Finance Sourcebook*, ed. Anthony Corrado, Thomas E. Mann, Daniel R. Ortiz, and Trevor Potter, 48–90. Washington, DC: Brookings Institution.

Presthus, Robert. 1973. *Elite Accommodation in Canadian Politics.* Toronto: Cambridge University Press.

Pross, A. Paul. 1975. "Pressure Groups: Adaptive Instruments of Political Communication." In *Pressure Group Behaviour in Canadian Politics*, ed. A. Paul Pross, 1–26. Toronto: McGraw-Hill Ryerson.

Pross, A. Paul. 1992. *Group Politics and Public Policy.* 2nd ed. Toronto: Oxford University Press.

Rich, Andrew. 2005. *Think Tanks, Public Policy, and the Politics of Expertise.* New York: Cambridge University Press.

Rich, Eric, and Theola Labbe. 2004. "Moms Unleash Their Anguish, Anger: Thousands March to End Gun Violence, Renew Assault Weapons Ban." *Washington Post*, May 10, B1.

Richards, Cecile. 2004. Comments at the Take Back America Conference, Washington, DC, June 3.

Rimmerman, Craig A. 1994. "'New Kids on the Block': WISH List and the Gay and Lesbian Victory Fund in the 1992 Elections." In *Risky Business? PAC Decisionmaking in Congressional Elections*, ed. Robert Biersack, Paul S. Herrnson, and Clyde Wilcox, 214–23. Armonk, NY: M. E. Sharpe.

Roese, Neal J. 2002. "Canadians' Shrinking Trust in Government: Causes and Consequences." In *Value Change and Governance in Canada*, ed. Neil Nevitte, 149–63. Toronto: University of Toronto Press.

Roof, Tracy. 2008. "Can the Democrats Deliver for the Base? Partisanship, Group Politics, and the Case of Organized Labor in the 110th Congress." *PS: Political Science* 41 (1): 83–87.

Rosenberg, Alyssa. 2009. "Business: It's Not Just Card Check." *National Journal*, February 14.

Rosenberg, David. 2002. "Broadening the Base: The Case for a New Federal Tax Credit for Political Contributions." Washington, DC: American Enterprise Institute.

Rosenthal, Steven. 2002. "Response to Malbin et al." *Election Law Journal* 1 (4): 546–47.

Rosenthal, Steven. 2004. "Okay, We Lost Ohio. The Question Is, Why?" *Washington Post*, December 5, B3.

Rozell, Mark J., Clyde Wilcox, and David Madlock. 2006. *Interest Groups in American Campaigns: The New Face of Electioneering*, 2nd ed. Washington, DC: Congressional Quarterly Press.

Russell, Peter H., and Lorne Sossin, eds. 2009. *Parliamentary Democracy in Crisis.* Toronto: University of Toronto Press.

Sabato, Larry J. 1984. *PAC Power: Inside the World of Political Action Committees.* New York: W. W. Norton.

Saletan, William. 2004. *Bearing Right: How the Conservatives Won the Abortion War.* Berkeley: University of California Press.

Salisbury, Robert H. 1969. "An Exchange Theory of Interest Groups." *Midwest Journal of Political Science* 13 (1): 1–32.

Salisbury, Robert H., John P. Heinz, Edward O. Laumann, and Robert L. Nelson. 1987. "Who Works with Whom? Group Alliances and Opposition." *American Political Science Review* 81 (4): 1217–34.

Salutin, Rick. 1989. *Waiting for Democracy.* Toronto: Penguin.

Samples, John. 2006. *The Fallacy of Campaign Finance Reform.* Chicago: University of Chicago Press.

Sandherr, Stephen. 2002. Deposition of Associated General Contractors of America in the U.S. District Court (District of Columbia) Three Judge Court, *McConnell et al. v. Federal Election Commission et al.,* Case 02-0582, September 30.

Sapiro, Virginia, Steven J. Rosenstone, and the National Election Studies. 2005. *1948–2004 Cumulative Data File* (data set). Ann Arbor: University of Michigan, Center for Political Studies (producer and distributor).

Savoie, Donald J. 1999. *Governing from the Centre: The Concentration of Power in Canadian Politics.* Toronto: University of Toronto Press.

Sawer, Marian. 2004. "Populism and Public Choice: Constructing Women as a 'Special Interest.'" Paper presented at the Annual Meeting of the Canadian Political Science Association, Winnipeg, Manitoba.

Sayers, Anthony M., and Lisa Young. 2004. "Election Campaign and Party Financing in Canada." Australian Democratic Audit. Canberra: Australian National University.

Scarrow, Susan. 2004. "Explaining Political Finance Reforms: Competition and Context." *Party Politics* 10:653–75.

Scarrow, Susan. 2006. "Party Subsidies and the Freezing of Party Competition: Do Cartels Work?" *West European Politics* 29 (3): 619–39.

Scarrow, Susan. 2007. "Political Finance in Comparative Perspective." *Annual Review of Political Science* 10:193–210.

Schadler, Holly. 2003. Comments at the Take Back America Conference, Washington, DC, June 3.

Schultz, Richard J. 1980. *Federalism, Bureaucracy, and Public Policy: The Politics of Highway Transport Regulation.* Montreal: McGill-Queens University Press.

Schwartz, Mildred A. 2006. *Party Movements in the United States and Canada: Strategies of Persistence.* Lanham, MD: Rowman and Littlefield.

Shaiko, Ronald G., and Marc A. Wallace. 1999. "From Wall Street to Main Street: The National Federation of Independent Businesses and the New Republican Majority." In *After the Revolution,* ed. Robert Biersack, Paul S. Herrnson, and Clyde Wilcox, 18–35. New York: Allyn & Bacon.

Sharpe, Sydney, and Don Braid. 1992. *Storming Babylon: Preston Manning and the Rise of the Reform Party.* Toronto: Key Porter Books.

Shull, Darrell. 2004. "P2 Wrap-Up." *BIPAC Elections Insight* 32 (3): 3.

Simpson, Jeffrey. 2002. *The Friendly Dictatorship.* Toronto: McClelland and Stewart.

Skinner, Richard M. 2005. "Do 527s Add Up to a Party? Thinking about the 'Shadows' of Politics." *The Forum* 3 (3), article 5.

Smith, Ben. 2010. "Ginsberg et al.: A Drastically Altered Landscape." *Politico,* January 21. http://www.politico.com/blogs/bensmith/0110/Ginsberg_et_al_A_drastically_altered_landscape.html.

Smith, Bradley. 2001. *Unfree Speech: The Folly of Campaign Finance Reform.* Princeton: Princeton University Press.

Smith, Bradley. 2010. "Newsflash: First Amendment Upheld." *Wall Street Journal*, January 22.

Smith, Jennifer. 2004. *Federalism: The Canadian Democratic Audit.* Vancouver: University of British Columbia Press.

Smith, Miriam. 2005. *A Civil Society? Collective Actors in Canadian Political Life.* Toronto: Broadview Press.

Smith, Miriam. 2008. "Theories of Group and Movement Organizing." In *Group Politics and Social Movements in Canada,* ed. Miriam Smith, 15–32. Toronto: Broadview Press.

Smith, Richard A. 1995. "Interest Group Influence in the U.S. Congress." *Legislative Studies Quarterly* 20 (1): 89–139.

Sperling, Valerie. 1999. *Organizing Women in Contemporary Russia: Engendering Transition.* New York: Cambridge University Press.

Spitzer, Robert. 1995. *The Politics of Gun Control.* Chatham, NJ: Chatham House.

Squire, Peverill, Keith E. Hamm, Ronald D. Hedlund, and Gary Moncrief. 2005. "Electoral Reforms, Membership Stability, and the Existence of Committee Property Rights in American State Legislatures." *British Journal of Political Science* 35:169–81.

Stanbury, William T. 1989. "Financing Federal Parties in Canada, 1974–1986." In *Canadian Parties in Transition,* ed. Alain-G. Gagnon and A. Brian Tanguay, 354–83. Scarborough, ON: Nelson Canada.

Stanbury, William T. 1991. *Money in Politics: Financing Federal Political Parties in Canada.* Toronto: Dundurn Press.

Steen, Jennifer. 2003. "The 'Millionaire's Amendment.'" In *Life after Reform: When the Bipartisan Campaign Reform Act Meets Politics,* ed. Michael J. Malbin, 159–74. Lanham, MD: Rowman and Littlefield.

Stewart, Ian. 2005. "Bill C24: Replacing the Market with the State?" *Electoral Insight,* January. http://www.elections.ca/eca/eim/article_search/article.asp?id=127&lang=e&frmPageSize=&textonly=false.

Stewart-Patterson, David. 2003. Testimony to the Standing Committee on Procedure and House Affairs, 37th Parliament, 2nd sess., May 1.

Stone, Peter H. 2003. "The Texan's Rangers." *National Journal*, October 25, 3260–63.

Strom, Stephanie. 2003. "A Debt of $100 Million Is Confronting the NRA." *New York Times,* December 21.

Strope, Leigh. 2004. "Labor Unions Fail to Deliver Votes for Kerry Candidacy." Associated Press, November 5.

Tanguay, A. Brian. 2002. "Parties, Organized Interests, and Electoral Democracy: The 1999 Ontario Provincial Election." In *Political Parties, Representation, and Electoral Democracy in Canada,* ed. William P. Cross, 145–60. Toronto: Oxford University Press.

Tanguay, A. Brian. 2009. "What's So Bad about Cultivating Our Own Theoretical Gardens? The Study of Political Parties in Canada." In *The Comparative Turn in Canadian Political Science,* ed. Linda A. White, Richard Simeon, Robert Vipond, and Jennifer Wallner, 177–93. Vancouver: University of British Columbia Press.

Tanguay, A. Brian, and Barry J. Kay. 1991. "Political Activity of Local Interest Groups." In *Interest Groups and Elections in Canada,* ed. F. Leslie Seidle, 77–115. Toronto: Dundurn Press.

Teachout, Zephyr. 2010. "Supreme Injustice: The Campaign Finance Decision Puts Democracy up to the Highest Bidders." *Slate*, January 21. http://www.thebig money.com/articles/judgments/2010/01/21/supreme-injustice.

Thomas, Stephen W. 1980. "Interest Groups: Inside Perspectives." In *Parties, Interest Groups, and Campaign Finance Laws*, ed. Michael J. Malbin, 82–85. Washington, DC: American Enterprise Institute.

Thomas, Sue. 1999. "NARAL PAC: Battling for Women's Reproductive Rights." In *After the Revolution*, ed. Robert Biersack, Paul S. Herrnson, and Clyde Wilcox, 134–43. New York: Allyn & Bacon.

Thorburn, Hugh G. 1985. *Interest Groups in the Canadian Federal System*. Toronto: University of Toronto Press.

Totten, Gloria. 2003. Comments at the Take Back America Conference, Washington, DC, June 3.

Traugott, Michael W. 2003. "The 2000 Michigan Senate Race." In *The Other Campaign: Soft Money and Issue Advocacy in the 2000 Elections*, ed. David B. Magleby, 97–110. Lanham, MD: Rowman and Littlefield.

Truman, David B. 1951. *The Governmental Process: Political Interests and Public Opinion*. New York: Alfred A. Knopf.

Tuohy, Carolyn J. 1992. *Policy and Politics in Canada: Institutionalized Ambivalence*. Philadelphia: Temple University Press.

Valpy, Michael. 2009. "Liberals Import Obama Software for Election Preparation." *Globe and Mail*, April 16.

van Biezen, Ingrid. 2004. "Political Parties as Public Utilities." *Party Politics* 10 (4): 701–22.

Vandehei, Jim. 2006. "Democrats Scrambling to Organize Voter Turnout." *Washington Post*, August 2, A1.

Vandehei, Jim, and Chris Cillizza. 2006. "A New Alliance of Democrats Spreads Funding." *Washington Post*, July 17, A1.

Van Nijnatten, Debora L. 1996. "Environmental Governance in an Era of Participatory Decision Making: Canadian and American Approaches." *American Review of Canadian Studies* 26 (3): 405–23.

Van Nijnatten, Debora L. 2003. "Analyzing the Canada-U.S. Environmental Relationship: A Multi-faceted Approach." *American Review of Canadian Studies* 33 (1): 93–120.

Van Nijnatten, Debora L. 2004. "Canadian-American Environmental Relations and Politics." *American Review of Canadian Studies* 34 (4): 649–64.

Vickers, Jill, Pauline Rankin, and Christine Appelle. 1993. *Politics as If Women Mattered: A Political Analysis of the National Action Committee on the Status of Women*. Toronto: University of Toronto Press.

Vizzard, William J. 2000. *Shot in the Dark: The Policy, Politics, and Symbolism of Gun Control*. Lanham, MD: Rowman and Littlefield.

Vogel, Kenneth P. 2007. "SCOTUS Loosens McCain-Feingold Provision." *Politico*, June 25. http://www.politico.com/news/stories/0607/4633.html.

Vogel, Kenneth P. 2010. "Court Decision Opens Floodgates for Corporate Cash." *Politico*, January 21. http://www.politico.com/news/stories/0110/31786.html.

Walker, Jack. 1991. *Mobilizing Interest Groups in America*. Ann Arbor: University of Michigan Press.

Wallace, Donald C. 1989. "Friends and Foes: Prime Ministers and Premiers in Intergovernmental Relations." In *Prime Ministers and Premiers: Political Leadership and Public Policy in Canada,* ed. Leslie Pal and David Taras, 69–86. Scarborough, ON: Prentice-Hall.

Wattenberg, Martin P. 2001. "The Decline of Party Mobilization." In *Parties without Partisans: Political Change in Advanced Industrial Democracies,* ed. Russell Dalton and Martin P. Wattenberg, 64–78. New York: Oxford University Press.

Wayne, Leslie. 2008. "Democratic Groups Turn to Foot Soldiers." *New York Times,* September 21.

Weissman, Steve, and Ruth Hassan. 2006. "527 Groups and BCRA." In *The Election after Reform: Money, Politics, and the Bipartisan Campaign Reform Act,* ed. Michael J. Malbin, 79–111. Lanham, MD: Rowman and Littlefield.

Whitehorn, Alan. 1992. *Canadian Socialism: Essays on the CCF-NDP.* Toronto: Oxford University Press.

Williams, Vanessa. 2004. "Democrats Aim to Organize the Union Vote: Labor Leaders Predict Record Turnout as they Rally Members for Kerry in Battleground States." *Washington Post,* October 23, A8.

Willis, Derek. 2000. "The 75 Percent Dissolution." *Congressional Quarterly,* September 23, 2193–94.

Wilson, Graham. 1981. *Interest Groups in the United States.* New York: Oxford University Press.

Wilson, James Q. 1973. *Political Organizations.* New York: Basic Books.

Winterhof, Jo Dee. 2004. Comments at the Take Back America Conference, Washington, DC, June 3.

Wiseman, Nelson. 2007. *In Search of Canadian Political Culture.* Vancouver: University of British Columbia Press.

Woll, Cornelia. 2008. *Firm Interests: How Governments Shape Business Lobbying on Global Trade.* Ithaca: Cornell University Press.

Wright, John R. 1996. *Interest Groups and Congress: Lobbying, Contributions, and Influence.* New York: MacMillan.

Yates, Charlotte A. B. 1993. *From Plant to Politics: The Autoworkers Union in Postwar Canada.* Philadelphia: Temple University Press.

Yates, Charlotte A. B. 2008. "Organized Labour in Canadian Politics: Hugging the Middle or Pushing the Margins?" In *Group Politics and Social Movements in Canada,* ed. Miriam Smith, 85–106. Toronto: Broadview Press.

Young, Lisa. 2000. *Feminists and Party Politics.* Vancouver: University of British Columbia Press.

Young, Lisa. 2004. "Regulating Campaign Finance in Canada: Strengths and Weaknesses." *Election Law Journal* 3 (3): 444–62.

Young, Lisa, and Joanna Everitt. 2004. *Advocacy Groups.* Vancouver: University of British Columbia Press.

Yussuff, Hassan. 2003. Testimony to the Standing Committee on Procedure and House Affairs, 37th Parliament, 2nd sess., May 1.

Zenilman, Avi, and Ben Smith. 2008. "Labor Confronts Race Issue." *Politico,* November 2. http://www.politico.com/news/stories/1108/15176.html.

Zuberi, Dan. 2006. *Differences That Matter: Social Policy and the Working Poor in the United States and Canada.* Ithaca: Cornell University Press.

Zullo, Roland. 2004. "Labor Council Outreach and Union Member Voter Turnout: A Microanalysis from the 2000 Election." *Industrial Relations* 43 (2): 324–38.

Index

Note: Page numbers in italic indicate tables or figures.

Edwards Brothers Inc.
Ann Arbor MI. USA
February 23, 2011